First World War

and Army of Occupation

War Diary

France, Belgium and Germany

35 DIVISION
106 Infantry Brigade,
Brigade Machine Gun Company
24 April 1916 - 30 January 1918

WO95/2490/6

The Naval & Military Press Ltd
www.nmarchive.com
Published in association with The National Archives

Published by

The Naval & Military Press Ltd

Unit 10 Ridgewood Industrial Park,

Uckfield, East Sussex,

TN22 5QE England

Tel: +44 (0) 1825 749494

www.naval-military-press.com

www.nmarchive.com

This diary has been reprinted in facsimile from the original. Any imperfections are inevitably reproduced and the quality may fall short of modern type and cartographic standards.

Contents

Document type	Place/Title	Date From	Date To
Heading	WO95/2490/6		
Heading	35th Division 106th Infy Bde 106th Machine Gun Coy Apr 1916-Jan 1918		
Miscellaneous	From O/C 106 Coy Machine Gun Corps D of G. 3rd Echelon.		
War Diary	Grantham	24/04/1916	24/04/1916
War Diary	Fouthampin	25/04/1916	25/04/1916
War Diary	Le Harve	27/04/1916	27/04/1916
War Diary	Lestrum	28/04/1916	28/04/1916
War Diary	Zelobes	29/04/1916	29/04/1916
War Diary	In The Line	05/05/1916	22/05/1916
War Diary	Farbus	22/05/1916	27/05/1916
War Diary	In The Line	28/05/1916	30/05/1916
War Diary	Festubert.	01/06/1916	11/06/1916
War Diary	Fauquessart.	11/06/1916	27/06/1916
Heading	106th Bde. 35th Div. War Diary 106th Brigade Machine Gun Company 1st to 31st July 1916.		
War Diary		02/07/1916	31/07/1916
Heading	106th Brigade. 35th Division. 106th Brigade Machine Gun Company August 1916.		
War Diary		01/08/1916	31/08/1916
War Diary	Sus St Ledger.	01/09/1916	01/09/1916
War Diary	Agnez.	02/09/1916	12/09/1916
War Diary	Arras	14/09/1916	30/09/1916
War Diary	Appendix 1.	07/09/1916	07/09/1916
War Diary	Appendix 2.	11/09/1916	11/09/1916
War Diary	Appendix 3.	12/09/1916	12/09/1916
War Diary	Appendix 4.	13/09/1916	13/09/1916
War Diary	Appendix 5.	14/09/1916	14/09/1916
War Diary	Appendix 6.	21/09/1916	21/09/1916
War Diary	Appendix 7.	27/09/1916	27/09/1916
War Diary	Arras.	01/10/1916	31/10/1916
Miscellaneous	Operation Order No 11	09/10/1916	09/10/1916
Operation(al) Order(s)	Operation Order No. 12	12/10/1916	12/10/1916
Operation(al) Order(s)	Operation Order No. 13	16/10/1916	16/10/1916
Operation(al) Order(s)	Operation Order No.14.	20/10/1916	20/10/1916
Operation(al) Order(s)	Operation Order No 15	24/10/1916	24/10/1916
Operation(al) Order(s)	Operation Order No. 16.	28/10/1916	28/10/1916
Operation(al) Order(s)	Machine Gun Operation Order No.17.	31/10/1916	31/10/1916
Operation(al) Order(s)	Operation Order No. 18.	31/10/1916	31/10/1916
Operation(al) Order(s)	Operation Order No.20	07/11/1916	07/11/1916
War Diary	Arras.	01/11/1916	30/11/1916
Operation(al) Order(s)	Operation Order No.19.	01/11/1916	01/11/1916
Operation(al) Order(s)	Operation Order No.20		
Operation(al) Order(s)	Operation Order No.21		
Miscellaneous	O.C. Map. Left. 2nd Lt. H.N. Fisher		
Operation(al) Order(s)	Operation Order No.22.	15/11/1916	15/11/1916
Miscellaneous	O.C. Map. Left 2nd Lt F.A. Hooper		
Operation(al) Order(s)	Operation Order No 23	16/11/1916	16/11/1916
Operation(al) Order(s)	Operation Order No 24.	19/11/1916	19/11/1916

Miscellaneous	O.C. Map Left. 2nd Lt. F.A. Hooper		
Operation(al) Order(s)	Operation Order No. 25	19/11/1916	19/11/1916
Operation(al) Order(s)	Operation Order No. 26	21/11/1916	21/11/1916
Operation(al) Order(s)	Operation Order No. 27.		
Miscellaneous	O.C. Map Left. 2nd Lt. F.A. Hooper.		
Operation(al) Order(s)	Operation Order No 28	24/11/1916	24/11/1916
Operation(al) Order(s)	Operation Order No. 29		
Operation(al) Order(s)	Operation Order No.30	28/11/1916	28/11/1916
War Diary	Arras.	01/12/1916	31/12/1916
War Diary	Foyfflin Ricametz	01/02/1917	01/02/1917
Miscellaneous	106th M.G. Coy Programme of Work	12/01/1917	12/01/1917
Miscellaneous	106th M.G. Coy Programme of Work.	06/01/1917	06/01/1917
Miscellaneous	Programme of Work. 106th M.G. Coy.	30/12/1916	30/12/1916
Miscellaneous	Programme of Work. 106th Machine Gun Coy.	19/01/1917	19/01/1917
Miscellaneous	106th M.G. Coy Programme of Work	29/01/1917	29/01/1917
War Diary	Foufflin Ricametz.	01/02/1917	27/02/1917
War Diary	Field	27/02/1917	27/02/1917
Operation(al) Order(s)	Operation Order No.33 by Capt C.W. Merison Comdg 106 MG Coy		
Operation(al) Order(s)	Operation Order No.34		
Operation(al) Order(s)	Operation Order No.35		
Operation(al) Order(s)	Operation Order No.37. by. Capt. C.W. Merison Comdg. 106th Machine Gun Co.		
Operation(al) Order(s)	Operation Order No.38		
Operation(al) Order(s)	Operation Order No.39.	26/02/1917	26/02/1917
War Diary	Field	03/03/1917	16/03/1917
War Diary	Caix	16/03/1917	16/03/1917
War Diary	Rosieres	17/03/1917	17/03/1917
War Diary	Field	18/03/1917	21/03/1917
War Diary	Rodieres	21/03/1917	28/03/1917
War Diary	Licourt	29/03/1917	31/03/1917
Operation(al) Order(s)	Operation Order No.40	02/03/1917	02/03/1917
Operation(al) Order(s)	Operation Order No.41	06/03/1917	06/03/1917
Operation(al) Order(s)	Operation Order No.42.	08/03/1917	08/03/1917
Operation(al) Order(s)	Operation Order No.43.	10/03/1917	10/03/1917
Operation(al) Order(s)	Operation Order No.44.	10/03/1917	10/03/1917
Operation(al) Order(s)	Operation Order No.45	14/03/1917	14/03/1917
Operation(al) Order(s)	Operation Order No.46.	17/03/1917	17/03/1917
Operation(al) Order(s)	Operation Order No.47.	18/03/1917	18/03/1917
Operation(al) Order(s)	Operation Order No.48.	21/03/1917	21/03/1917
Operation(al) Order(s)	Operation Order No.49.	28/03/1917	28/03/1917
War Diary	Licourt	01/04/1917	05/04/1917
War Diary	Athies	03/04/1917	08/04/1917
War Diary	Meraucourt	09/04/1917	09/04/1917
War Diary	Vermand	10/04/1917	20/04/1917
War Diary	Villeveque	22/04/1917	29/04/1917
Operation(al) Order(s)	Operation Order No.50		
Operation(al) Order(s)	Operation Order No.51	09/04/1917	09/04/1917
Operation(al) Order(s)	Operation Order No.51A	10/04/1917	10/04/1917
Operation(al) Order(s)	Operation Order No.52	11/04/1917	11/04/1917
Operation(al) Order(s)	Operation Order No.53	12/04/1917	12/04/1917
Operation(al) Order(s)	Operation Order No.54.	14/04/1917	14/04/1917
Operation(al) Order(s)	Operation Order No.55	14/04/1917	14/04/1917
Operation(al) Order(s)	Operation Order No.56	16/04/1917	16/04/1917
Operation(al) Order(s)	Operation Order No.57	19/04/1917	19/04/1917
Operation(al) Order(s)	Operation Order No.58	19/04/1917	19/04/1917

Operation(al) Order(s)	Operation Order No. 59	22/04/1917	22/04/1917
Operation(al) Order(s)	Operation Order No.60.	29/04/1917	29/04/1917
War Diary	Field	01/05/1917	20/05/1917
Operation(al) Order(s)	Peronne	21/05/1917	21/05/1917
War Diary	Field	22/05/1917	01/06/1917
Operation(al) Order(s)	Operation Order No.61.	05/05/1917	05/05/1917
Operation(al) Order(s)	Operation Order No.62.	06/05/1917	06/05/1917
Miscellaneous			
Operation(al) Order(s)	Operation Order No.63	09/05/1917	09/05/1917
Operation(al) Order(s)	Operation Order No 64	13/05/1917	13/05/1917
Operation(al) Order(s)	Operation Order No. 65 Refce. O.O. 64.	14/05/1917	14/05/1917
Operation(al) Order(s)	Operation Order No. 66	18/05/1917	18/05/1917
Operation(al) Order(s)	Operation Order No.67.	20/05/1917	20/05/1917
Operation(al) Order(s)	Operation Order No.68	22/05/1917	22/05/1917
Operation(al) Order(s)	Operation Order No.69	28/05/1917	28/05/1917
Operation(al) Order(s)	Operation Order No.70	31/05/1917	31/05/1917
Operation(al) Order(s)	In The Field	01/06/1917	01/06/1917
War Diary	Aizecourt Le Bas	02/06/1917	09/06/1917
War Diary	In The Field	09/06/1917	26/06/1917
Operation(al) Order(s)	Operation Order No.71	31/05/1917	31/05/1917
Operation(al) Order(s)	Operation Order No. 72.	08/06/1917	08/06/1917
Operation(al) Order(s)	Operation Order No.73	12/06/1917	12/06/1917
Operation(al) Order(s)	Operation Order No.74	16/06/1917	16/06/1917
Operation(al) Order(s)	Operation Order No.75	18/06/1917	18/06/1917
Operation(al) Order(s)	Operation Order No.76	20/06/1917	20/06/1917
Operation(al) Order(s)	Operation Order No.77	23/06/1917	23/06/1917
Operation(al) Order(s)	Operation Order No.78	25/06/1917	25/06/1917
Operation(al) Order(s)	Operation Order No.79	25/06/1917	25/06/1917
Operation(al) Order(s)	Operation Order No.101	30/08/1917	30/08/1917
War Diary	Field	01/07/1917	31/07/1917
Operation(al) Order(s)	Operation Order No.80		
Operation(al) Order(s)	Operation Order No.81	01/07/1917	01/07/1917
Operation(al) Order(s)	Operation Order No.82.	05/07/1917	05/07/1917
Operation(al) Order(s)	Operation Order No.83.	06/07/1917	06/07/1917
Operation(al) Order(s)	Operation Order No.84	07/07/1917	07/07/1917
Operation(al) Order(s)	Operation Order No.85	08/07/1917	08/07/1917
Operation(al) Order(s)	Operation Order No.86	13/07/1917	13/07/1917
Operation(al) Order(s)	Operation Order No.87.	15/07/1917	15/07/1917
Operation(al) Order(s)	Operation Order No.88	22/07/1917	22/07/1917
Heading			
Operation(al) Order(s)	Operation Order No 89.	28/07/1917	28/07/1917
War Diary	In The Field	01/08/1917	18/08/1917
War Diary	In The Field	15/08/1917	17/08/1917
War Diary	In The Field	18/08/1917	31/08/1917
Operation(al) Order(s)	Operation Order No.90	01/08/1917	01/08/1917
Operation(al) Order(s)	Operation Order No.91	02/08/1917	02/08/1917
Operation(al) Order(s)	Operation Order No.92	06/08/1918	06/08/1918
Operation(al) Order(s)	Operation Order No.93		
Operation(al) Order(s)	Operation Order No.94.	09/08/1917	09/08/1917
Operation(al) Order(s)	Operation Order No.95	18/08/1917	18/08/1917
Miscellaneous	Appendix B.		
Miscellaneous	Appendix C		
Operation(al) Order(s)	Operation Order No 96	21/08/1917	21/08/1917
Operation(al) Order(s)	Operation Order No 97.	23/08/1917	23/08/1917
Operation(al) Order(s)	Operation Order No 98		
Operation(al) Order(s)	Operation Order No.99	26/08/1917	26/08/1917

Operation(al) Order(s)	Operation Order No.100	27/08/1917	27/08/1917
War Diary		02/09/1917	16/09/1917
War Diary		15/08/1917	30/08/1917
Operation(al) Order(s)	Operation Order No.102	02/09/1917	02/09/1917
Operation(al) Order(s)	Operation Order No.103.	04/09/1917	04/09/1917
Operation(al) Order(s)	Operation Order No.104	07/09/1917	07/09/1917
Operation(al) Order(s)	Operation Order No.105	10/09/1917	10/09/1917
Operation(al) Order(s)	Operation Order No.106.	12/09/1917	12/09/1917
Operation(al) Order(s)	Operation Order No.107	13/09/1917	13/09/1917
Miscellaneous	Appendix "A"		
Operation(al) Order(s)	Operation Order No.108	14/09/1917	14/09/1917
Operation(al) Order(s)	Operation Order No.108 (A)	15/09/1917	15/09/1917
Miscellaneous	Appendix "A"		
Miscellaneous	Appendix B.		
Map	Map France		
Operation(al) Order(s)	Operation Order No.109	17/09/1917	17/09/1917
Operation(al) Order(s)	Operation Order No.110	18/09/1917	18/09/1917
Operation(al) Order(s)	Operation Order No.111	21/09/1917	21/09/1917
War Diary		01/10/1917	29/10/1917
Operation(al) Order(s)	Operation Order No 112	01/10/1917	01/10/1917
Miscellaneous	Appendix "A"		
Operation(al) Order(s)	Operation Order No.113.	01/10/1917	01/10/1917
Operation(al) Order(s)	Operation Order No.114.	02/10/1917	02/10/1917
Operation(al) Order(s)	Operation Order No.115.	02/10/1917	02/10/1917
Operation(al) Order(s)	Operation Order No.116	12/10/1917	12/10/1917
Operation(al) Order(s)	Operation Order No.117	15/10/1917	15/10/1917
Operation(al) Order(s)	Operation Order No.118	18/10/1917	18/10/1917
Operation(al) Order(s)	Operation Order No.119	20/10/1917	20/10/1917
Operation(al) Order(s)	Operation Order No.120	21/10/1917	21/10/1917
Operation(al) Order(s)	Operation Order No.120 (A)	23/10/1917	23/10/1917
Operation(al) Order(s)	Operation Order No.121	24/10/1917	24/10/1917
War Diary		01/11/1917	30/11/1917
Operation(al) Order(s)	Operation Order No.122	31/10/1917	31/10/1917
Operation(al) Order(s)	Operation Order No.123	04/11/1917	04/11/1917
Operation(al) Order(s)	Operation Order No.124	07/11/1917	07/11/1917
Operation(al) Order(s)	Operation Order No.125	14/11/1917	14/11/1917
Operation(al) Order(s)	Operation Order No.126	14/11/1917	14/11/1917
Operation(al) Order(s)	Operation Order No.127	15/11/1917	15/11/1917
Operation(al) Order(s)	Operation Order No.128	17/11/1917	17/11/1917
Operation(al) Order(s)	Operation Order No.129	18/11/1917	18/11/1917
Operation(al) Order(s)	Operation Order No 130	20/11/1917	20/11/1917
Operation(al) Order(s)	Operation Order No 131	27/11/1917	27/11/1917
War Diary	In The Field	02/12/1917	31/12/1917
Operation(al) Order(s)	Operation Order No.133	01/12/1917	01/12/1917
Operation(al) Order(s)	Operation Order No.134.	02/11/1917	02/11/1917
Operation(al) Order(s)	Operation Order No.135	06/12/1917	06/12/1917
Operation(al) Order(s)	Operation Order No.136	10/12/1917	10/12/1917
War Diary	Road Camp.	01/01/1918	07/01/1918
War Diary	Poelcappelle Sector	08/01/1918	16/01/1918
War Diary	Klober Farm.	17/01/1918	22/01/1918
War Diary	Westroosbeke Sector.	22/01/1918	30/01/1918
Operation(al) Order(s)	Operation Order No 137.	07/01/1918	07/01/1918
Operation(al) Order(s)	Operation Order No 138.	07/01/1918	07/01/1918
Operation(al) Order(s)	Operation Order No 139.	11/01/1918	11/01/1918
Operation(al) Order(s)	Operation Order No 140	15/01/1918	15/01/1918
Operation(al) Order(s)	Operation Order No.141.	20/01/1918	20/01/1918

Operation(al) Order(s)	Operation Order No.142	24/01/1918	24/01/1918
Operation(al) Order(s)	Operation Order No.143	28/01/1918	28/01/1918
Heading	18th H.L.I. Vol I 35 1916 Feb'16. Feb'19		

35TH DIVISION
106TH INFY BDE

106TH MACHINE GUN COY

APR 1916 - JAN 1918

[827] W13345/4182 500m 12/15R G & S 77 77 Forms C. 348 61

Army Form C. 348.

MEMORANDUM.

From
O/C 106 Coy
Machine Gun Corps

To
D A G
3rd Echelon

5 6 1916.

Herewith War Diary
from date of Embarkation
to 31st May.
I regret this has not
been sent earlier

C W Morrison
Capt
O/C 106 Coy
Machine Gun Corps

From

To

ANSWER.

191 .

Apr '16
|
Jan '18

Instructions regarding War Diaries and Intelligence Summaries are contained in F. S. Regs., Part II. and the Staff Manual respectively. Title Pages will be prepared in manuscript.

WAR DIARY ~~or INTELLIGENCE SUMMARY~~

(Erase heading not required.)

Army Form C. 2118.

XXV

106 Coy Machine Gun Corps

Vol I

Place	Date	Hour	Summary of Events and Information	Remarks and references to Appendices
Grantham	24.4.16		Left for Southampton	
Southampton	25		Sailed for Le Havre	
Le Havre	27		Left for Lestrem	
Lestrem	28		Arrived	
Zelobes	29		In billets	
In the Line	5.5.16		Sgt. McDade wounded by shrapnel	
	6.		A & D Sections Front Line and Keeps B Indirect C Reserve took over by 4pm	
	7.		Indirect Fire from S3C6.3. at S17A83 and from S ~~3C6~~ 9A06 at S17A ~~..~~ 56 between 5 and 6 am about 1000 rounds. B Section	
	8		Further Indirect Fire from S8A33 at S16D38 between 9-10pm about 100 rounds C Section	
	8		Indirect Firing from S9A06 at S17A87 between 3-3.40 am about 250 rounds and from S3C63 at SD87 between 12.15am-6.30pm about 250 rounds	
			Sergt Tunny wounded by shrapnel	
			Shell fell on S.3C63 at about 11pm on the billet wounding L/Cpl. Rockett in both feet. I desire to recommend him B Section	
			Richebourg St Vaast was also shelled but no damage	
	9		Hostile M.G. fired at S3C63 at about 7pm until midnight	

2449 Wt. W14957/M90 750,000 1/16 J.B.C. & A. Forms/C.2118/12.

Instructions regarding War Diaries and Intelligence Summaries are contained in F. S. Regs., Part II. and the Staff Manual respectively. Title Pages will be prepared in manuscript.

WAR DIARY
or
~~INTELLIGENCE~~ SUMMARY

(Erase heading not required.)

Place	Date	Hour	Summary of Events and Information	Remarks and references to Appendices
In the Line	10.5.16		Indirect firing from S 3 C 63 at ~~about 7 am until midnight~~ S 16 D 87 between 11.30 pm & 12.30 pm about 11 30 pm & 12 30 am about 250 rounds and from S 9 A 06 at S 17 A 87 between 3.45 & 4 am. 50 rounds A Section Hostile m gs on S 3 C 63 Following reliefs took place by 12 noon – B relieved D and C relieved A Windy Corner, 1 Sub Section at Hqrs. D Reserve Got rid of M.M.G. & Bde guns collected Signallers sent to Trenches. Line connected up Pte Mc Nelly B Section wounded 10.30 pm	
	11		Ptes Hunter & Jones C Section wounded Indirect firing from S 9 A 06 at S 16 D 21 about 500 rounds A Section	
	12		Indirect firing A Section from S 20 B 88 at S 22 D 15 one thousand rounds, gun going very well, emplacement completed enough to fire in one day	
	13		Indirect fire took place between 10 pm & mn from S 3 C 63 on S 16 B 42 about 1500 rounds. From S ~~17 A 87~~ 9 A 06 on S 17 A 87 about 1750 rounds From S 20 B 88 on S 22 D 14 about 1000 rounds New site for Indirect chosen at S 20 D 63	
	14		S 20 B 88 rendered untenable by shell fire; new site chosen at S 10 B 37	
	15		Vickers fired indirect from S 3 C 63 at S 17 A 87 from about 1.30 am &	

2449 Wt. W14957/M90 750,000 1/16 J.B.C. & A. Forms/C.2118/12.

Army Form C. 2118.

WAR DIARY
or
~~INTELLIGENCE~~ SUMMARY
(Erase heading not required.)

Instructions regarding War Diaries and Intelligence Summaries are contained in F. S. Regs., Part II. and the Staff Manual respectively. Title Pages will be prepared in manuscript.

Place	Date	Hour	Summary of Events and Information	Remarks and references to Appendices
			2.30 p.m. about 1000 rounds; no retaliation. Great activity on our left	
	16.5.16		Nothing to report	
	17.		Officers tour for taking over 2 Lt Morris wounded in the knee. bottom of arm. Pte Rennie wounded, hand blown off	
	18		D Section relieved C in Front Line. A Section relieved B in Front Line. B to Rich[?] Billets Richebourg. C - 1 Sub Sec. Windy Corner, 1 Sub Sec [illegible]	
	19.		Indirect fire took place between 10 p.m. & 11.30 p.m. at S 22 D 1 4 from S 20 B 4 7 about 900 rounds was fired.	
			Rope Keep emplacement improved	
			104 Coy M G C came to Richebourg[?]	
	20.		M G fired from near No 6 emplacement over the parapet between 9 a.m. & 10 a.m. at a hostile aeroplane.	
			Indirect fire took place from S 3 C 6 3 at S 10 D 7 3 about 1000 rounds, also from S 9 A 0 6 at S 17 A 8 8 about 1750 rounds both from 8.30 p.m. to 9.30 p.m. in conjunction with D L I fire scheme	
			Shell destroyed dug out in Rope Keep	
	21		Officers of 104 Coy took over from 106 Coy. Indirect fire took place between 9 p.m. & 10 p.m. from S 20 B 4 7 at S 22 D 1 4 about 1400 rounds. From S 16 D 6 4 at S 22 D 8 9½ about 500 rounds. ~~From~~ Also between 9 p.m. & 11 p.m. from S 9 A 0 6 at S 16 D 8 7 200 rounds. From S 3 C 6 3 at S 16 D 6 8½ 2000 rounds	

2449 Wt. W14957/M90 750,000 1/16 J.B.C. & A. Forms/C.2118/12.

Instructions regarding War Diaries and Intelligence Summaries are contained in F. S. Regs., Part II. and the Staff Manual respectively. Title Pages will be prepared in manuscript.

WAR DIARY
or
INTELLIGENCE SUMMARY

(Erase heading not required.)

Army Form C. 2118.

Place	Date	Hour	Summary of Events and Information	Remarks and references to Appendices
In the Line	2?.5.16		Relieved. Pte Ryan wounded.	
[illegible]			Billets	
"	27		In rest till 27th inst	
In the Line	28		Took over Festubert Sector D Sec. 4 guns in O.B.L. C Section 2 guns in O.B.L	
			A Sec. 2 guns Festubert Central 2 guns Le Plantin. B Section 2 guns	
			Festubert East. These equal village line	
			B Sec 2 guns } in reserve C Sec 2 guns }	
	29		Personal reconnaissance of O.B.L	
	30		Personal reconnaissance of village line	

O.H. [illegible] Lieut
for [illegible] M.G.C

2449 Wt. W14957/M90 750,000 1/16 J.B.C. & A. Forms/C.2118/12.

Instructions regarding War Diaries and Intelligence Summaries are contained in F. S. Regs., Part II. and the Staff Manual respectively. Title Pages will be prepared in manuscript.

Army Form C. 2118.

35 June 106 M.G.C. Vol 2

WAR DIARY
or
INTELLIGENCE SUMMARY

(Erase heading not required.)

Place	Date	Hour	Summary of Events and Information	Remarks and references to Appendices
Festubert	1/6/16		New defence scheme in force	
			1 gun A section Richmond Terrace	
			2 guns C section } Old British Line	
			4 guns D section }	
			3 guns A section } Village Line	
			2 guns B section }	
			4 guns (2 B Section + 2 C Section) Reserve at Le Hamel	
	2/6/16		Indirect fire scheme approved	
	3/6/16		Emplacements commenced for "Indirect Fire Positions"	
	4/6/16		Nothing to record	
	5/6/16		Nothing to record	
	6/6/16		Nothing to record	
	7/6/16		Changed village line	
	8/6/16		} Nothing to record	
	9/6/16		}	
	10/6/16		Left the line for rest at Les Lobes.	
Fauquissart	11/6/16		Moved in the evening to the 184 Brigade and took up dispositions in the Fauquissart sector.	
			4 guns } Front line	
			1 gun C.R.A + Road Bend post	
			1 " Elgin post	
			1 " Flleux post.	Blomenson Capt O.C. 106 M.G. Coy

2449 Wt. W14957/M90 750,000 1/16 J.B.C. & A. Forms/C.2118/12.

Instructions regarding War Diaries and Intelligence Summaries are contained in F. S. Regs., Part II. and the Staff Manual respectively. Title Pages will be prepared in manuscript.

WAR DIARY
or
INTELLIGENCE SUMMARY
(Erase heading not required.)

Army Form C. 2118.

2

Place	Date	Hour	Summary of Events and Information	Remarks and references to Appendices
	1916			
Fauquissart	June 11		1 gun ... A.1. post 2 guns ... Masselot post 2 " ... Jocks post 1 gun ... Hougomont post 1 " ... Fauquissart post 1 " ... Reserve at Laventie (dispositions unsuitable) C Section fired 250 rounds about 8.30 pm and dispersed a hostile working party. D Section fired about 500 rounds.	
"	June 12		100 men attached for instruction joined us at 2 pm and were sent to Masselot, Road Bend & Jock's Posts. Scheme obtained from Divisional Office Line reconnoitred for purpose of a new scheme. D Section fired from "Open Emplacement" No 3 from 9 to 11 pm. traversing enemy's parapet. A gun of this section also fired from No 2 Open Emplacement. C Section fired from No 8 Open Emplacement at a suspected enemy machine gun which at once retaliated.	
	June 13		Personal reconnaissance of front line and Keeps continued. Gun at No 3 (N.13.C.3½.3½) swept enemy's parapet from 9 to 11 pm. " " No 2 (M.24.4) fired doing likewise from 9 to 2.15 am. Indirect fire from No 5 Indirect Fire Position (which is a useless emplacement) (N.7.a.2.1.) at N.20.a.7.9 to N.20.d.7.5. from 9.30 pm till 10.30 pm about 1500 rounds fired.	

2449 Wt. W14957/M90 750,000 1/16 J.B.C. & A. Forms/C.2118/12.

Army Form C. 2118.

WAR DIARY
or
INTELLIGENCE SUMMARY

(Erase heading not required.)

Instructions regarding War Diaries and Intelligence Summaries are contained in F. S. Regs., Part II. and the Staff Manual respectively. Title Pages will be prepared in manuscript.

3

Place	Date	Hour	Summary of Events and Information	Remarks and references to Appendices
Fauquissart	June 3		Hostile gun opposite No 2 Emplacement changed his position or stopped firing owing to our fire	
			2 Lieut Talbot wounded in finger	
	June 4		Guns from No 2 + 3 Battle Emplacements swept the hostile parapet about 750 rounds fired	
			Indirect fire from No 2 "Indirect Fire Position" at (M 18 b. 0.4.) to (N 20. c. 1. 6) between 8.30 pm and 10 p.m. about 1000 rounds fired.	
	June 5		Indirect Fire from No 3 Indirect Fire Position from 9pm to 12pm at (M 18 c 6 6) traversing from N 14 b 6 2 to N 15 a. 1 2.) about 3000 rounds expended	
			Sectional Relief:–	
			A from Jocks + Hougomont Posts and Headquarters to front line Flank posts and A.1. post.	
			B from C.R.A., Masselot and Elgin posts to front line, Fauquissart and Seton post.	
			C from where A is to where B was	
			D from where B is to Jocks + Hougomont posts and headquarters	
	June 6		A section from near Battle Emplacement 3 2 for a short time during the night along enemy parapet.	
			B section fired from near Battle Emplacement 3 at a suspected Machine gun at N 19 a 7½ 9½ from 9pm to 10p.m.	

2449 Wt. W14957/M90 750,000 1/16 J.B.C. & A. Forms/C.2118/12.

Army Form C. 2118.

Instructions regarding War Diaries and Intelligence Summaries are contained in F. S. Regs., Part II. and the Staff Manual respectively. Title Pages will be prepared in manuscript.

WAR DIARY
or
INTELLIGENCE SUMMARY

(Erase heading not required.)

4

Place	Date	Hour	Summary of Events and Information	Remarks and references to Appendices
Fauquissart	June 17		A section fired 1000 rounds from 1 am (N14 a 2½ 3) on a target (gap in wire) at N 14 a 4½ 3.	
	June 18		Same as 17th inst 1800 rounds fired. Pte Barrow wounded.	
	June 19		A section fired from N14 a 2½ 3 at gap at N 14 a 4½ 9½ from 10.30 pm to 3 am. 1000 rounds fired at another gap from M24 d 49 to N19 a 35 to N 19 a 4 9½.	
			Another gun traversed the enemys' parapet firing from M24 a 65 Indirect Fire.	
			Indirect Fire Position 3. at N 15 a 0 8½ to N15 a 4 8½ from 10.10 pm to 10.30 p.m. 750 rounds.	
			" " " 4 at the road running east of Delevac ~~Farm~~ from 9.30 pm to 9.55 pm from 10 pm to 10.30 target changed to No 3 target. 1450 rounds.	
			Pte Hawley killed.	
	June 20		Gun at N14 a 2 3 traversed from N14 a 50 to N14 a 83 from 10.30 pm to 11.5 p.m. 300 rounds.	
			Gun at M 24 b 5.3. traversed from N 19 a 3 2½ to N 19 c 2½ 9½ 7000 rounds fired	
			Gun at N13 c 8½ 9 traversed from N13 d ½ 6 to N13 d 0 2½ 1000 rounds fired. All firing from 10.30 p.m. to 11.5 p.m.	

2449 Wt. W14957/M90 750,000 1/16 J.B.C. & A. Forms/C.2118/12.

Army Form C. 2118.

Instructions regarding War Diaries and Intelligence Summaries are contained in F. S. Regs., Part II. and the Staff Manual respectively. Title Pages will be prepared in manuscript.

WAR DIARY
or
INTELLIGENCE SUMMARY
(Erase heading not required.)

5

Place	Date	Hour	Summary of Events and Information	Remarks and references to Appendices
Fauquissart	June 20		Two guns indirect. One from Indirect Fire Position No1 and 2 on Barrages I, II, III & IV N 25 b 4 3 / N 19 d 4 5 / N 20 a 9 8 / N 14 d 8 6.	
			7100 rounds fired from 10.30 p.m. to 11.15 p.m.	
			Pte Stoolley Killed	
			Sergeant Nixon wounded	
	June 21		Relief completed. C Relieved A, D relieved B. 6 guns in front line.	
			No1 gun traversed enemy parapet,	
			No2 gun ~~from N xx a x x~~ at gap in wire N19a 7½ 9½	2000 rounds fired per gun.
			No5 gun. at gap in wire N14 a 7½ .3.	
	June 22		No4 gun traversed from N13 d ½ 6½ to N d 3½ 6½ all night about 2000 rounds fired.	
			No5 gun kept gap open at N14 a 6 1½ and located a hostile machine gun at N 14 a 5.0 which was silenced.	
			No1 gun swept parapet all night	
			No3 gun kept open gap in wire at N13 d 27	
			No2 gun fired on Point 36	

2449 Wt. W14957/M90 750,000 1/16 J.B.C. & A. Forms/C.2118/12.

Commanding Coy

Instructions regarding War Diaries and Intelligence Summaries are contained in F. S. Regs., Part II. and the Staff Manual respectively. Title Pages will be prepared in manuscript.

WAR DIARY
or
INTELLIGENCE SUMMARY

(Erase heading not required.)

Army Form C. 2118.

6

Place	Date	Hour	Summary of Events and Information	Remarks and references to Appendices
Fauquissart	June 22	8.30 pm to 10 pm	Indirect fire position No 1. Fire opened searching the Rue Enfer & rounds fired about 2000.	
	June 23		No 1 gun believed to have dispersed a working party. It fired all night traversing enemy's parapet and wire. No 2 gun fired at enemy's parapet and wire at point 36. No 3 gun kept open gap at N13 d 27; No 5 gun at gap N14 A 6½. Guns fired all night 4500 rounds expended	
		9 pm to 10.30 pm	Indirect fire position No 1. on Rue Enfer, 2000 rounds fired	
		9.30 pm to 10.30 pm	Indirect fire position No 4 on road running E from Fme Delaval about 250 rounds fired.	
	June 24		Nos 1, 5, & 6 guns traversed enemy wire near Red Lamp. No 3 gun kept gap open at N14 a 6½	
		8.30 pm to 10 pm	Indirect fire from No 4 Indirect Fire Position on Le Pietre 750 rounds	
		9 pm to 10 pm	" " " No 1 " " " on Rue Enfer 1000 "	
			" " " No 3 " " " on back of German Line 1000 "	
			" " " No 1 " " " as a barrage on the gap N13 d 27, 3000 rounds being fired.	

Army Form C. 2118.

Instructions regarding War Diaries and Intelligence Summaries are contained in F. S. Regs., Part II. and the Staff Manual respectively. Title Pages will be prepared in manuscript.

WAR DIARY
or
INTELLIGENCE SUMMARY
(Erase heading not required.)

7

Place	Date	Hour	Summary of Events and Information	Remarks and references to Appendices
Fauquissart	June 25		No1 gun kept gap in wire open at N13 c 7 0 4 " " " " " " N13 d 2 7 5 " " " " " " N14 a 7½ 3	
			Indirect fire.	
			No1 at Rue Enfer about 2000 rounds	
			No2. on track running from Rue Delevat also on Barrage III near Fme Delevat, also Aubers was traversed and searched. 2500 rounds fired.	
			No 3. trench N of Fme Delaporte running East 1250 rounds	
			No 4 track running from Fme Delevat 1750 rounds	
			Lieut Curry wounded. Pte Kellaway wounded.	
	June 26		Relief completed; Company withdrawn to Laventie; Church parade.	
	June 27		Company marched to Lanhoy.	

2449 Wt. W14957/M90 750,000 1/16 J.B.C. & A. Forms/C.2118/12.

106th Bde.
35th Div.

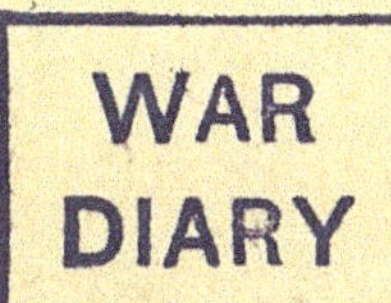

106th BRIGADE

MACHINE GUN COMPANY

1st to 31st JULY 1916.

Instructions regarding War Diaries and Intelligence Summaries are contained in F. S. Regs., Part II. and the Staff Manual respectively. Title Pages will be prepared in manuscript.

WAR DIARY
or
INTELLIGENCE SUMMARY
(Erase heading not required.)

Army Form C. 2118.

35 JULY
106 MGC
Vol 3

Place	Date	Hour	Summary of Events and Information	Remarks and references to Appendices
	1916			
	July 2		Entrained at CHOCQUES	
	July 3		Detrained at Frevent and marched to Ivergny	
	" 5		night march to Authie.	
	" 10		Marched to Varennes	
	" 13		marched to Bresle	
	" 14		marched to Billon Wood and bivouaced, in reserve to a big attack	
	" 15		Marched to Talus Boisé	
	" 16		Prepared for an attack 2nd Lt Jenkins, Talbot and A Section went in error to Longueval and assisted the Gordons and Seaforths. Sergt. Gooth and Lance Corporal Barker wounded. Gooth since died of wounds	
	" 17		Reconnoitred Delville Wood, accompanied by Lieut. Dineen, 2/Lts. Ling, Grabham and Lee. A hot place. Lee very slightly hit on return journey at Longueval, a very hot place. Operations cancelled.	
	" 19		Lieut. Dineen and 2nd Lieut. Talbot went again to reconnoitre Delville Wood. On return assisted Lewis guns of the Gordons, who expected counter attack. Lieut. Dineen wounded in the arm, near shoulder.	
	" 20		Moved to valley near Carnoy	
	" 21-23		At Carnoy. Caftet Wood.	

Cl. W. Emerson Capt.
O.C. No 106 M.G. Coy

2449 Wt. W14957/M90 750,000 1/16 J.B.C. & A. Forms/C.2118/12.

Instructions regarding War Diaries and Intelligence Summaries are contained in F. S. Regs., Part II. and the Staff Manual respectively. Title Pages will be prepared in manuscript.

WAR DIARY
or
INTELLIGENCE SUMMARY

(Erase heading not required.)

Army Form C. 2118.

Place	Date	Hour	Summary of Events and Information	Remarks and references to Appendices
	July 24		moved at about 1 A.M. to Montauban Quarry. One section E. of sunken road. One sub-section S.E. of Quarry. One section S.E. of gun pits. One and a half sections in German gun pits. Shelling intense. 2nd Lt V.S.M. KENDRICK ~~[illegible]~~ hit by shell splinter	
	" 25		withdrew to Caftet Wood at about 8 P.M.	
	" 26		At Carnoy	
	" 27		At Carnoy	
	" 28		Standing by to assist 2nd Division.	
	" 29		Reconnoitred near Favière Wood. At about 8. P.M. moved to position of assembly in SILESIA trench.	
	" 30/31		Big attack from DELVILLE to GUILLEMONT. Supporting 89th Infantry Brigade. D Section accompanied West Yorks and reached front line trenches near MALT HORN FARM	
			C Section with Royal Scots at Dublin Trench and half company in support at Hair pin bend. Later at night C Section attached to Royal Scots Fusiliers. Two guns on	
			[illegible signature] Capt O.C. No 106 [illegible]	

2449 Wt. W14957/M90 750,000 1/16 J.B.C. & A. Forms/C.2118/12.

Army Form C. 2118.

Instructions regarding War Diaries and Intelligence Summaries are contained in F. S. Regs., Part II. and the Staff Manual respectively. Title Pages will be prepared in manuscript.

WAR DIARY
or
INTELLIGENCE SUMMARY

(Erase heading not required.)

Place	Date	Hour	Summary of Events and Information	Remarks and references to Appendices
			Trones – Guillemont road and one at Arrow Head Copse. Withdrew at about 5.A.M.	

C.W. Morrison Capt. O.C. No 106 M.G.C.

2449 Wt. W14957/M90 750,000 1/16 J.B.C. & A. Forms/C.2118/12.

106th Brigade.

35th Division.

106th BRIGADE

MACHINE GUN COMPANY

AUGUST 1 9 1 6

Instructions regarding War Diaries and Intelligence Summaries are contained in F. S. Regs., Part II. and the Staff Manual respectively. Title Pages will be prepared in manuscript.

WAR DIARY
or
INTELLIGENCE SUMMARY
(Erase heading not required.)

Army Form C. 2118.

Place	Date	Hour	Summary of Events and Information	Remarks and references to Appendices
	Aug 1		Marched from CAFTET WOOD to SANDPIT VALLEY	
	Aug 2		" " SANDPIT VALLEY to MORLANCOURT	
	Aug 2-4		MORLANCOURT	
	" 5		Marched to MERICOURT Stn & entrained for SALEUX	
	" 6		" " LE MESGE	
	" 9		Transport returned by road under 2nd Lt Lee	
	" 10		Entrained at HANGESTE	
	" 11		Detrained at MERICOURT at about 2.30 am & marched to MORLANCOURT	
	" 15		Marched from MORLANCOURT to SANDPIT Bivouac	
	" 19		" " SANDPIT to CONTOUR WOOD	
	" 22		Relieve 3rd Div in trenches between GUILLEMONT & ANGLE WOOD. A Section followed the D. L. I & took up position three guns in Lonely Trench & one in BANTAM Trench. B Section occupied EDWARDS Trench, D Sec in Reserve LANCASTER Trench, C Sect remained in SILESIA Trench. Transport moved to CITADEL	
	" 23		One gun in BANTAM Trench fired about 250 rounds in the direction of Strong point T25c 6.5. During the night 23/24 this gun was damaged by shrapnel	
	" 24		About 11 a.m a gun of D Sect was damaged by Shell fire. During the day arrangements were made to cooperate with the H. L. I & D. L. I for an attack. These arrangements consisted of withdrawing B Section to TRONES WOOD – MALTHORN FARM SUNKEN ROAD where it is crossed by DANIEL Trench (A6a.7.6). This Section made emplacements in the embankment & dug cover trenches for the detachment 7 feet deep. No casualties occurred here although the road was shelled, due to the depth & narrowness of these trenches	

2449 Wt. W14957/M90 750,000 1/16 J.B.C. & A. Forms/C.2118/12.

Instructions regarding War Diaries and Intelligence Summaries are contained in F. S. Regs., Part II. and the Staff Manual respectively. Title Pages will be prepared in manuscript.

WAR DIARY or INTELLIGENCE SUMMARY

(Erase heading not required.)

Army Form C. 2118.

..85

Vol 4

106. MG Coy

Place	Date	Hour	Summary of Events and Information	Remarks and references to Appendices
	Aug 24	Contd	C. Sect was brought up from SILESIA Trench to LANCASTER Trench to complete the dispositions for the attack. On attack not taking place further arrangements were made for cooperating with an attack with the H. L. I.	
			B. Section (A 6. a. 7. 6) fired about 4000 rds between 6 p.m. & 7 p.m. during our bombardment placing a barrage on Guillemont - FALFEMONT ridge & 1 gun engaged supposed hostile M.G.S at T. 25. d 8. 2. & T. 26 a. 0. 4	
	Aug 24/25 Night		A. Section was relieved by C. Section in the front line & B. Section by D. Section at (A. 6. a. 7. 6)	
	Aug 25		Officer i/c C. Section & 2 N. C. O's having been wounded this Section was reinforced by 1 off & 1 N. C. O. Dispositions in the front line were as under 1 gun LONELY Trench at extreme left 1 gun junction of LONELY & BANTAM TRENCHES 1 gun BANTAM trench. about 8 p.m orders were received to engage a contemplated counter attack on GUILLEMONT D. Section at A 6 a 7. 6 was reinforced by 1 sub-section of B, 1 Sub. Section of A was sent to Brigade H. Q. The guns at (A 6 a 7. 6) fired indirect on WEDGEWOOD - GINCHY road & GUILLEMONT - LEUZE Wood road barraging this vicinity from 9 P.M. until 6 am about 13000 rounds were expended. At 9 P.M. orders were received to relieve 2 guns of 73rd Brigade, 1 sub section of A. was sent & occupied positions as S. 30 d 6. 9 & T 25. C. 2. 6	
	Aug 25/26 Night		Relief reported correct by 1 am. The Sub Section of A. at Bdge H. Q returned to LANCASTER trench at 1 am	

2449 Wt. W14957/M90 750,000 1/16 J.B.C. & A. Forms/C.2118/12.

Army Form C. 2118.

WAR DIARY
or
INTELLIGENCE SUMMARY

(Erase heading not required.)

Instructions regarding War Diaries and Intelligence Summaries are contained in F. S. Regs., Part II. and the Staff Manual respectively. Title Pages will be prepared in manuscript.

Place	Date	Hour	Summary of Events and Information	Remarks and references to Appendices
	Aug 26		About 6 a.m. Indirect fire ceased + 1 Sub. Section B. returned to LANCASTER trench. Relief of 93rd M.G. Coy commenced at 5.30 P.M + the last Section left for camp at 8.45 P.M. arriving HAPPY VALLEY midnight 26/27	
	" 29		Transport left at 10.45 am for CARDONETTE	
	" 30		Marched to HEILLY + there entrained for CANDAS detraining there at 8 P.M.	
	"		" " AUTHEUX	
	" 31		" " SUS-St LEGER	

[illegible] O.C. No 106 M.G. Coy

Army Form C. 2118.

WAR DIARY
or
INTELLIGENCE SUMMARY
(Erase heading not required.)

Instructions regarding War Diaries and Intelligence Summaries are contained in F. S. Regs., Part II. and the Staff Manual respectively. Title Pages will be prepared in manuscript.

106 Machine Gun Coy

Vol 5

Place	Date	Hour	Summary of Events and Information	Remarks and references to Appendices
SUS ST LEDGER	1st Sept		Reorganized.	
AGNEZ.	2nd		Moved by Motor-lorry. Transport by Road.	
	3rd 4th		Went into the line at ROCLINCOURT Section. Front line 2 guns D Section.	
			Work-line. 2 guns B Section, 2 guns D Section, 2 guns C Section,	
			Support line. 2 " A " , 2 " B " , 2 " C " .	
	5th		Slight shelling near M.G. 4 + 5. B Section guns.	
	6th		Intermittent H.E. Shelling near M.G. 5. Coy Relief. Dispositions as follows.	
			Front line, 1 gun D Section. 1 gun C Section.	
			Work-line, 2 guns B " , 2 " A " , 1 gun C section, 1 gun D Section.	
			Support line. 2 " A " , 2 " B " , 2 " C " .	
	7th		M.G. 6. D Section fired about 200 rounds at a hostile working party.	
	9th		Coy relief. Front line. 1 gun C Section, 1 gun B. Section.	
			Work line 1 gun C Section, 1 " A " , 3 " B, " , 1 gun D Section.	
			Support line 3 " A " , 1 " B " , 1 " D " .	
			Indirect fire took place on TELUS ROAD from 8 to 10 pm. 2000 rounds were fired.	
	10th		Small bombing raid made on KATIE Crater M.G. 1 unable to fire (no target.)	
	11th		Scheme for Cross bands of fire for covering front line brought into operation.	
	12th		Coy Relief. Front line. 1 gun C Section, 1 gun B Section.	
			Works line. 1 gun C Section, 1 " A Se " , 2 " B " , 2 gun D Section.	
			Support line. 3 " A " , 2 " D " , 1 " B " .	

Capt. C.W. Merrison

2449 Wt. W14957/M90 750,000 1/16 J.B.C. & A. Forms/C.2118/12.

Army Form C. 2118.

WAR DIARY
or
~~INTELLIGENCE~~ SUMMARY

(Erase heading not required.)

Instructions regarding War Diaries and Intelligence Summaries are contained in F. S. Regs., Part II. and the Staff Manual respectively. Title Pages will be prepared in manuscript.

106 Machine Gun Coy

Place	Date	Hour	Summary of Events and Information	Remarks and references to Appendices
ARRAS	14 Sept		Trench 40 was shelled during the morning & later during the evening.	
	18 "		M.G.C. fired at a hostile M.G. mounted on the parapet which was firing at a working party, gun silenced.	
			Coy Relief Front line, 2 guns C. Section,	
			Work line. 1 gun A Section, 2 " C ", 2 guns D Section, 1 gun B Section.	
			Support line 3 guns A ", 2 " D ", 1 " B ".	
	21st		Coy Relief Front line 1 gun A Section. 1 gun B Section.	
			Work line 2 guns C Section, 2 " A ", 2 " D ".	
			Support line. 2 " C ", 3 " B ", 1 " A ".	
	22nd		Indirect fire took place from I.F.P. near OBSERVATORY REDOUBT from 12-45 pm. till 2-15 am Barraging the following points:	
			H. 1 a 9 3. — H. 1. b 3 6. — H. 1 b. 3. 8. — B. 25. d. 9. 1. 2250 Rounds expended	
	24th		Coy Relief. Front line, 1 gun A Section, 1 gun B Section,	
			~~Work~~ line, 2 guns C Section 1 " B ", 2 " A ", 1 gun D Section.	
			Support line. 2 " C ", 3 " B ", 1 " A ".	
			Indirect fire took place from I.F.P. near OBSERVATORY REDOUBT from 8 pm till 10 pm barraging, H. 1 a 9 3. — H. 1 b. 3. 6. — H. 1 b. 3. 8. — B. 25 d 9. 1	
			2500 rounds expended.	

Capt. C. W. Mason

Army Form C. 2118.

Instructions regarding War Diaries and Intelligence Summaries are contained in F. S. Regs., Part II. and the Staff Manual respectively. Title Pages will be prepared in manuscript.

WAR DIARY
or
INTELLIGENCE SUMMARY

(Erase heading not required.)

106 Machine Gun Coy

Place	Date	Hour	Summary of Events and Information	Remarks and references to Appendices
ARRAS	27th Sept.		Coy Relief Front line 1 gun B Sect. 1 gun D section Works Line 2 guns C section 2 guns D Section, 2 guns B Section Support line 2 guns C " 1 gun D Section, 1 gun B Section. Relief complete by 4 pm Machine Gun in S. 5, & S 3. withdrawn to Brigade Reserve.	
	28th			
	29th		Indirect fire took place from I.F.P. 3. Traget Road & trench tramway Rounds expended 2500.	
	30th		Reconnaissance of trenches for alternative position.	

H. Y. Russell 2/Lt for
Capt. Morrison
106 Machine Gun Coy.

2449 Wt. W14957/M90 750,000 1/16 J.B.C. & A. Forms/C 2118/12.

WAR DIARY

Appendix 1. 7.9.16	2nd./Lt.R.Law reported for duty from 23rd.D.L.I. and posted to W Coy. 2nd./Lt.W.S.Cauvin reported for duty from 23rd.D.L.I.and posted to Y Coy.
Appendix 2. 11.9.16	2nd./Lt.W.G.Wiseman reported for duty from 3rd.D.L.I. and posted to W.Coy. 2nd./Lt.R.H.Meacock reported for duty from 21st.D.L.I. and posted to X Coy.
Appendix 3. 12.9.16	Lt.Col.B.C.Dent assumed command of Battalion.
Appendix 4. 13.9.16	2nd./Lt.G.W.Johnson reported for duty from 21st.D.L.I. and posted to Y Coy. 2nd./Lt.R.C.J.Allen reported for duty from 21st.D.L.I. and posted to Z.Coy. Draft of 29 men reported from Base.
Appendix 5. 14.9.16	Draft of 11 men reported from Base.
Appendix 6. 21.9.16	Draft of 9 men reported from Base
Appendix 7. 27.9.16	Draft of 10 men reported from Base.

E Cameron Capt
Adjt 19 D.L.I. 3/10/16

Instructions regarding War Diaries and Intelligence Summaries are contained in F. S. Regs., Part II. and the Staff Manual respectively. Title Pages will be prepared in manuscript.

WAR DIARY
or
~~INTELLIGENCE~~ SUMMARY
(Erase heading not required.)

Army Form C. 2118.

Vol 6

106. Machine Gun Coy

Place	Date	Hour	Summary of Events and Information	Remarks and references to Appendices
ARRAS.	1-10-16		Inter Company relief carried out by day-light. Winter time came into force, all clocks put back during the night one hour at 1.00am.	Map Ref 51b NW Roclincourt 1/10000
	2nd		Indirect fire carried out during the night on roads behind enemy's lines. Rounds expended 3,000.	
	3rd		A Vickers gun was damaged while mounted in the front line during the night by a stray bullet. No indirect fire was carried out this night.	51b NW 3 ARRAS 1/10000
	4th		Making necessary preparations for the Gas operation. Gas being now installed in our front line and ready for discharge tomorrow or next suitable wind at night. Indirect fire carried out from 1 F.P. LICE PIT on C.T.s leading to enemy's trenches. Rounds expended 2,000.	
	5th		Inter Company relief carried out by daylight. four guns & team in Brigade Reserve Billets.	
	6th		Received code at 7.30pm word ~~for~~ gas operation to commence by DUNCAN 9.30pm at 9.00 received code word JACK meaning operations cancelled. Coy. Hqrs moved up to advanced H.Q. at Wednesday Cave.	
	7th		Received at 7.00pm. code word DUNCAN 8.15. Coy H.Q. again moved up to advanced H.Qrs. at 7-45 Received at 7.45pm code word JACK mg operations cancelled, wind unfavourable.	

C.W. Menerson Capt
Comdg no 106 M.G. Coy.

2449 Wt. W14957/M90 750,000 1/16 J.B.C. & A. Forms/C.2118/12.

Instructions regarding War Diaries and Intelligence Summaries are contained in F. S. Regs., Part II. and the Staff Manual respectively. Title Pages will be prepared in manuscript.

WAR DIARY
or
~~INTELLIGENCE~~ SUMMARY
(Erase heading not required.)

Army Form C. 2118.

106 Machine Gun Coy

Place	Date	Hour	Summary of Events and Information	Remarks and references to Appendices
ARRAS	8 Oct. 1916		Received at 7.15 pm code word DUNCAN 8.45 pm. Coy H.Q again moved to advanced H.Q. all guns in readiness standing by at 7.50 pm. Gas discharged at 8.45 pm. Four machine guns firing indirect on special targets, roads, barrages etc. for two hours during & after cloud gas attack. Rounds expended 15,000.	Map Ref 51b N.W.1 Roclincourt 1/10000
	9th Oct.		Inter Company relief carried out by daylight. 4 guns & teams sent back on relief to Brigade Reserve Billets.	51b N.W.3 ARRAS 1/10000
	10th Oct		Indirect fire carried out from I.F.P. LICEPIT on SPECIAL target. Rounds expended 2,500.	
	11th "		Two Vickers guns in front line were relieved by two Lewis guns, Vickers guns moved back to position in Novels line (support line). Indirect fire carried out from I.F.P.3 on targets ranging 41°36 + 103°. Rounds expended 1,500.	
	12th "		Indirect fire carried out from LICEPIT position. Rounds expended 2,000	
	13th "		Inter Company relief carried out by daylight.	
	14th "		Indirect fire carried out from I.F.P. 1 & 3 on to roads behind enemy lines supposed to be used by his transport. Rounds expended 3,500	

Clemenson Capt
Comdg No 106 M G Coy

2449 Wt. W14957/M90 750,000 1/16 J.B.C. & A. Forms/C.2118/12.

Instructions regarding War Diaries and Intelligence Summaries are contained in F. S. Regs., Part II. and the Staff Manual respectively. Title Pages will be prepared in manuscript.

WAR DIARY
or
~~INTELLIGENCE SUMMARY~~
(Erase heading not required.)

Army Form C. 2118.

106th Machine Gun Coy.

Place	Date	Hour	Summary of Events and Information	Remarks and references to Appendices
ARRAS	16th Oct. 16		Indirect fire was carried out between 7 pm + 10 pm on road A17 b 8 1 and barraging following points: B.25 c 9.1, H 1 b 3.7 + H 1 a 9.5. Rounds expended 5,000	Map Ref 51b N.W.1 Roclincourt 1/10,000
	17th Oct.		The defence system reorganized, new scheme submitted.	51b N.W.3 ARRAS 1/10,000
	18th Oct.		Inter Coy Relief carried out during the day.	
	19th Oct.		Indirect machine gun fire carried out between 7 pm + midnight on points behind enemy's line. Rounds expended 4,000.	
	20th	"	Firing indirect on one of our aeroplanes that had come down behind enemy lines at B. 27 d. 2.4. Fire continued all night. 6,000 rounds expended.	
	21st	"	Inter Coy relief carried out during the day.	
	22nd		Indirect fire carried out between 10.30 pm till dawn on fallen aeroplane which enemy were ~~attempting~~ to carry away. Rounds expended 16,000 Target.	
	23rd		Continued at night to fire in vicinity of fallen aeroplane where much movement was reported.	

C W Menson Capt.
Comdg no 106 M G Coy

2449 Wt. W14957/M90 750,000 1/16 J.B.C. & A. Forms/C.2118/12.

Army Form C. 2118.

Instructions regarding War Diaries and Intelligence Summaries are contained in F. S. Regs., Part II. and the Staff Manual respectively. Title Pages will be prepared in manuscript.

WAR DIARY
or
INTELLIGENCE SUMMARY
(Erase heading not required.)

106 Machine Gun Coy.

Place	Date	Hour	Summary of Events and Information	Remarks and references to Appendices
	1916			
ARRAS	26th Oct		Indirect fire took place as under from three guns.	Map Ref.
			(1) From 7 till 9 pm the following points were barraged.	51b NW1
			H.1a.9.3, H.1b.3.6, H.1b.3.7, B.25.d.91.	Roclincourt
			(2) From 9 to midnight the Sunken road running to THELUS at A.18 was swept.	1/10,000
			(3) From 2 till 5 am the SUNKEN road running from B.13.c.10.1 to	51b NW3
			COMMANDANT'S HOUSE was swept.	ARRAS
	27th		Firing indirect from I.F.P. 2 Barraging H.1a.9.3, H.1b.3.6,	1/10,000
			H.1b.3.8, B.25.d.9.1. Rounds expended 3,500.	
	29th		Inter Coy Relief carried out by day, four guns & teams on relief	
			moved back to Brigade Reserve at Coy. Hdqrs.	
	30th		Two Vickers guns moved up to front line to fire at enemy parapet	
			during the hours of 1 and 3 am in accordance with plans for	
			a future enterprise.	
	31st		Two Vickers guns firing from front line and support line at G.6.b.1	
			G.6.d	

C W Merriman Capt
Comdg No 106 M.G. Coy.

2449 Wt. W14957/M90 750,000 1/16 J.B.C. & A. Forms/C.2118/12.

COPY No 5

SECRET

OPERATION ORDER No 11

The following Reliefs will take place within the Company on 9th October 1916

TEAM AT GUN POSITION	S.4	WILL STAND FAST.
"	M.G.5.	WILL STAND FAST.
" " "	S.2	" PROCEED AT 1.00 PM TO M.G.4
"	M.G.4	" ON RELIEF " S.2
"	M.G.1	STAND FAST
"	M.G.3	PROCEED AT 10.00 AM TO M.G.2
"	M.G.2	" ON RELIEF " M.G.3.
"	S.1	STAND FAST.
"	H.Q.B.5	" PROCEED AT 10.00 AM TO M.G.6
"	H.Q.B.6	" 10.00 AM " S.6
"	H.Q.B.7.	NOON M.G.8.
"	H.Q.B.8	NOON M.G.7.
"	M.G.7. M.G.8. M.G.6: S.6:	ON RELIEF TO BILLETS

2 (a)

Gun Teams at the following positions S.2 and M.G.3. will move off at times stated leaving one man behind to hand over Gun Position: Trench Stores &c.

(b)

Teams B.5 and B.6 will move off at 10.00 am Teams B.7 and B.8 will move off at Noon.

3 Only Guns and spare-parts will be taken with Guns to new positions

Copy No. 6

4. On Relief all Gun Teams will see that everything is handed over in a thorough manner to the incoming team

5. Section Officers will arrange for guides if required

6 Teams from M.G.7 and M.G.8. while at Billets will be ready to move off at once to S.3 and S.5 if required

7. The Emplacements of S.3 will be under O.C. NAP CENTRE and will be visited once daily by the N.C.O. from S.4.

8. The Emplacement of S.5 will be under O.C. NAP LEFT and will be visited once daily by the N.C.O. from S6.

These Emplacements will be kept clean and in good order

9. Teams will come under command of officers as follows.

O.C. NAP RIGHT.

2nd LIEUT W.A.R. RICHARDSON.

POSITIONS.	HEADQUARTERS.	SECTION.
M.G1: M.G2: M.G3. S1.	TELUS.	'A'

COPY. No 6 3.

9 (CONTD) O.C. NAP CENTRE

2nd LIEUT B.A.K NORMAN

POSITIONS	H.Q	SECTION
M.G.4: M.G.5: S2. S4	"WEDNESDAY"	"C"

O.C. NAP LEFT

2nd LIEUT. H.J. LEE.

POSITIONS	H.Q.	SECTION
MG6. MG7. MG8. S6	"ROCLINCOURT"	"B"

10. REPORTS will be rendered to H.Q by each Section Officer viz. O.C. NAP RIGHT. O.C. NAP CENTRE. O.C. NAP LEFT.

11. Completion of Relief to be reported to me at Coy. H.Q. by word "DONE" by wire

COPIES 1-2-3-4 to Section Officers
5 - War Diary
6 - File
7 - Brigade

ACKNOWLEDGE.

[signature] Lt. for O.C. 106. M.G. Coy.

8-10-16

Copy No 6

SECRET

OPERATION ORDER No 12

The following Relief will take place within the Companies on 13th October 1916

1. Team at Gun Position S.1 will proceed at Noon to M.G.2
" " " " M.G.2 " on Relief " S.1
" " " " M.G.3 " Stand Fast
" " " " M.G.1 " "
" " " " S.6 " Proceed at Noon to M.G.8
" " " " M.G.8 " on Relief " S.6
" " " " M.G.7 " Stand Fast
" " " " M.G.6 " "
" " " " H.Q. D.13 " Proceed at 10.00 A.M. to S.2
" " " " H.Q. D.14 " " 10.00 A.M. " S.4
" " " " H.Q. D.15 " " Noon " S.3
" " " " H.Q. D.16 " " Noon " M.G.4
Positions S2. S4. S3. M.G.4 " on Relief " Billets.

2 (a) Gun Teams at the following positions S1. and S6. will move off at times stated, leaving one man behind to hand over Gun Position Trench Stores &c

(b) Teams D 13 and D 14 will move off at 10.00 A.M. Teams D 15 and D 16 will move off at Noon

3 Only Guns and spare parts will be taken with Gun Team to new positions

4 On Relief all gun teams will see that everything is handed over in a thorough manner to the incoming team

Copy No. 5

5. Section Officers will arrange for guides if required

6. The Emplacement of S.5. will be under O.C. NAP LEFT, and will be visited once daily by the N.C.O. from S.6.

This Emplacement must be kept clean and in good order.

7. Teams will come under Command of Officers as follows.

O.C. NAP RIGHT

2nd LIEUT. H.A.R. RICHARDSON.

POSITIONS	H.Q.	SECTION
M.G.1: M.G.2: M.G.3. S1:	TELUS	'A'

O.C. NAP CENTRE

2nd LIEUT. F.A. HOOPER.

POSITIONS.	H.Q.	SECTION.
M.G.4: M.G.5: S2: S.4:	WEDNESDAY	'D'

O.C. NAP LEFT

2nd LIEUT. B.A.K. NORMAN

POSITIONS	H.Q.	SECTION
M.G.6: M.G.7: M.G.8: S6:	ROCLINCOURT.	'B'

8. Reports will be rendered to H.Q. by each Section Officer. viz. O.C. NAP RIGHT; O.C. NAP CENTRE. AND O.C. NAP LEFT.

9. Completion of Relief to be reported to me at Coy. H.Q. by word 'CLEAR' by wire

COPIES 1-2-3-4 TO SECTION OFFICERS
5 . WAR DIARY
6 . FILE
7 . BRIGADE.

H.M. Bell Lt. for
O.C. 106. M.G. Coy

12-10-16

Copy No. 5

SECRET.

OPERATION ORDER No. 13

1. The Following Relief will take place within the Coy. on 17th October 1916.

TEAMS AT GUN POSITIONS OF "B" SECT. WILL STAND FAST. — NO CHANGE —

" " " "D" " STAND FAST. — NO CHANGE —

" " "	H.Q. "C" 9.	WILL PROCEED AT.	2.30 P.M. TO	OBSERVATORY. RED. M.G. 1.
" " "	H.Q. "C" 10	" "	2.30. P.M. "	M.G. 2
" " "	H.Q. "C" 11	" "	3.30. P.M. "	M.G. 3
" " "	H.Q. "C" 12	" "	3.30. P.M. "	S. 1

On RELIEF TEAMS AT. M.G.1. M.G.2. M.G.3. S1. will PROCEED TO BILLETS.

2. Teams "C" 9 and "C" 10 will move off at 2-30 P.M. Teams "C" 11 and "C" 12 will move off at 3.30 p.m.

3. Only Guns and spare-parts will bee taken with Gun-Teams to new position

4. On Relief, all Gun-Teams will see that everything is handed over in a thorough manner to the incoming teams

Copy 2

5. The Emplacement of S.5 will be under O.C J.K. 25L. and will be visited once daily by the N.C.O. from S.6.

This Emplacement must be kept clean and in good order

6. Teams will come under command of Officers as follows.

"O.C. J.K. 25 R."

2nd LIEUT. H.E. TALBOT

POSITIONS.	H.Q.	SECTION.
M.G.1: M.G.2: M.G.3: S.1.	TELUS	'C'

"O.C. J.K. 25 C"

2nd LIEUT: B.A.K. NORMAN

POSITIONS.	H.Q.	SECTION
M.G.5. M.G.4. S2. S3	'WEDNESDAY'	'D'

O.C. "J.K. 25 L"

2nd LIEUT: H.J. LEE

POSITIONS.	H.Q.	SECTION
M.G.7: M.G.8: ~~4.~~ S6: S4:	ROCLINCOURT.	'B'

7. Reports will be rendered to H.Q. by each Section Officer O.C. "J.K. 25 R": O.C. "J.K. 25.C" & O.C. J.K 25L.

8. Completion of Relief to be reported to me at Coy. H.Q. by word "MONK" by wire

COPIES 1-2-3-4 TO SECTION OFFICERS
5 - WAR DIARY
6 - FILE
7. - BRIGADE.

16-10-16.

[illegible signature] for O.C. 106 M.G. Coy

COPY No 5

SECRET

OPERATION ORDER No 14

1 THE FOLLOWING RELIEFS WILL TAKE PLACE WITHIN THE COMPANY ON 21ST OCTOBER 1916.

~~TEAM AT GUN POSITION~~ ~~WILL PROCEED AT~~ TO

TEAMS OF 'D' SECT. WILL STAND FAST - NO CHANGE -

'C' SECT. WILL STAND FAST - NO CHANGE -

AT H.Q. A1 WILL PROCEED AT 8 30 AM TO S6

H.Q. A2 " " 8 30 AM TO S4

H.Q. A3 " " 8 30 AM TO M.G.7

H.Q. A4 " " 8 30 AM TO M.G.8

S6: S4: M.G.7: M.G.8 WILL PROCEED ON RELIEF TO BILLETS.

2 Teams A1: A2: A3: A4: will move off at 8 30 A.M.

3 Only Guns and Spare-Parts will be taken with Gun-Teams to new positions.

4 On Relief all Gun Teams will see that everything is handed over in a thorough manner to the incoming teams.

Copy 5

5. The Emplacement of S.5 will be under O.C. T.K. 25L and will be visited once daily by the N.C.O from S.6.
This Emplacement must be kept clean and in good order.

6 Teams will come under command of Officers as follows.

O.C. T.K. 25. R.
2nd LIEUT B.A.K. NORMAN

POSITIONS. H.Q. SECTION
M.G.1. M.G.2: M.G.3. S.1. TELUS. "C"

O.C. T.K. 25. C.
2nd LIEUT F.A. HOOPER.

POSITIONS. H.Q. SECTION
M.G.4. M.G.5. S.2. S.3. WEDNESDAY. "D"

O.C. T.K. 25 L.
2nd LIEUT H.E. TALBOT.

POSITIONS
M.G.8. M.G.7. S.6. S.4. ROCLINCOURT. "A"

7 Reports will be rendered to H.Q. by each Section Officer viz: O.C. T.K. 25 R: O.C. T.K. 25C. O.C. T.K. 25 L.

8 Completion of Relief to be reported to me at Coy. H.Q. by word by wire

COPIES 1-2-3-4 To Section Officers
5. To WAR DIARY
6 - FILE
7. - BRIGADE.

20-10-16.

[signature] Lt.

COPY. No. 5

SECRET.

OPERATION ORDER No 15

1 The following Relief will take place within the Company on 25th October 1916

TEAM AT GUN POSITION	S6	HILL PROCEED	AT 11.00 AM.	TO M.G.7.
" " " "	S4	" "	" 1.00 PM.	" M.G 8.
" " " "	M.G.7.	" "	ON RELIEF	" S6.
" " " "	M.G.8	" "	"	" S4.
" " " "	M.G.1.	" "	AT 10.30 AM.	" M.G.3
" " " "	S1.	" "	" NOON	" M.G.2
" " " "	M.G.3	" "	ON RELIEF	" M.G.1
" " " "	M.G.2.	" "	"	" S.1.
" " " "	H.Q. "B" 5	" "	AT 1.00 PM.	" S2.
" " " "	H.Q. "B" 6	" "	" 1.00 PM.	" M.G.5.
" " " "	H.Q. "B" 7.	" "	" 1.00 PM.	" M.G.4.
" " " "	H.Q. "B" 8	" "	" 1.00 PM.	" S.3.
" " " "	S2; M.G5; M.G4; S3.	"	ON RELIEF	" BILLETS.

2 Teams S6; S4; M.G.1, and S.1. will move off at times stated, leaving one man behind to hand over Gun Position, Tripod, Trench-Stores &c.

Teams "B" 5; "B" 6; "B" 7; and "B" 8. will move off at 1-00 PM.

3. Guide from M.G.4; will be at WEDNESDAY AVE H.Q. at 2 pm. to guide relieving team to new position

Other Guides will be arranged for by Section Officers if required.

Copy 4.

4 Only Guns and and Spare Parts will be taken with Gun Teams to new position

5. On Relief all Gun Teams will see that everything is handed over in a through manner to the incoming team

6. The Emplacement of S.5 will be under O.C. J.K. 25 L and will be visited once daily by the N.C.O. from S.6.

This Emplacement must be kept clean and in good order.

7. Teams will come under command of Officers as follows.

O.C. J.K. 25 R.

2nd LIEUT. B.A.K. NORMAN.

POSITIONS	HEADQUARTERS.	SECTION
M.G.1; M.G.2; M.G.3: S1:	TELUS	C

O.C. J.K. 25 C.

2nd LIEUT. H.J. LEE

2nd LIEUT. R. SKEVINGTON

POSITIONS.	HEADQUARTERS.	SECTION
M.G.4; M.G.5; S2: S3:	WEDNESDAY.	B

O.C. J.K. 25 L.

2nd LIEUT. H.E. TALBOT.

POSITIONS.	HEADQUARTERS.	SECTION
M.G.8: M.G.7: S6: S4:	ROLLINCOURT.	A

Appx 'H'

3

8 Reports will be rendered to H.Q. by each Section officer viz: O.C. T.K. 25 R: O.C. T.K. 25 C and O.C. T.K. 25 L.

9. Completion of Relief to be reported to me at Coy. H.Q. by word 'CIRCUS' by wire

COPIES. 1 - SECTION OFFICER.
2 " "
3 " "
4 " "
5 WAR DIARY.
6 FILE
7. BRIGADE.

24/10/16

[illegible] Lieut.
O.C. NAPIER.

COPY No 5

SECRET

OPERATION ORDER No. 16.

1/ The following Reliefs will take place within the Company on the 29-10-16.

TEAM AT GUN POSITION	S3	WILL PROCEED AT 1.00P.M.	TO MG 4
" " " "	MG 4	" " ON RELIEF	TO S3
" " " H.Q.	"D" 13	" " AT 1.00P.M.	" MG 3
" " " "	"D" 14	" " " 1.00P.M.	" MG 2
" " " "	"D" 15	" " " 1.00P.M.	" MG 1
" " " "	"D" 16.	" " " 1.00P.M.	" S1
" " " POSITIONS. MG 3 MG 2. MG 1 S1. ON RELIEF WILL PROCEED TO BILLETS.			

2/ Teams "D" 13, "D" 14, "D" 15, "D" 16, will move off at 1.00P.M.

Team at S.3 will move off at time stated leaving one man behind to hand over Gun Position, Trench Stores etc.

3/ Only Guns, Tripods, and Spare-parts will be taken with Gun-teams to new positions.

4/ On Relief all Gun-teams will see that everything is handed over in a thorough manner to the incoming team.

Copy No. 5.

SECRET.

5/ The emplacement of S5. will be under O.C. MAP. LEFT and will be visited once daily by the N.C.O. from S6.

This emplacement must be kept clean and in good order.

6/ The teams will come under Command of Officers as follows:—

O.C. MAP. RIGHT.

2ND LT. F.A. HOOPER.

POSITIONS.	H.Q.	SECTION.
M.G1. MG3. MG2. S1.	TELLUS.	'D'

O.C. MAP. RIGHT.

2ND LT. R. SKEVINGTON.

POSITIONS.	H.Q.	SECTION
MG.4 MG5 S2 S3	WEDNESDAY.	"B"

O.C. MAP. LEFT.

2ND LT. H.E. TALBOT.

POSITIONS.	H.Q	SECTION.
MG8, MG7, S6. S4.	ROCLINCOURT.	"A"

7/ Reports will be rendered to H.Q. by each Section Officer viz:—

O.C. MAP. LEFT.
O.C. MAP CENTRE
O.C. MAP RIGHT.

COPY. NO. 5

3

8 | Completion of Relief to be reported to me at Coy H.Q. by word "ENCORE" by wire.

COPIES. 1 SECTION OFFICER.
2 " "
3 " "
4 " "
5 WAR DIARY
6 FILE
7 BRIGADE.

28/10/16.

[signature] Lt.
O.C. 106 M.G. Coy

SECRET

COPY No. 5

MACHINE GUN OPERATION ORDER No. 17.

1/ The M.G. Coy will combine with a scheme of the WEST YORKS for a minor operation.

2/ Two Guns 'D' section under 2nd LIEUT F.A. HOOPER will fire from Trench 104 in the direction of KENT CRATER at the enemy's wire and parapet from 1 a.m. until the explosion of the Bangaline Torpedo.

One Gun will fire at a time, the second Gun opening fire as soon as the first ceases, they will fire at the rate of 400 rds: per minute.

Maximum Expenditure 3000 rds:

3/ 3 Guns will fire indirect sweeping the hostile support line and Communication Trenches.

1 Gun from No. 2 L.F.P. off FISH AVENUE under 2nd Lieut H.E. TALBOT will fire on Barrage M.

[(B. 25. a6. ½) (B25. a9. ½) (B25. b4. 3) (B25. b1. 6)]

1 Gun from A29. C3½. 1½ under 2nd LIEUT R. SKEVINGTON will fire on Barrage N.

[(A30. d9. 4) (B25. C3. 5.) (H1. a1. 6) (H1. a4½. 9) (G6 b 8½. 4)]

COPY. No. 5

3 (Contd.)
1 Gun from Trench 40 (G5 c.2.8) under 2ND LIEUT. B.A.K. NORMAN will fire on Barrage O.

[[G6. d3. 2)(G6. d5. 1)(G6. d9. 1)(H1. c2. 1)]]

4. These guns will fire on three (3) red rockets ascending and cease on the Artillery ceasing.

5. Maxim expenditure of ammunition 10,000 rds per gun.

6. These guns will be controlled by the Coy. Commander from advanced Coy Hd.qrs.

7. All messages, reports to be sent to advanced Coy Hd.qrs.

WEDNESDAY AVENUE (Telephone P.C. exchange J.A. 34)

Acknowledge please. Commission Cmdg No 6 M G Coy

COPY	No 1.	2ND LT. H.E. TALBOT
"	" 2	2ND LT. R. SKEVINGTON
"	" 3	2ND LT. B.A.K. NORMAN.
"	" 4	2ND LT. F.A. HOOPER
"	" 5	WAR DIARY.
"	" 6	FILE
"	" 7	BDE Hd qrs.
"	" 8	RT. BN.
"	" 9	T.M.B.

31—10—16

ISSUED AT 8.30 P.M.

SECRET. COPY. NO. 5

OPERATION ORDER NO. 18.

1. From receipt of this order the Anti-aircraft Emplacements will be manned from dawn to dusk

2. Guns, tripods, aircraft mountings, rangefinders, telescopes or field glasses and 500 rounds in metallic belts will be taken daily.

3. One N.C.O. one machine Gunner and one range finder will be on duty daily.

4. The N.C.O. will fire on receiving information from the observer that a hostile aeroplane is approaching.

5 The Range-taker will give the range direction and approximate angle of the machine.

6. No angle less than 20° or more than 80° will be attempted

7. The N.C.O. will verify the nature of the plane before firing.

8. 1000 Rds. of S.A.A. will be kept in each emplacement as a reserve

9. The emplacements will be occupied on the word WHITE from Hdqrs; and not occupied on the word DARK.

IN THE FIELD.
31-10-16.
ISSUED AT 10PM.

Clemenson Capt
Comdg 1st M.G. Coy

COPY No. 1 RT. SECTOR NAPIER.
" No. 2. CENTRE SECTOR NAPIER.
" No. 3. LEFT SECTOR NAPIER.
" No 4 ———
" No 5 WAR DIARY.
" No 6 FILE
" No. 7. BDE HD. QRS.

Copy No 7

SECRET.

Operation Order No 20

1/ The following Reliefs will take place within the Company on the 7-11-16

Team at H.Q "A1 will proceed at 2pm to MGR4 - S3

" " 2 " " 2.00pm MGR3 - S2

" " 3 " " 2.00pm MG4 - MG4

" " 4 " " 2.00pm MG3 - MG5

2 Teams at MGR4, MGR3, MG4, MG3. on Relief will proceed to H. Q. Billets

All other teams stand fast

2 Teams A1, A2, A3, A4 will move off at 2.00pm taking with them Guns Spare parts and Tripods

3 Only Guns Tripods and Spare-parts will be taken with Gun teams to new positions

4 On Relief all Gun teams will see that everything is handed over in a thorough manner. to the incoming team

5 All teams moving to and from Trenches to Billets must not use Bridge over Canal near GAS WORKS

— by order

2

6 The teams will come under Command of Officers as follows

O.C. NAP RIGHT

2ND LT F.A. HOOPER.

POSITIONS.	H.Q	SECTION
MGR1, MG2, MG1, MGR2. IFP.4, IFP6 AAP3	TELUS	"D"

O.C. NAP. CENTRE

2ND LT H.E. TALBOT.

POSITIONS	HQ	SECTION.
MG4, MG3, MGR3, MGR4 IFP3, IFP5, AAP2.	WEDNESDAY	A.

O.C. LEFT.

2ND LT R. SKEVINGTON.

POSITIONS.	H.Q.	SECTION.
MG6, MG5, MGR6, MGR5 IFP1, IFP2, AAP1	ROCLINCOURT	C

7 Reliefs will be reported to H.Q. by each Section Officer viz:—

O.C. NAP LEFT

O.C. NAP CENTRE

O.C. NAP RIGHT.

3/

Completion of Relief to be reported to me at my H.Q by word "CHASE" by wire.

COPIES 1 SECTION OFFICER
2 " "
3 " "
4 " "
5 WAR DIARY
6 FILE
7 BRIGADE.

ACKNOWLEDGE.

[signature] Lt.
for
7.11.16. O.C. NAPIER.

Instructions regarding War Diaries and Intelligence Summaries are contained in F. S. Regs., Part II. and the Staff Manual respectively. Title Pages will be prepared in manuscript.

WAR DIARY
or
~~INTELLIGENCE SUMMARY~~
(Erase heading not required.)

Army Form C. 2118.

106. M. G. Coy.

Vol 7

Place	Date	Hour	Summary of Events and Information	Remarks and references to Appendices
ARRAS.	1 Nov.	1916.	Two Guns firing indirect between the hours of 1 am & 4 am. on enemys Support line G.6.b. and G.6.d. where movement had been seen during day. 1500 rounds.	Map. Ref. Sheet 51B NW1.
	Nov 2.	..	Three Vickers guns firing indirect throughout the night cooperating with a raiding party which successfully entered the Enemys Lines. Barraging B.25b. A30d H1 + G6. 12000 rounds	
	No 3.	..	Inter Coy. relief took place during the hours of daylight. COMMANDANTS HOUSE Rd. + TELLYS Rd. swept by indirect fire, from 6 to 10 pm. 5000 rounds	
	Nov. 4.		Two Vickers guns firing indirect between the hours of 9 pm & 2 am. along the Sunken TELLUS ROAD. and A18.c.7.2. to A.12.d.6.5. 5000 rounds.	
	No 5.		BAILIEUL Rd. & Commandants HOUSE Rd swept from 6 pm to 1 am. by indirect fire. 10000 rounds.	
	Nov 6.		Three Vickers guns firing indirect between hours of 6 pm & 1 am on points 14.1 B.25. and B.25. central. 2500 rounds.	
	Nov. 7.		Inter Company relief took place during the day. BAILIEUL Rd. barraged 1500 rounds	
	Nov. 8.		Three guns firing indirect during the night from 5 to 9 pm. barraging the BAILIEUL ROAD, B 19.c. central. + road leading to COMMANDANTS. HOUSE. 3000 rounds.	
	Nov. 9.		Three Vickers guns firing indirect from 8 pm to midnight on B.13.c.2.3 B.13.c.7.9. B.19.a.8.6, B.19.b.3.9. 2000 rounds.	
	No 10.		Hostile Aeroplanes driven off by our Anti Aircraft Vickers guns. Indirect fire BAILIEUL Rd. from 10 to midnight. 3000 rounds.	
	No 11.		Inter Company relief took place during the hours of daylight. Indirect fire onto TELLUS Rd. Commandants House Rd. between 8 & 10 pm. 4000 rounds	

2449 Wt. W14957/M90 750,000 1/16 J.B.C. & A. Forms/C.2118/12.

Instructions regarding War Diaries and Intelligence Summaries are contained in F. S. Regs., Part II. and the Staff Manual respectively. Title Pages will be prepared in manuscript.

WAR DIARY
or
~~INTELLIGENCE~~ SUMMARY

(Erase heading not required.)

Army Form C. 2118.

106. M. G. Coy.

Place	Date	Hour	Summary of Events and Information	Remarks and references to Appendices
ARRAS	Nov. 12	1916	Vickers gun firing indirect from 5 pm to 1.00 am. barraging H. 1 a 9 3 H. 1. b 3 8. B. 25. d. 9. 1. H. 1 b. 3. 6. and H. 14. a. 9. and sweeping trolley lines and Barraging points B. 13 a. 2 3, B. 13. a. 7. 9. B. 19. b 8. 3. B. 19. b. 8. 9. 5000 rounds	Map. Ref 51B N.W. Sheet.
	Nov. 13		Enemys tracks & roads swept during the night A. 18. c. 7. 2. to A. 18. b. 7. 9. 8000 rounds Commandants House Rd & Telus Rd	
	Nov. 14		After dark indirect machine gun fire was brought to bear on the enemy trolley lines and the area about. A 17 d. & Bailleul Rd. 5000 rounds	
	Nov. 15		Inter Coy. relief took place & indirect fire on Bailleul Rd. 1500 rounds	
	Nov. 16		Vickers gun fired during the night at intervals on tracks visible in Air photos about H. 1 & B. 25 & during afternoon combining with Artillery fired indirect. 4000 rounds	
	Nov. 17		During the night Vickers gun played on the ARRAS - BAILIEUL ROAD and the ground between B. 26. c 4 3. & B. 25. b. 3. 4. & Telus & Commandants Ho. Rd. 7000 rounds	
	Nov. 18		Indirect M. G. fire was directed on the roads & trolley lines leading to TELUS & COMMANDANTS HOUSE between 7 & 10 pm. 2000 rounds	
	Nov. 19		Inter. Company relief took place during the hours of daylight. Indirect fire in connection with Artillery strafe on communication trenches between 3.20 & 4.15 pm	5000 rounds
	Nov. 20	/	The BAILIEUL ROAD and the road in A. 18. b. were swept by two Vickers M. G. during the night. 1000 rounds.	
	Nov. 21		Three Vickers gun firing on enemy tracks & roads during the night; A 30 b. 3 2 to B. 19 c 3. 2, B. 25. a 0 1, to B. 19 b. 4. 4., B. 25. c. 1. 8. to B. 25 d. 9 7. H. 1. a. 3 9. to B. 25. d 3. 2. 8000 rounds.	

[signature] Commdg. No. 106 M.G.C.

2449 Wt. W14957/M90 750,000 1/16 J.B.C. & A. Forms/C.2118/12.

Army Form C. 2118.

WAR DIARY
or
~~INTELLIGENCE SUMMARY~~
(Erase heading not required.)

Instructions regarding War Diaries and Intelligence Summaries are contained in F. S. Regs., Part II. and the Staff Manual respectively. Title Pages will be prepared in manuscript.

106th M.G. Coy.

Place	Date	Hour	Summary of Events and Information	Remarks and references to Appendices
ARRAS.	Nov. 23 1916		Inter. Coy. Relief took place during the hours of daylight. Indirect fire onto Road at point 9 21 from 6 to 7 pm. 1000 rounds	Map Ref. Sheet 51B N.W.1
	Nov. 24		Two Machine Guns fire indirect and swept the road from A.18 central & the SUNKEN ROAD to COMMANDANT'S HOUSE. 6,000 rounds	
	Nov. 25.		Three M.G.s firing indirect on the road junction ARRAS BAILIEUL ROAD at H.1.6.0.3. H.1.6.3.8. H.16.5.6. 3000 rounds	
	Nov. 26.		In conjunction with a raid made by the 19th D.L.I. on the enemy trench at A.29.6.9.9. Indirect M.G. fire was brought to bear on the enemy's support line, strong points & tracks about B 19 a & A 24 a. 8500 rounds	
	Nov. 27th		Inter. Coy. relief took place during the hours of daylight. & indirect fire on Telus Rd. Commandant's House & point 121 — 6000 rounds	
	Nov. 28th		Indirect machine gun fire carried out between 7 pm & 9 pm upon the ARRAS—BAILIEUL ROAD. 1500 rounds	
	Nov. ~~29~~ 30th		The following points were barraged by indirect M.G. fire between 10 pm & 1 am. A.30.d.9.4, B.25.a.1.6, G.6.b.9.5, H.1.a.4.9. 9000 rounds.	
	~~Nov 31st~~		~~Inter Coy. relief took place during the hours of daylight~~	

Commanding No 106 M.G. Coy.

2449 Wt. W14957/M90 750,000 1/16 J.B.C. & A. Forms/C.2118/12.

COPY. No. [illegible]

SECRET

OPERATION ORDER No 19.

1/ The following Reliefs will take place within the Company on the 3-11-16.

Team at H.Q. "C" 9. will proceed at 2pm to S4
" " "C" 10 " " " 2.00 pm to S.6
" " "C" 11 " " " 2.00 pm to MG.8
" " "C" 12 " " " 2.00 pm to MG.7

Teams at positions S4; S6; MG8; MG7; on Relief will proceed to H.Q. Billets
All other teams stand fast.

2/ Teams "C" 9; "C" 10; "C" 11; "C" 12; will move off at 2.00 p.m taking with them Guns Spare parts and Tripods.

3/ Only Guns, Tripods and Spare parts will be taken with Gun teams to new positions

4 On Relief all Gun Teams will see that everything is handed over in a thorough manner to the incoming team.

OVER.

5/ The teams will come under command of Officers as follows:-

O.C. NAP. RIGHT.

2ND LT. F.A. HOOPER.

POSITIONS.	H.Q	SECTION
MG1; MG3; MG2; S1.	TELUS	"D"

O.C. NAP. CENTRE.

2ND LT. R. SKEVINGTON.

POSITIONS	H.Q.	SECTION
MG.4; MG5; S2; S3	WEDNESDAY.	"B"

O.C. NAP. LEFT.

2ND LT. B.A.K. NORMAN.

POSITIONS.	H.Q.	SECTION.
MG8; MG,7; S6; S4;	ROCLINCOURT.	"C"

6/ Reports will be rendered to H.Q. by each Section Officer viz:-

O.C. NAP. LEFT.
O.C. NAP. CENTRE.
O.C. NAP RIGHT.

3.

7 Completion of Relief to be reported to me at Coy H.Q. by word "HUNT" by wire

COPIES 1 SECTION OFFICER
2 " "
3 " "
4 " "
5 WAR DIARY
6 FILE
7 BRIGADE

1-11-16

[signature] Lt.
for O.C. NAPIER.

ACKNOWLEDGE

COPY NO 4

SECRET

OPERATION ORDER No 20

1/ The following Reliefs will take place within the Company on the 7-11-16

Team at H.Q. "A" 1 will proceed at 2pm to MGR4 = S3
"	"	2	"	"	2.00pm " MGR3 = S2
"	"	3	"	"	2.00pm " MG4 = MG4
"	"	4	"	"	2.00pm " MG3 = MG5

2 Teams at MGR4, MGR3, MG4, MG3, on Relief will proceed to H.Q. Billets

All other teams stand fast

2 Teams A1, A2, A3, A4 will move off at 2.00 pm taking with them Guns Spare parts and Tripods

3 Only Guns Tripods and Spare-parts will be taken with Gun teams to new positions

4/ On Relief all Gun teams will see that everything is handed over in a thorough manner. to the incoming team

5/ All teams moving to and from Trenches to Billets must not use Bridge over Canal near GAS WORKS

– by order

2

6 The teams will come under Command of Officers as follows

O.C. MAP RIGHT

2ND Lt. F.A. HOOPER

POSITIONS.	H.Q	SECTION
MGR1, MG2, MG1, MGR2 IFP.4, IFP6 AAP3	TELUS	"D"

O.C. MAP. CENTRE

2ND Lt. H.E. TALBOT.

POSITIONS	HQ	SECTION.
MG4, MG.3, MGR.3, MGR4 IFP3, IFP5, AAP2.	WEDNESDAY	A.

O.C. LEFT.

2ND Lt. R. SKEVINGTON.

POSITIONS	H.Q.	SECTION.
MG6, MG5, MGR6, MGR5 IFP1, IFP2, AAP1.	ROCLINCOURT	C

7 Reports will be rendered to H.Q by each Section Officer viz:—

O.C. MAP LEFT

O.C. MAP CENTRE

O.C. MAP RIGHT

3

Completion of Relief to be reported to me at Coy H Q by word "CHASE" by wire.

COPIES	1	SECTION OFFICER
	2	" "
	3	" "
	4	" "
	5	WAR DIARY
	6	FILE
	7	BRIGADE.

ACKNOWLEDGE

COPY No 5

SECRET.

OPERATION ORDER No 21

MAP REF

1/ The following Reliefs will take place within the Company on the 11 — 11 — 16

Team at H.Q B 5 will proceed at 2 pm to MGR 1
" " B 6 " " 2 pm " MGR 2
" " B 7 " " 2 pm " MG 1
" " B 8 " " 2 pm " MG 2

Gun team D13, D14, D15, D16 on Relief will proceed to H.Q. Billets.

All other teams stand fast.

2/ Only Guns Tripods & Spare-parts will be taken with Gun teams to new positions

3/ On Relief all Gun teams will see that everything is handed over in a thorough manner to the incoming team

4/ All teams moving to and from Trenches to Billets must not use Bridge over Canal near GAS WORKS —

BY ORDER.

5/ The teams will come under Command of Officers as follows:—

O.C. MAP RIGHT

2ND LT R SKEVINGTON.

POSITIONS	H.Q	SECTION.
M.GR1, MG2, MG1, MGR2, IFP 4, IFP 6, AAP 3	TELUS	'B'

O.C. MAP CENTRE

2ND LT H E TALBOT.

POSITIONS.	H Q.	SECTION.
MG4, MG3, MGR 3, MGR4, IFP 3, IFP5, AAP2	WEDNESDAY.	"F"

3

O.C. MAP. LEFT.

2ND LT. H.N. FISHER

POSITIONS	H.Q.	SECTION.
MG1, MG5, MGR6, MGR5, IFP1, IFP2, GAP1.	ROCLINCOURT	"C"

5/ (contd.)

6 Reports will be rendered to H.Q. by each section officer viz:—
O.C. MAP. LEFT
O.C. MAP. CENTRE
O.C. MAP. RIGHT

Completion of Relief to be reported at Coy H.Q. by word HOUND by wire

Clomeran Capt
Comdg No 106 M.G.C.

COPIES 1 SECTION OFFICER.
2 " "
3 " "
4 " "
5 WAR DIARY.
6 FILE.
7 BRIGADE.

ACKNOWLEDGE.

ISSUED AT 7-00PM

COPY. No 5

SECRET

1

OPERATION ORDER No. 22.

MAP REFERENCE. 51 b. N.W. 1 Ed. 4a.

1/ The following Reliefs will take place within the Company on the 15-11-16

Team at H.Q. D13. will proceed at 2pm. to M.GR. 5
" " 14 " " 2pm. " MGR 6
" " 15. " " 2pm. " MG. 6
" " 16. " " 2pm. " MG 5

Gun teams C9, C10, C11, C12 on Relief will proceed to H.Q. Billets.
All other teams stand fast.

2/ Only Guns, Tripods and Spare-parts will be taken with gun teams to new positions

3/ On Relief all gun teams will see that everything is handed over in a thorough manner to the incoming team.

4/ All teams moving to and from Trenches & Billets must not use Bridge over Canal near GAS WORKS – BY ORDER.

5/ Teams will come under Command of Officers as follows:–

O.C MAP RIGHT
2nd LT. H J. LEE.

POSITIONS	H.Q.	SECTION
MGR1, MG2, MG1, MGR2, IFP, 4 IFP6, AAP3.	TELUS	"B"

O.C. MAP CENTRE
2ND LT. H.E TALBOT – 2ND LT. ~~H.M. FISHER~~ C. J. THOMAS

POSITIONS.	H Q.	SECTION
MG4, MG3, MGR3, MGR4. IFP3, IFP5, AAP.2	WEDNESDAY.	A

2

O.C. MAP LEFT

2nd Lt F. A. HOOPER

POSITIONS	HQ	SECTION
MG6, MG5, MGR 6, MGR5 IFP1, IFP2, AAP1 ROCLINCOURT		D.

6 Reports will be rendered to H.Q. by each Section Officer viz:-

O.C. MAP LEFT

O.C. MAP CENTRE

O.C. MAP RIGHT

Completion of Relief will be reported at Coy H.Q. by word "WHIP" by wire

C W Menzies [illegible]

Comdg No 106 MG Coy.

COPIES 1 SECTION OFFICER
2 " "
3 " "

ACKNOWLEDGE.

4 " "
5 WAR DIARY
6 FILE

ISSUED AT 7.00P.m.

7 BRIGADE

Copy no. 6 Secret

Operation order No 23

1. The following scheme in cooperation with artillery will take place this afternoon at 4 pm.

2 Machine gun indirect fire will open on the artillery barrage commencing.

3 Guns as under will take part.

1.F.P.5. one gun of D. Section under 2nd Lt F.A. HOOPER Magnetic bearings. 87°. 89° and 93° Range 2400x search to 3000x

1.F.P.6 one gun of A Section under 2nd Lt H.E. TALBOT. Magnetic bearings. 60°. 63° and 68° Range 2100x search to 2800x

1.F.P.4. one gun of B. Section under 2nd Lt. R. SKEVINGTON Special Barrage.

4. Maximum no of rounds per gun 3000.

5. Fire will cease at 5 pm.

Issued at 11.30 pm.
16/11/16.

C W Merrison Capt
Comdg. M.G. Coy.

Copy No 1. Nap. Rt.   Copy no 5 War D.
" " 2 Nap. Cen.   " " 6 File
" " 3 Nap. Left.   " " 7. Bde.
" " 4 Reserve.   " " 8. War D.

COPY. No 5

SECRET.

OPERATION ORDER No 24.

MAP REFERENCE 51b. N.W.1 Ed 4a.

1/ The following Reliefs will take place within the Company on the 19–11–16

Team at H.Q. C9 will proceed at 1pm to MG 3
" " C10 " " 1pm " MG 4
" " C11 " " 1pm " MGR 3
" " C12 " " 1pm " MGR 4

Gun teams A1, A2, A3, A4 on Relief will proceed to H.Q. Billets

All other teams stand fast.

2/ Only, Guns, Tripods and Spare-parts will be taken with gun teams to new positions

3/ On Relief all gun-teams will see that everything is handed over in a thorough manner to the incoming team.

4/ Teams will come under command of Officers as follows:—

O.C. MAP RIGHT.

2nd Lt R. SKEVINGTON

POSITIONS	H Q	SECTION
MGR1, MG2, MG1, MGR2, IFP4, IFP6, AAP3.	TELUS	"B".

O.C. MAP CENTRE

2nd Lt H. N. FISHER.

POSITIONS.	H. O.	SECTION.
MG4, MG3, MGR3, MGR4, IFP3, IFP5, AAP2,	WEDNESDAY	"C"

2.

O.C. NAP LEFT.
2nd Lt F.A. HOOPER

POSITIONS.	H.Q	SECTION.
MG6, MG5, MGR6, MGR5, JFP1, JFP2, AAP1	ROCLINCOURT.	"D"

5/ Reports will be rendered as usual

Completion of relief will be reported at Coy H.Q by word "BONNE"

H. ... Lt
for CAPTAIN,
O.C. 100th MACHINE GUN COY.

COPIES 1. SECTION OFFICER
2. " "
ACKNOWLEDGE. 3. " "
4. " "
5. WAR DIARY
ISSUED AT 7 P.M 6. FILE
7. BRIGADE.

8

Copy No. [illegible]

Operation Order No. [illegible]

1. The following [illegible] [illegible] [illegible] [illegible] [illegible] [illegible] [illegible] [illegible] [illegible] [illegible] [illegible] [illegible] [illegible] [illegible] [illegible] [illegible] [illegible]

2. [illegible] [illegible] [illegible] [illegible] [illegible] [illegible] [illegible] [illegible] [illegible] [illegible] [illegible]

3. Guns [illegible] [illegible] will [illegible] [illegible]

1.F.P.5 One gun of "C" Section under 2nd Lt H. M. Fisher will [illegible] the following bearings

R { 9[illegible]° / 93° Magnetic / 9[illegible]° } Range 1900 / [illegible]00

S { 98° / 99° Magnetic / 101° } 1900 to 2900

1.F.P.6 One gun of "B" Section under 2nd Lt R. Shevington will [illegible] the following bearings

T { 6[illegible]° / 64° Magnetic / 65° / 6[illegible]° } Range 19[illegible] to 2[illegible]

V { 88° / 90° } 2[illegible]00 to 3000

4. No. of rounds [illegible] per gun.

5. Reports to be sent to F.A. 34.

[illegible] [illegible] [illegible] 19-11-16

Copies No. 1 [illegible] 5 [illegible]
2 [illegible] 6 [illegible]
3 [illegible] 7 [illegible]
4 [illegible] 8 [illegible]

[illegible] [signature]

Copy No. 4

Secret

Operation Order No. 26

1. [illegible] with [illegible] [illegible] [illegible] [illegible] Attack [illegible] flies [illegible] [illegible] [illegible]
2. [illegible] Gun [illegible] fire will commence at [illegible]
3. Guns are [illegible] [illegible]
   1FPB The guns of "D" section under 2nd Lt. F.H. HORNER will fire on the following targets
Object	Bearing	Range
STOLLWERK	93° Traverse 1° rt. left	1500 search & 2900
HASELMEYER WEG.	98° Traverse 1° rt. left	1800 search & 2900

   1FPE One gun of "C" Section under 2nd Lt. H.F. FISHER on following target
Objects	Bearing	Range
ZEHMER WEG	65° Traverse 1° rt. left	1900 search & 2800

   Swinging traverse 65° to 75° right at ranges 2050 2750

   1FP 4. One gun of "B" Section under 2nd Lt. R. SKEVINGTON on target
Object.	Bearing.	Range.
TA WEG	76° Traverse 1° rt. 1° left	1500 search 2700

   Swinging traverse 75° to 65° left at ranges 1500 2250

4. Maximum number of rounds per gun 5000.

Copy No. 4

OPERATION ORDER No 26

1. The following operation in connection with an Artillery [illegible] will take place tomorrow at [illegible]
2. Machine gun indirect fire will commence at [illegible]
3. Guns are [illegible] will [illegible]

IFP.5 One gun of "D" section under 2nd Lt. F.A. HOOPER will fire on the following targets.

OBJECT	BEARING	RANGE
GRALL WEG	92°	1800^x search
	TRAVERSE 1° RT 1° LEFT	to 2700^x
HASELMEYER WEG.	95°	1800^x search
	TRAVERSE 1° RT. 1° LEFT	to 2900

IFP.6 One gun of "C" Section under 2nd Lt H.M. FISHER on following targets

OBJECTS	BEARING	RANGE
ZEHNER WEG	65°	1900^x search
	TRAVERSE 1° RT & 1° LEFT	to 2800^x

Swinging traverse 65° to 75° right at ranges 2050 2750

IFP.14 One gun of "B" Section under 2nd Lt R. SKEVINGTON on targets.

OBJECTS.	BEARING.	RANGE.
TA WEG	76°	1500^x search
	TRAVERSE 1° RT 1° LEFT	2700^x

Swinging traverse 76° to 65° left at ranges 1800^x 2250^x

4. Maximum number of rounds per gun 5000.

8

Copy

OPERATION ORDER No. [illegible]

1. The following [illegible]
[illegible]

2. [illegible]
[illegible]

3. Guns [illegible]
1/P.S. one gun of C Section [illegible]
25 [illegible] F. S. [illegible]
[illegible] following
Bearings

R { [illegible]° / 85° magnetic [illegible] / [illegible]° [illegible] 00°

S { [illegible]° / 99° magnetic 1900 to / 101° 2900

One gun of B Section [illegible]
1/P.L. [illegible] SHREVINGTON
[illegible]
bearings

T { [illegible]° Range / 64° magnetic [illegible] / 55° [illegible]

V { [illegible]° / 68° 2,100 / 70° to 3000

4. No. of rounds [illegible] per gun.

5. Reports to be sent to [illegible]

Issued at [illegible] 29-11-[illegible]

Copies No. 1 [illegible] 5 [illegible]
2 [illegible] 6 [illegible]
3 [illegible] 7 [illegible]
4 [illegible] 8 [illegible]

8. Reports to [illegible] H.Q. [illegible]
opening at 1.15 pm

Issued at 6 pm.
28/11/16

[illegible] Capt
Comdg M.G.Coy

Copy No. 1 Map Right
2 Map Centre
3 Map Left
4 Reserve
5 War [illegible]
6 File
7 Brigade
8 War Diary
9 Rt Battn
10 Left Battn

COPY. No. 5

SECRET.

OPERATION ORDER No. 27.

1/ MAP REFERENCE 51 b N.W. 1 Ed 4A.

The following Reliefs will take place within the company on the 23-11-16

Team at H.Q. A1 will proceed at 12 noon to MG1
" " A2 " 12 " MG2
" " A3 " 12 " MGR2
" " A4 " 12 " MGR1

Gun teams B5, B6, B7, B8 on Relief will proceed to H.Q. Billets

All other teams stand fast

2/ Only Guns Tripods and Spare parts will be taken with gun teams to new positions

3 On Relief all gun teams will see that everything is handed over in a thorough manner to the incoming team.

4/ Teams will come under Command of Officers as follows:-

O.C. MAP. RIGHT

2ND LT H. E. TALBOT.

POSITIONS	H.Q.	SECTION
MGR1, MG2, MG1, MGR2, IFP4, IFP6, AAP3,	TELLUS.	"A".

O.C. MAP CENTRE

2ND LT. H. N. FISHER

POSITIONS	H.Q.	S
MG3, MG4, MGR3, MGR4. IFP.3. IFP5 AAP2.	WEDNESDAY.	"C"

O.C. NAP LEFT.

2ND LT F.A. HOOPER

POSITIONS	H.Q.	SECTION.
MG6, MG5, MGR6, MGR5, HFP1, HFP2, IFP1.	ROCLINCOURT.	"D"

5/ Reports will be rendered as usual.

Completion of Relief will be reported at H.Q. by word "JOY" by wire

H Place [illegible] Lt.
for

COPIES 1 SECTION OFFICER
2 " "
3 " "
4 " "
5 WAR DIARY
6 FILE
7 BRIGADE.

ACKNOWLEDGE

ISSUED AT 7.00pm

OPERATION ORDER NO 28

OPERATION 1 [illegible] with a minor [illegible]

MG FIRE 2 [illegible] indirect fire will [illegible]

[illegible] 3 [illegible] after three Very light [illegible] by H.Q.

GUNS 4
IN [illegible] IFP 1. [illegible]
ROCLINCOURT [illegible] will sweep the SUNKEN RD [illegible]

IFP 3 [illegible] of C Section under
LONGRECK [illegible] same [illegible] COMMANDANT H.Q.

IFP 2 [illegible] of D [illegible] under
[illegible] 2nd Lt. A.A. HOOPER will [illegible]

B19.a 9.6 600 [illegible] 23[illegible]
B19 [illegible] 2.9 [illegible] 2250
B19.b 2.6 [illegible]
B19.a 1.7 [illegible] 00
B19 [illegible] 2250
[illegible] 2200

IFP 6 [illegible] gun of A Section under 2nd
TRENCH 40 Lt. H.E. TOL[illegible]

A24 [illegible] 35 [illegible] 3[illegible]
[illegible] 38 [illegible] 2700
H21 [illegible] 41 [illegible] 27

RATE 5 From [illegible] fire 100 rounds [illegible] minutes then [illegible] guns will fire 250 rounds [illegible]

CESSATION OF FIRE. Fire will be [illegible] by Telephone from Adv. Coy Hd-qrs.

SIGNALS 7/ Red Rockets will be fired 5 minutes previous to the Machine Guns ceasing fire. Piper whistles will also indicate the same.

PRECAUTION 8/ All men in NAP. CENTRE and NAP. LEFT will stand to in their dugouts from 1 a.m. till 6 a.m.

WATCHES. 9/ Watches will be synchronised at 10 p.m. at Adv. Coy Hd-qrs.

AMMUNITION 10/ 2,500 rounds will be ready at each Gun.

HEADQUARTERS. O.C. NAPIER will establish his Hd-qrs at Adv. Coy Hd-qrs at 10 p.m.

Issued at 12 m.n. 24/25th-11-16. [illegible]

Copy No. 1 Nap Right
2 Nap Centre
3 Nap Left.
4 Reserve
5 War Diary
6 File
7 Brigade
8 War Diary
9 Left Batt.

Copy No. 5

SECRET

OPERATION ORDER No. 29

MAP REFERENCE. 51 b. NW 1 Ed 4a

1/ The following Reliefs will take place with in the Company on the 27-11-16

Team at HQ B5 will proceed at 1PM to MG5
" " B6 " " 1PM " MG6
" " B7 " " 1PM " MGR6
" " B8 " " 1PM " MGR5

Gun teams D13, D14, D15, D16 on Relief will proceed to H.Q. Billets.

All other teams stand fast

2/ Only Guns Tripods and Spare-parts will be taken with Gun teams to new positions

3/ On Relief all gun teams will see that everything is handed over in a thorough manner to the incoming team

4/ Teams will come under Command of Officers as follows

O.C. MAP RIGHT.

2ND LT. C. J. THOMAS.

POSITIONS.	H.Q.	SECTION
MGR 2, MGR1, MG1, MG2 IFP 4, IFP6, AAP3.	TELUS.	"A".

O.C. MAP CENTRE

2ND H.N. FISHER

POSITION	H.Q	SECTION
MG3. MG4, MGR3, MGR4. IFP 3, IFP5, AAP.2	WEDNESDAY.	"C"

O.C. MAP LEFT.

2ND LT. R. SKEVINGTON

POSITIONS	H.Q.	SECTION
MG6, MG5, MGR6, MGR5, IFP1, IFP2, AAP1.	ROCLINCOURT.	B

2

5 Reports will be rendered as usual

Completion of relief will be reported at H.Q by word "SPEED" by wire

H [illegible] Lieut
for [illegible]

ACKNOWLEDGE.

ISSUED AT 7 P.m.

COPIES 1 SECTION OFFICER
2 " "
3 " "
4 " "
5 WAR DIARY
6 FILE
7 BRIGADE

Copy No. 5

SECRET

OPERATION ORDER No. [illegible]

OPERATION 1. The following scheme in connection with an Artillery concentration will take place [illegible] the day 30/11/16

M.G. FIRE 2. Machine Gun indirect fire will commence at 2.20 pm and cease at 3.30 pm.

GUNS IN ACTION 3. [illegible] as under will take part.

I.F.P. 4. One gun of "A" Section under 2nd Lt C.J. THOMAS will sweep the communication Trench [illegible] WEG magnet. bearing 76°
RANGE 17[illegible]
SEARCH to 2[illegible]00x
TRAVERSE 1° RT and 1° LEFT

I.F.P. 6. One gun of "C" Section under 2nd Lt B.I. [illegible] NORMAN will sweep the HELFER GRABEN
Magnetic bearing [illegible]°
RANGE 1800x
SEARCH to 2100x
TRAVERSE 1° RT and 1° Left.

I.F.P. 5. One gun of B Section under 2nd Lt R. SKEVINGTON will barrage the BAILLEUL Road;

Magnetic bearings	Range
110	2500x
114	2350x
121	2350x
122	2050x
125	2300x
156	1900x

Ammunition 4. Maximum No. of rounds 3000 per gun.

Watches 5. Watches will be synchronised at [illegible] [illegible] [illegible] at 1.30 pm.

Hdqrs. 6 Hdqrs will open at adv. Bn Hdqrs at 1.30 pm.

Issued at 6pm.

28 - 11 - 16

Copy 1 Nap Right

2 Nap Centre

3 Nap Left

4 Reserve

5 War Diary

6 File

7 Brigade

8 War Diary

9 Rt Battn.

C W Merson Capt
Comdg M G Coy.

Instructions regarding War Diaries and Intelligence Summaries are contained in F. S. Regs., Part II. and the Staff Manual respectively. Title pages will be prepared in manuscript.

Vol 8

Army Form C. 2118.

WAR DIARY

or

~~INTELLIGENCE SUMMARY.~~

(Erase heading not required.)

106th M.G.Coy

Place	Date	Hour	Summary of Events and Information	Remarks and references to Appendices
ARRAS.	1/12/16.		Inter Coy relief took place during the hours of daylight.	
"	2/12/16.		The 106th M.G. Coy. were relieved by the 27th M.G. Coy. The relief was completed by 11.00 pm. without incident and after relief the whole Company marched to AGNEZ arriving there at 3.00 am. 9-00 am the Company marched off from AGNEZ to FOUFFLIN RICAMETZ. arriving there at 5.00 pm and proceeded to Billets.	
	3.12.16 To 31.12.16		Training and reorganising at FOUFFLIN RICAMETZ.	

[signature]

Captain. O.C. 106 Machine Gun Coy.

7/1/16

106 MACHINE GUN COY. Date 7/1/17 ORDERLY ROOM

A5834 Wt. W4973 M687 750,000 8/16 D. D. & L. Ltd. Forms/C.2118/13.

Instructions regarding War Diaries and Intelligence Summaries are contained in F. S. Regs., Part II. and the Staff Manual respectively. Title pages will be prepared in manuscript.

WAR DIARY
or
INTELLIGENCE SUMMARY.
(Erase heading not required.)

106th M.G.Co. Vol 9

Army Form C. 2118.

Place	Date	Hour	Summary of Events and Information	Remarks and references to Appendices
FOUFFLIN RICAMETZ	1/2/17		Training at FOUFFLIN RICAMETZ from 1st to 31st January as per attached programmes.	LENS. 11

A5834 Wt. W4973 M687 750,000 8/16 D. D. & L. Ltd. Forms/C.2118/13.

106th M. G. Coy

Programme of Work

Day	Date	Subject	Time
Monday	15/1/17	Gun Drill in Box Respirators for A+B Sections Night Firing Gun Drill under C.O. Revolver Drill for A+B. Bombing for Nos 3&4. Bandaging for First Class under Lt H E Talbot.	9.15 A.M. 10.30 A.M. 11.45 A.M. 2.00 P.M. [illegible] P.M.
Tuesday.	16/1/17	Filling Belts. Cleaning Billets Washing and Packing Limbers Tactical Ride for Officers Bandaging for First Class	9.15 Am 9.15 Am till 4 P.m. 10.00 Am. – 5.00 pm.
Wednesday	17/1/17	Inspection by C.O.	11.30 A.M.
Thursday.	18/1/17	Elementary Tests. Firing on Range (Traversing & Elevating Box) Revolver Drill Bombing for Nos 3&4 A+B Sections Lecture by C.O. to men from Infantry Batts.	9.15 A.M. 11.00 A.M. 2.00 P.M. 2.00 P.M. 5.00 P.M.
Friday	19/1/17	Indirect Fire and Anti-Aircraft Work Testing Levels, Clinometers Compass. Revolver Practice on Range A+B Sections Bombing for Nos 3&4 C and D " Bandaging for First Class under Lt H.E. Talbot	9.15 A.M. 9.45 A.M. 10.30 A.M. 2.00 P.M. 5.00 P.M.
Saturday	20/1/17	Firing on Range 'C' and 'D' Sections Traversing & Elevating	10.00 A.M.

106 MACHINE GUN COY.
Date [illegible]
ORDERLY ROOM.

[signature] CAPTAIN.
O.C. 106 MACHINE GUN COY.

106th M. G. Coy

PROGRAMME OF WORK

DAY	DATE	SUBJECT	TIME
Monday	8/1/17	Gun Drill and Elementary Tests for Class. Bombing for No 3 and 4 – C and D Sections Immediate Action for Class Course of Firing on Range – Grouping. Revolver Drill for Class. Lecture by C.O. to all men from Infantry units	9.15 AM. 9.15 AM. 11 AM. 2 PM. 2 PM. 3 PM.
Tuesday.	9/1/17.	Gun Drill and Elementary Test for Class, C & D Sections. Immediate Action for Class Course of firing on Range for C and D Sects Traversing (2 [illegible]) Revolver Drill for C and D Sections Lecture on "First Aid" by Lt H E Talbot (To Second Class)	9.15 AM. 11.00 AM. 11.00 AM. 2.00 PM. 5.00 PM.
Wednesday	10/1/17.	Gun Drill & Elementary Tests for Class, C & D Sections. Course of firing on Range for Class – Traversing & Elevating Course of firing on Range for C & D Sects – Elevating & [illegible] Revolver Practice on Range. Lecture to Second Class on "First Aid" by Lt Talbot	9.15 AM. 11.00 AM. 11.00 AM. 2.00 PM. 5.00 PM.
Thursday	11/1/17	Gun Drill in Box Respirators Whole Company on Range – Long Distance	9.15 AM. 11.00 AM.
Friday	12/1/17	Elementary Tests – All Sections Gun Drill under C.O. Lecture to all late Infantry men by C.O. Lecture on First Aid by Lt Talbot – Second Class	9.45 AM. 11.30 AM. 2.00 PM. 5.00 PM.
Saturday	13/1/17	Test inspection by Sect Officers & C.Q.M.S. [illegible] Cleaning Billets, improvements to Billets & [illegible] Tactical Ride for All Officers	9.15 AM. 10.30 AM. 10.30 AM.

106 MACHINE GUN COY.
Date 6/1/17
ORDERLY ROOM.

[illegible]
CAPTAIN.
O.C. 106 MACHINE GUN COY.

PROGRAMME OF WORK. 106th M. G. Coy.

DAY	DATE.	SUBJECT.	TIME
Monday.	1/1/17	NEW YEAR'S DAY (HOLIDAY) FOOTBALL.	
Tuesday	2/1/17	GUN DRILL And Elementary Tests for CLASS COURSE of FIRING FOR CLASS under Orderly Officer (GROUPING) Immediate Action Revolver Drill GUN DRILL And Elementary Tests BUNKING Lecture on "First Aid" by Lieut Talbot - (both Classes)	9.15 am - 10.15 am 11 am - 1 pm 9.15 am - 10 am 10 am - 11 am 12 noon - 12.45 pm 2 pm - 4.30 pm 5.30 pm - 6.15 pm
Wednesday	3/1/17	GUN DRILL And Elementary Tests COURSE of firing on Range - GROUPING - Revolver "C" and "D" Morning - A and B Afternoon Class same as Tuesday - (TRAVERSING) Lecture on "First Aid" (First Class)	9.15 am - 10.30 am (A & B) 11 am - 1 pm (C & D) 2 pm - 4 pm 5.30 pm.
THURSDAY	4/1/17.	GUN DRILL And Elementary Tests COURSE of firing on Range - Traversing - (2 Practices) Revolver Same as Wednesday Class Same as TUESDAY (ELEVATING) Lecture on "First Aid" - (Second CLASS)	9.15 am - 10.30 am C & D 11 am - 1 pm A & B 2 pm - 4 pm 5 - 30 pm.
FRIDAY	5/1/17	DRILL under C.O. COURSE of firing on RANGE - (Elevating & Stoppage) Revolver And Class - Same as Above. Lecture on "FIRST AID" - Second Class	9 - 15 am - 10.15 am A & B 11 am - 1 pm C & D 2 pm - 4 pm 5 - 30 pm
SATURDAY	6/1/17	Cleaning Equipment - Bunking and improvements to Billets Tactical Ride for All Officers	9 am 1 pm 9 am 1 pm

106 MACHINE GUN COY.
30-12-16
ORDERLY ROOM.

H. G. Bell Lt.
for Captain
O.C. 106 MACHINE GUN COY.

Programme of Work.

106th Machine Gun Coy.

Day	Date	Subject	Time
Monday,	22-1-17	Firing on Range 400x 30 Rounds Grouping 60 Rounds Traversing	9.00 A.M. till 4.30 P.M.
Tuesday	23-1-17	Route March to Tinques. Attack scheme on Guestreville.	9.30 A.M. till 4.30 P.M.
Wednesday	24-1-17	Firing on Range 400x Details who did not fire on Monday. Bandaging under Lieut. H.E. Talbot	10. A.M. till 11.00 A.M. 5.00 P.M.
Thursday.	25-1-17	Belt filling and Cleaning. Foot Inspection and Haircutting Bandaging under Lieut. H.E. Talbot	9.15 A.M. 2.00 P.M. 5.00 P.M.
Friday.	26-1-17	Indirect and Night Firing, and Anti-Aircraft Work. Elementary Tests Coy. S. M. Parade for N.C.O.s	9.15 A.M. 10.30 A.M. 6.00 P.M.
Saturday	27-1-17	Kit Inspections. Billet Inspections.	9.15 A.M. 10.30 P.M.

106 MACHINE GUN COY.
Date [illegible]
ORDERLY ROOM.

[illegible] CAPTAIN,
O.C. 106 MACHINE GUN COY.

106th M.G. Coy

Programme of Work

Day	Date	Subject	Time
Monday	29-1-17	Lecture by Officers to Sections on the Attack, Tactics, communication, Indirect and Covering fire, consolidation, Fields of Fire etc. etc. Practice the Above. Revolver Drill for Coy including Transport & Hdqrs.	9 AM to 11 AM. 11 AM to 1 PM 2.30 PM to 4 PM
Tuesday	30-1-17	Coy to practice the Attack, Ammunition Supply communication and the rapid building of Emplacements in the captured position. Revolver Drill for all Sections including Transport and H.Q. Ords.	9 AM to 1 PM 2.30 PM to 3.30 PM
Wednesday	31-1-17	Overhauling Limbers, Cleaning Gun Equipment. Washing Limbers Revolver Practice on Range	9 AM to 11.30 AM. 11.30 AM to 1.00 P.M. 2.30 PM to 4.00 P.M.
Thursday	1-2-17	Route March to Tingues, Attack on Quesreville	9.00 AM to 3.30 PM
Friday	2-2-17	Drill Parade Gun Drill Transport Inspection Coy S.M. Parade for N.C.Os Box Respirator Drill	9 [illegible] to 11 AM. 11.00 AM to 1 PM. 2.00 PM to 2 PM. 3.00 PM to 3.30 PM [illegible] 9.00 PM.
Saturday	3-2-17	Tactical Ride for all Officers Coy Drill Parade under S.M. Kit & Clothing Inspection C/QMS.	[illegible] 9.00 AM to 11.00 AM. 11.00 AM to 1 PM.

Instructions regarding War Diaries and Intelligence Summaries are contained in F. S. Regs., Part II. and the Staff Manual respectively. Title pages will be prepared in manuscript.

WAR DIARY
or
INTELLIGENCE SUMMARY.
(Erase heading not required.)

Vol 10

Army Form C. 2118.

106th M. G. Co

Place	Date	Hour	Summary of Events and Information	Remarks and references to Appendices
FOUFFLIN RICAMETZ.	1/2/17		Training at FOUFFLIN RICAMETZ	MAP. REF.
	6-2-17.		Left FOUFFLIN RICAMETZ for LIGNY-SUR-CHANCE about 8 miles.	LENS. 11 1/100,000
	7-2-17		Left LIGNY-SUR-CHANCE for OCCOCHES about 9 miles Billeted in huts.	
	8-2-17		Left OCCOCHES for VIGNACOURT about 12 miles (good marching)	AMIENS 1/100,000
	9-2-17		At VIGNACOURT.	
	18-2-17		Transport moved by road to AUBIGNY from VIGNACOURT. Personnel by train from VIGNACOURT to MARCELCAVE, marched to AUBERCOURT.	
	23-2-17		Left AUBERCOURT for Divisional Reserve at CAIX.	
	25-2-17		Reconnoitred LIHONS Sector	
	27/2/17		Marched to ROSSERES.	

CWG

A5834 Wt. W4973 M687 750,000 8/16 D. D. & L. Ltd. Forms/C.2118/13.

Army Form C. 2118.

Instructions regarding War Diaries and Intelligence Summaries are contained in F. S. Regs., Part II. and the Staff Manual respectively. Title pages will be prepared in manuscript.

WAR DIARY
or
~~INTELLIGENCE SUMMARY.~~
(Erase heading not required.)

106th M. G. Co.

Place	Date	Hour	Summary of Events and Information	Remarks and references to Appendices
FIELD	27/2/17		Relieved 104 M. G. Coy Dispositions which were French & not in accordance with English ideas of Machine Gunnery. C Section 2 guns BRUNIG TR. 2 guns TOUROTT TR. A Section 2 guns TOUROT TR. covering DEMI-LUNE 1 gun CAROLINE TR. 1 gun KUSS TR. D Section. 2 guns Tr BOIS TRIANGULAIRE. 2 guns Tr BOIS IV. B Section 4 guns in reserve ROSIÈRES.	MAP REF AMIENS 1/100,000

106 MACHINE GUN CO.
Date 7/3/17
ORDERLY ROOM

[signature] Capt
CAPTAIN.
O.C. 106 MACHINE GUN CO.

A5834 Wt. W4973 M687 750,000 8/16 D. D. & L. Ltd. Forms/C.2118/13.

5

OPERATION ORDER No. [illegible]

by Capt C. W. Morrison Comdg [illegible] M.G. Coy

I. Move — The Company will move [illegible] by Route March to LIGNY-SUR-CANCHE.

II. Hour — Company will pass the starting point — POST OFFICE - West end of Village at 10.30 am.

III. Order of March — Signallers, Headquarters, A. B. C. D. [illegible] formation.

IV. Transport — Transport in the following order. Battle Wagons A. B. C. D. & Headquarters Wagon, Water Cart, Mess Cart.

I. Dress — Marching order, Packs to be carried, leather jerkins underneath the pack, waterproof sheet under flap of Pack & under straps.
OFFICERS Drill order. British Warms only to be worn.
Box Respirators over the Coat.

Rations — The unconsumed portion of the days Rations except meat & Potatoes will be carried by the men.
All horses [illegible] carry feeds.

Hour of arrival — Probable hour of arrival 2.30 pm

C W Morrison Capt
Comdg

Copy No. 1 Section Officer
2 "
3 "
4 "
5 War Diary
6 File
7 Brigade
8 War Diary

Secret.

Copy No. 5

OPERATION ORDER No 34

MOVE. The Company will move from LIGNY-SUR-CHANCE to OCCOCHES by Route march passing the starting point at 8.15 am. (S in pt-BOUBERS)

HOUR The Coy will Parade at 7.45 am and march off at 8 am.

ORDER OF MARCH. Signallers A.B.C.D. Headquarters. Limbers will assemble at head of Column at Road junction South of LIGNY Church by 7.45 am. Battle Wagons A.B.C.D. Nos 3 A.B.C.D. Headquarters Wagon, Water Cart and Mess Cart.

ROUTE. VACQUERIE, FORTEL, BONNIERS, BARLY.

HOUR of ARRIVAL. Probable hour of arrival 1 pm

REVEILLE 6.00 A.M.

BREAKFAST. 6.30 A.M

BLANKETS & DIXCIES. All Blankets and Dixcies to move off from Billets at 7.00 am and packed properly in the Limbers on main Road by 7.15 am.

RATIONS. The unconsumed portion of the days Rations will be carried on the man. All Horses will carry feeds.

[signature] Capt.

Copy No. 1 Section Officer
2 " "
3 " "
4 " "
5 War Diary
6 File
7 Brigade
8 War Diary

SECRET.

Copy No. 5

OPERATION ORDER No. 35

MOVE. The Company will move from OCCOCHES by Route March passing the Starting point at 9.45 am

HOUR. The Company will parade at 9.15 am. and march off at 9.30 am.

ORDER of MARCH. Signallers A.B.C.D. Headquarters. Limbers will assemble at the Starting Point. Battle Wagons A.B.C.D No's 3 A.B.C.D, Headqrs Wagon, Water Cart and Mess Cart.

HOUR of ARRIVAL. Probable hour of arrival 3 pm.

REVEILLE. 7.00 A.M.

BREAKFAST. 7.45 A.M.

BLANKETS & DIXCIES. All Blankets and Dixcies to move off from Billets and be properly Packed in Limbers by 8.30 am.

RATIONS. The unconsumed portion of the days rations will be carried on the man.

All horses will carry feeds.

Edw Menson Capt

Copy No 1 Section Officer
2 " "
3 " "
4 " "
5 War Diary.
6 File.
7 Brigade
8 War Diary

SECRET.

Copy No. 5.

OPERATION ORDER No. 37.

by CAPT. C.W. MERISON Comdg.

106th MACHINE GUN Co.

MOVE. The Unit will move from VIGNACOURT to MARCELCAVE by Route & Rail.

TRANSPORT The Transport under Lt. S.W. Kindred will move by March Route to AUBIGNY on the 18th inst. Starting point 1 Mile S. of VIGNACOURT on the VIGNACOURT ST. VAAST Road.

ROUTE ST. VAAST, AMIENS, VECQUEMONT.

PARADE 7.15 A.M.

MOVE OFF 7.45 A.M.

On the 19th inst Transport will move from AUBIGNY to MARCELCAVE via VILLERS under arrangements of the Brigade Transport Officer.

Sections & H.Q. will detail the following Brakesmen:—

H.Q 3 men.
SECTIONS 3 "
TOTAL 15 men.

All Grooms & Officers horses will accompany the Transport.

SIGNALLERS Four Signallers will accompany the Transport

BILLETING PARTY Lt. F.H. Hooper & Sgt. Haskell are detailed as a billeting party. They will leave VIGNACOURT Station at 9am. on the 18th inst. They will report to B.H.Q. at 8.45 am. and will provide themselves with two days rations. On arrival at MARCELCAVE they will report at 3pm. to the Staff. Capt. at MARCELCAVE Church.

MOVE by RAIL. The Unit will move by rail from VIGNACOURT Station at 10am. on the 19th inst.

PARADE 8.20am. Dress. Marching Order. Blankets rolled and carried on three sides of the pack. The unconsumed portion of the days rations will be carried on the man.

OPERATION ORDER No 37. Cont.

BAGGAGE. The Dixies & Mess equipment will be carried in the Motor lorry. The time of packing & parade will be notified later.

OPERATION ORDER No. 37. Cont.

BAGGAGE. The Dixcies & Mess equipment will be carried in the motor lorry. The time of packing & parade will be notified later.

[signature] Lt.
for CAPTAIN,
O.C. 106 MACHINE GUN Co

Copy. No.

1 Section Officer.
2 " "
3 " "
4 " "
5 War Diary.
6 File.
7 Brigade
8 War Diary.

106 MACHINE GUN CO.
Date 17-2-1917
ORDERLY ROOM.

SECRET.

Copy No. 5

OPERATION ORDER No. 38

MOVE The Unit will move from AUBERCOURT to CAIX on the 22-2-17.

ROUTE. IGNACOURT, CAYEUX.

STARTING POINT. Head of the Column will pass the Road Junction S of the I in AUBERCOURT at 12.32 pm.

TIME OF PARADE. The Company will parade at 12.15 pm. Marching Order with Waterproof Sheets slung over the Shoulder.

ORDER OF MARCH. Signallers. A.B.C.D Headqrs.

TRANSPORT. Battle Wagons C.D.A.B and Nos 3 C.D.A.B. Headquarters Wagon Water Cart and Mess Cart.

BLANKETS. Blankets will be rolled in bundles of ten and packed as previously. No Blankets will be carried on the man.

RATIONS. The unconsumed portion of the days Rations will be carried on the man.

All Horses will carry feeds

DINNERS. Dinners will be served on arrival at the new destination.

BILLETS. All men will be clear of Billets by 11.45 a.m.

C W menon Capt

Copy No 1 Section Officer
2 " "
3 " "
4 " "
5 War Diary
6 File
7 Brigade
8 War Diary

SECRET.

OPERATION ORDER No. 39.

RELIEF The 106th M.G.Co. will relieve the [illegible] M.G.C. in the LIHONS Sector on the night of 27/28th Feby 1917.

ORDER of BATTLE. D Section Left, A Section Centre, C Section Right and B Section in Reserve.

ORDER of MARCH Advance party - B Section, Headquarters (less Signallers) and Sergeant under 2/Lt J. [illegible] 2/Lt [illegible] will accompany this party. They will leave CAIX at 8.30 a.m. Remaining Sections in the following order - "A" Section 10.15 a.m. "D" Section [illegible] "C" Section [illegible] Battle formations.
Signallers - 11.00 a.m.
Q.M. Stores, No. 3 Limbers, Hd.Qrs Limber and "B" Sections Battle Limbers 1.00 p.m.

DRESS. Marching Order

BLANKETS Blankets will be packed on Battle Wagons.

MARCH TO THE TRENCHES. Centre Sector. "A" Section will leave ROSIERES at 1.30 p.m. and march to LIHONS.
LEFT SECTOR. "D" Section will leave ROSIERES at 3.00 p.m. and march to LIHONS.
RIGHT SECTOR. "C" Section will leave ROSIERES at 11.00 a.m. and march to the Right Ration Dump.

GUIDES. LEFT SECTOR. One Guide at LIHONS.
2 Guides at Sector Hd.Qrs.
CENTRE SECTOR. One Guide at LIHONS.
3 Guides at Sector Hd.Qrs.
RIGHT SECTOR 2 Guides at Right Ration Dump.

ROUTE TO SECTOR HEADQUARTERS.
LEFT SECTOR. CAIN Trench, IRIS Trench, PRESSOIRE Trench to [illegible] Wood.
CENTRE SECTOR. CAIN Trench, IRIS Trench to SELENITES Trench.
RIGHT SECTOR. Railway Line to HOLLAND Trench. [illegible] Sub Sections to move together.

LEAVING SECTOR HEADQUARTERS. No man of the Right and Left Sections is to leave Sector Hd.Qrs until enemy's line is invisible.

DRESS. Fighting Order. Greatcoats [illegible] and Waterproof Sheets.

RATIONS. "A" Section will draw Rations at 9.30 a.m. from Q.M.S. Stores. Remaining Sections will draw Rations at ROSIERES.
"C" and "D" Sections will as far as possible carry 2 days Rations.

Ammunition. Every man proceeding to the line will carry Two Bandoliers of S.A.A.

GUM BOOTS. Every man will carry a pair of Gum Boots to the line slung over the shoulder. These will be issued at ROSIERES.
Glycerine & Oil will also be carried on the man.

RATION PARTIES. 106th T.M. Batt. will carry Rations for the 106th M.G.C. Guides will report at Hd.Qrs. ROSIERES at 1.00 p.m.
Arrangements will be made for carrying parties by O.C. 106th T.M. Batt.

DRAG ROPES. One drag rope per [illegible] section will be carried to the line.

CERTIFICATES. A signed copy will be retained by each Gun Team Commander of all items and stores handed over.
Duplicate copies will be signed and given to the outgoing Gun Team Commanders.

RELIEF. The relief will be reported complete and correct by Section Commanders by message by word SQUIBS which will be brought back by the relieved Officers.

TRANSPORT. On completion of duty Transport will return to CAYEUX.

[illegible]

26/2/17

Issued at 6.30p.m.

Copy No. 1 Section Officer.
2 " "
3 " "
4 " "
5 War Diary
6 File
7 Brigade
8 War Diary.
9 C.Q.M.S.
10 O.C. 104th T.M. Batt.
11 Transport Officer
12 O.C. 104th M.G. Co.

Instructions regarding War Diaries and Intelligence Summaries are contained in F. S. Regs., Part II. and the Staff Manual respectively. Title Pages will be prepared in manuscript.

WAR DIARY
or
~~INTELLIGENCE SUMMARY~~
(Erase heading not required.)

Army Form C. 2118.

106th M.G. Co.

Vol XI

Place	Date	Hour	Summary of Events and Information	Remarks and references to Appendices
Field	3.3.17		One gun captured by raiding party of Germans	Map Ref. AMIENS 1/100000
	4.3.17		B section relieved C section right. Disposition now	
			B section 1 gun Tourot, 1 gun BRISBANE, 1 gun LUNETTE, 1 gun KUSS trenches	
			C section reserve in ROSIERES	
			A section 2 guns TOUROT, 1 gun CAROLINE, 1 gun KUSS.	
			D section 1 gun BOIS TRIANGULAIRE, 2 guns BOIS IV, 1 gun BOIS TRIANGULAIRE HQ	
	7/8.3.17		C section relieved A section	
	9/10.3.17		183 Coy relieved 3 guns of D section. D section complete came to HQ.	
	10.3.17		4 guns D section 1 gun C section relieved 104 Coy:- 1 gun TROCHU, 2 guns PIERRE I and GOUDERT, 1 gun EVACUATION and GOUDERT, 1 gun C section GOUDERT left of EVACUATION relief delayed owing to loss of guide.	
	11.3.17		Subsection of D relieved B section 1 TOUROT, 1 gun BRISBANE trenches	
	13.3.17		Subsection of B relieved subsection D as above	
	15/16.3.17		106 M.G. Coy relieved by 105 M.G. Coy	
CAIX	16.3.17		Coy moved to billets in CAIX as brigade in reserve.	
ROSIERES	17.3.17	9.45pm	Coy moved up to billets in ROSIERES at 9.45pm	
Field	18.3.17		Coy moved from ROSIERES to IRIS and DINARD trenches	
	19.3.17		Coy moved up to old German Front Line	
	20.3.17		Bridging trenches and making tracks	
	21.3.17		Cutting wire at PUNCHY and cleaning road to HALLU	
ROSIERES		5.30pm	Moved to billets at ROSIERES	
	to 28.3.17		Supplied working parties	

[signature]

2449 Wt. W14957/M90 750,000 1/16 J.B.C. & A. Forms/C.2118/12.

Instructions regarding War Diaries and Intelligence Summaries are contained in F. S. Regs., Part II. and the Staff Manual respectively. Title pages will be prepared in manuscript.

WAR DIARY

~~or~~

~~INTELLIGENCE SUMMARY.~~

(Erase heading not required.)

Army Form C. 2118.

106th M. G. Co.

Place	Date	Hour	Summary of Events and Information	Remarks and references to Appendices
LICOURT	29.3.17 to 31.3.17		Moved to Billets at LICOURT Billeted in the Factory Training and working parties	Map Ref. AMIENS 1/100000

Clowmerman Capt
Comdg No 106 M G Co

In the Field
6/4/17

A5834 Wt. W4973/M687 750,000 8/16 D. D. & L. Ltd. Forms/C.2118/13.

8.

OPERATION ORDER No. [illegible]

The following Reliefs will take place within the Company on the night 3rd/4th Feb 1917.

"A" and "D" Sections will stand fast — no change.

"B" Section will relieve "C" Section in the RIGHT SECTOR of LIHONS.

GUIDES. One Guide from each Gun Team will be at Right Ration Dump at 6.30 P.M. to guide teams to the new positions. "B" Section will leave Headqrs at 5.00 P.M. Intervals of 50 yards per Gun Team to be maintained.

DRESS. Fighting Order, Jerkins, Greatcoat and Waterproof Sheets. Water bottles will be filled.

Ammunition. Each man will carry 100 Rounds S.A.A. The two forward Gun Teams will carry one Box of BOMBS each.

RATIONS. The Rations for the following day will be carried.

RELIEF. On Relief all Gun Teams will see that everything is handed over in a thorough manner to the incoming teams. Signed copies of all Stores and Equipment handed over will be brought to Headquarters by outgoing teams.

On Relief "C" Section will march back to H.Q. moving by Gun Teams 50 yards interval.

Completion of Relief to be reported by Runners to Headquarters by word "TORCH"

2-3-17

Issued at 11.45 P.M.

Copy No 1 Section Officer.
2 " "
3 " "
4 " "
5 War Diary.
6 File.
7 Brigade.
8 War Diary.

Secret.

OPERATION ORDER No. 41

Copy 8

The following Reliefs will take place within the Company on the night 7th/8th March 1917.
"D" and "B" Sections will stand fast.
"C" Section will relieve "A" Section in the Centre Section of LIHONS.

GUIDES. One Guide from each Gun Team will be at Left Ration Dump at 6.30 pm. to guide teams to new positions.
"C" Section will leave Headquarters at 5.30 p.m. Intervals of 50 yards between Gun Teams is to be maintained.

DRESS. Fighting Order, Jerkins, Greatcoats and Waterproof Sheets.

AMMUNITION. Each man will carry two Bandoliers S.A.A. – 100 rounds. The forward Gun Team will carry one box of Bombs each.

RATIONS. The Rations for the following day will be carried.

RELIEF. On Relief all Gun Teams will see that everything is handed over in a thorough manner to the incoming teams. Signed copies of all stores and equipment handed over will be brought to Headquarters by outgoing teams.

On Relief "A" Section will march back to Headquarters moving by Gun Teams 50 yards interval.

Completion of Relief is to be reported by runners to Headquarters by word "LIGHT."

6-3-17

Issued at 8.00 P.M.

[signature illegible]

Copy No. 1 Section Officer
" " 2 " "
" " 3 " "
" " 4 " "
" " 5 War Diary
" " 6 File
" " 7 Brigade
" " 8 War Diary.

SECRET.

OPERATION ORDER No 42.

'D' SECTION of 106th M.G.Co. will be Relieved by three Guns of 183rd M.G.Co. on the night of 9th and 10th MARCH 1917.

DISPOSITIONS. The following dispositions will be handed over:- TWO GUN POSITIONS IN Trench BOIS IV, ONE GUN POSITION Sector Hd.QRS. Section Officer will point out to incoming Officer the position at the junction of KUSS Trench and PRESSOIRE Trench. Direction of fire South west corner of TRIANGULAIRE Wood. This Gun to cover the BRIGADE on the Right of Relieving Company.

GUIDES. One Guide from each Gun Position to be at LIHONS Ration dump at 4 P.M.

ROUTE. BOYAU, CAIN, IRIS Trench and PRESSOIRE Trench to Sector HEADQUARTERS.
Gun teams will move off at ten minutes interval from RATION DUMP. They will not move from Sector HEADQUARTERS until DARK.

EQUIPMENT Everything except Gun and Spare parts will be handed over at the three Positions. The fourth team will bring back everything except AMMUNITION AND Bombs.

RELIEF On Relief all Gun teams will see that everything is handed over in a thorough manner to incoming team. Signed copies of all stores handed over will be brought to Co. Hd.QRS.
On Relief "D" Section complete will march back to Hd.QRS at 50 Yards interval.
Limbers will pick up equipment at the LIHONS Ration Dump
Completion of Relief to be reported by wire by word "DARKNESS!"
On the 10th March equipment of 183 M.G.C. will be handed over according to Receipt at Hd.QRS 106th M.G.Co.
Times to be ARRANGED by 2nd in-Command concerned.

8-3-17

Issued at

C.W. Merrison Capt.
Cmdg No 106 M.G. Co.

COPY No. 1 'D' Section
2 Relieving Section Officer.
3 183. M.G.Co.
4 Transport Sergt.
5 WAR DIARY
6 File
7 Brigade
8 WAR DIARY

SECRET.

Copy No. 8

OPERATION ORDER No. 43.

"A" Section and 1 Gun of "C" Section of 100th M.G.Co will Relieve 5 Guns of 104th M.G. Co. on the 10th March 1917.

DISPOSITIONS. "A" Section will take up the following dispositions:-
One Gun COUDERT trench right of EVACUATION trench
Two Guns COUDERT trench near PIERRE. I.
One Gun TROCHU trench.
One Gun of 'C' Section COUDERT trench left of EVACUATION trench

WITHDRAWAL. At 7.00 p.m. one gun of 'C' Section now at TOURNOT trench will withdraw complete to Junction of RAILWAY and IRIS trench where guide will meet them at 9.00 P.M.

COMMAND. One Gun of "C" Section will temporarily come under the Command of O.C. "A" Section for tactical purposes, discipline, organization and trench routine.

GUIDES. 2 Guides will be at Hd.Qrs. at 2.30 p.m. for 2 Guns of 'A' Section EVACUATION and TROCHU trenches. 1 Guide will be at Hd.Qrs. at 2.30 P.M to lead the remaining 2 teams of "A" Section to MEHARICOURT where 2 Guides will meet them to Guide them to the NEW positions. 1 Guide will be at the junction of IRIS trench at 9.00 pm to guide team of "C" to NEW POSITION.

ROUTE. Left Party Railway Line, DUCKBOARDS, LUNETTE II trench to COUDERT trench
Right party MEHARICOURT MAUCOURT to COUDERT trench.
Gun teams will move at 200 paces interval.
The Gun for TROCHU trench will not leave COUDERT trench

EQUIPMENT. Spare parts, Spare barrels, Very Light pistols, will be taken into the Line. All other stores boxes of Bombs will be handed over.
Gun Team Commanders will sign one Receipt Form and hand over to outgoing Gun-team commanders retaining one signed copy.
Section Officer will render a complete list of Stores handed over which will be brought back by outgoing Section Officer.

DRESS. Fighting order, Greatcoats, Leather Jerkins and Waterproof sheets.

AMMUNITION. 2 Bandoliers per man will be carried into the line.

RELIEF. Completion of Relief to be reported by wire by word "CLOUD" from HANNEQUIN Hd.Qrs.

HANDING OVER. All stores will be handed over to 2nd-in-C. on the morning of the 11th according to signed receipt.

10-3-17
Issued at 10. A.M.

Copy No. 1 O.C A Section
2 " B "
3 " C "
4 " D "
5 War Diary
6 File
7 Brigade
8. War Diary
9 104th M.G.Co.
10 O.C. Left Bn

SECRET. Copy No 8...

OPERATION ORDER No. 44.

The following Relief will take place within the Company on THE 11th MARCH 1917.

Sub-section of "D" Section under Sergt Payne will relieve sub-section of 'B' Section in the Centre Sector.

DISPOSITIONS. 1 Gun TUROT Trench, 1 Gun BROWNIG Trench and junction of BRISBANE Trench.

GUIDES. One Guide will meet "D" Sub-section at the Ration Dump at 3-30 P.M. and guide teams to Junction of LUNETTE III and KLUSS Trenches where two guides will guide teams to new positions.

ROUTE. Railway Line, FLORENT Trench, IRIS Trench to LUNETTE III Trench.

DRESS. Fighting Order, Jerkins, Greatcoats, and Waterproof Sheets.

AMMUNITION. Each man will carry 2 Bandoliers S.A.F and each team will carry one Box of Bombs to each position.

PARADE. Sub-section will leave HQ.QRS at 2.00pm and teams will march 5 minutes interval to Ration Dump & 150 yards interval from there.

COMMAND. 2nd Lt. FISHER will assume command of Centre Sector consisting of Sub-section "B" and Sub-section 'D'.

RELIEF. On relief all Gun teams will see that everything is handed over in a thorough manner to incoming team. Signed copies of all stores handed over will be brought to Co. HQ.QRS.

Completion of Relief will be reported by wire by word 'LIGHTENING'.

10-3-17

ISSUED AT 8.00 P.M.

[signature] Capt
Comdg [illegible]

Copy No. 1 Section Officer
2 " "
3 " "
4 " "
5 War Diary
6 File
7 Brigade
8 War Diary

SECRET. COPY No 8

OPERATION ORDER No. 45

The 106th M.G.Co. WILL BE RELIEVED BY THE 105th M.G.Co. IN LIHONS SECTOR ON THE NIGHT 15/16th MARCH. 1917

DISPOSITIONS. Right Sector No 1, 5, 6, 7 AND 8 GUN POSITIONS. HEADQUARTERS PIERRE. 1.
CENTRE SECTOR. No. 2, 3, 9 & 10 GUN POSITIONS. HEADQUARTERS LUNETTE 3.
LEFT SECTOR. No. 4, 11 AND 12 GUN POSITIONS.

GUIDES. RIGHT SECTOR. Guides for 17 & 8 GUN POSITIONS will be AT SECTION HEADQUARTERS AT 6.00 P.M.
CENTRE SECTOR. ONE GUIDE FROM EACH GUN TEAM will be AT RATION DUMP RAILWAY AT 5.30 P.M.
LEFT SECTOR. ONE Guide from EACH GUN TEAM to be AT THE RATION DUMP RAILWAY AT 6.00 P.M.

ROUTE. RIGHT SECTOR - AS MUTUALLY ARRANGED.
CENTRE SECTOR - RAILWAY LINE IRIS TRENCH to LUNETTE 3.
LEFT SECTOR - FLORENT Trench, IRIS Trench to SELENITES Trench.

EQUIPMENT. EVERYTHING EXCEPT SPARE PARTS, VERY PISTOLS, CLEANING RODS AND PERISCOPES WILL BE HANDED OVER TO INCOMING TEAM.

GUM BOOTS. All Gum Boots will be brought out of the LINE CARRIED BY THE MEN. BOOTS AND PUTTEES WILL BE WORN.

RELIEF. ON RELIEF ALL GUN TEAMS WILL SEE THAT EVERYTHING IS HANDED OVER IN A THOROUGH MANNER. GUN TEAM COMMANDERS WILL BRING BACK TO SECTION HD.QRS. A SIGNED COPY OF ALL STORES HANDED OVER. SECTIONS WILL BRING BACK A COMPLETE LIST OF STORES HANDED OVER SIGNED BY RELIEVING SECTION OFFICER TO HEADQUARTERS.
GUN TEAMS WILL MOVE BACK AT 50 YDS INTERVAL.

ROUTE. RIGHT SECTOR. VIA - MAUCOURT, MEHARICOURT to HEADQUARTERS.
CENTRE SECTOR. VIA - LUNETTE 2, DUCKBOARDS, RAILWAY LINE to HEADQUARTERS.
LEFT SECTOR. VIA - FLORENT Trench, RAILWAY LINE to HEADQUARTERS.

COMPLETION OF RELIEF. COMPLETION of Relief to be Reported by WIRE by WORD "THUNDER".

STORES. All STORES will be taken over AT 10.00 A.M. on THE 16th MARCH.

TRANSPORT. All Mules, No 3 Limbers will be at HEADQUARTERS ROSIERES, by NOON 16th March. FEEDS WILL BE CARRIED.

MOVE. The Company WILL LEAVE for the RESERVE AREA AT 2.00 p.m. on the 16th. SECTIONS MOVING ¼ HOUR INTERVALS. BATTLE FORMATIONS.

14-3-17

ISSUED AT 9.00 P.M.

[signature] Capt
Comdg No 106 MGCo

COPY No 1 SECTION OFFICER
2 " "
3 " "
4 " "
5 WAR DIARY
6 File
7 BRIGADE
8 WAR DIARY
9 105th M.G.Co.
10 104th M.G.C.
11 Transport Officer.

SECRET.

COPY No 8

OPERATION ORDER No 46.

1. MOVE. 106th M.G.Co. WILL MOVE TO BILLETS AT ROSIERES TO-NIGHT.

2. PARADE. THE COMPANY WILL PARADE AT 9.45 P.M. (IN FULL MARCHING ORDER.) MOVING OFF IN THE FOLLOWING ORDER: BATTLE FORMATIONS "D" 10.00 P.M. "C" 10.5 P.M. "B" 10.10 P.M. "A" 10.15 P.M. H.Q.RS 10.20 P.M. No 3 LIMBERS WILL ACCOMPANY THE BATTLE WAGONS. SIGNALLERS WILL MOVE WITH "D" SECTION.

3. ADVANCE PARTY. LIEUT. F. A. HOOPER & PTE HANLEY WILL CYCLE FORWARD AS AN ADVANCE PARTY FOR THE UNIT.

4. BAGGAGE PARTY. CPL KNOWLES WITH 1 MAN FROM A. B. C. D SECTION & HEADQUARTERS WILL clean up Billets AND WILL PROCEED AT 7.00 A.M. TO-MORROW.

5. MEAL. Section Cooks WILL PARADE WITH Dixies & MOVE OFF WITH "D" Section & PREPARE A HOT MEAL OF TEA AT ROSIERES.

[signature] Capt
Comdg 106 M.G.Co

17/3/17

SECRET

COPY No 8

OPERATION ORDER No 47.

The advance is being continued. 104 & 105th Bde moving forward to HATTENCOURT - PUNCH

1. Move. 106th Brigade will move to the British & German front line.

2. Parade. The Co. will move off in the following order at 9.00 am. Battle formations - D. B. C. A. - 200 yards interval and will follow the Royal Scots. The Co. will occupy the DINARD line

'D' on the Right
'B' centre at DINARD
'C' on the left
'A' in Reserve.

Headquarters DINARD.

3. Transport & Depot. No 3 Limbers will remain ~~here~~ at ROSIERES. Battle wagons will return to ROSIERES. All surplus stores will be left there.

18-3-17

C W Mennon Capt
Comdg No 106 M G Co.

Copy No 1 Section Officer
" 2 " "
" 3 " "
" 4 " "
" 5 War Diary
" 6 File
" 7 Brigade
" 8 War Diary

SECRET.

COPY No. 8

OPERATION ORDER No. 48

The Company will withdraw to ROSIERES AT 5.30 P.M.

ORDER OF MARCH. D. C. B. A. Battle formations.

TRANSPORT. Transport will withdraw to ROSIERES to Billet No. 34 on receipt of this order. All stores equipment etc. from MEHARICOURT will be withdrawn.

SIGNALLERS. Signal communication will cease with 'BEAUTY'. All lines will be reeled in immediately.

21/3/17

[signature] Lt.
for O.C. NAPIER.

Copy No. 1 Section Officer
2 " "
3 " "
4 " "
5 WAR DIARY
6 FILE
7 BRIGADE
8 WAR DIARY.
9 Transport Officer.

COPY No. 8

OPERATION ORDER No. 45

Reference. [illegible] Map 100,000 AMIENS ST. QUENTIN

1. MOVE. The 100th M.G.C. will move to the following area to billets in LICOURT on the 29th March.

2. ROUTE. LIHONS – CHAULNES – MARCHELEPOT to LICOURT

3. PARADE. [illegible] The Co. will parade at 8.20 a.m.
   DRESS. Fighting order, blankets rolled in G.S. waterproof sheet & carried under haversack.

4. ORDER OF MARCH. D, B, C, A, Headqrs, No. 1 Limbers, Water cart, Cooks cart, G.S. wagon. Battle formations moving off at 8.50 a.m.

5. BAGGAGE. All transport to be packed by 8.00 a.m. Packs will be carried on battle wagons. Officers valises on No. 3.

6. BREAKFAST. 7.00 a.m.

7. RATIONS. The unconsumed portion of the days rations will be carried on the sections No. [illegible].
   All horses will carry feeds. Helmets will be carried in correct positions (full) [illegible].

Issued at 7.30 pm
28-3-17

[illegible signature]

Copy No. 1 Section Officer
2 " "
3 " "
4 " "
5 War Diary
6 File.
7 Brigade.
8 War Diary.

106 MACHINE GUN Co.

Instructions regarding War Diaries and Intelligence Summaries are contained in F. S. Regs., Part II. and the Staff Manual respectively. Title pages will be prepared in manuscript.

WAR DIARY
or
~~INTELLIGENCE SUMMARY.~~
(Erase heading not required.)

April 1917

Army Form C. 2118.

Vol 12

Place	Date	Hour	Summary of Events and Information	Remarks and references to Appendices
LICOURT	1.4.17		Training in carrying out a barrage and attacks combined with infantry – open warfare	
	2.4.17		Parties furnished for work to fill in a crater.	
	3.4.17		C.O. accompanied by Capt. J. Bostock left to reconnoitre the area in which fighting had been taking place by 32nd Div	
	4.4.17		Visited O.C.s 96 M.G.Co 97 M.G.Co and 14 M.G.Co. also Bde. H.Qs. 96 and 97. ascertained their plans of action.	
	5.4.17		C.O. returned to unit.	
	3.4.17 to 5.4.17		Training continued	
ATHIES			Moved to ATHIES	
	to 8.4.17		Training and working parties as on 1st and 2nd inst.	
MERAUCOURT	9.4.17		Moved to MERAUCOURT	
VERMAND	10.4.17		Moved to VERMAND and relieved 184 M.G.Co in VADENCOURT area – two sections in positions, two sections in reserve at VERMAND	
	11.4.17		Dispositions altered and now as under two guns COPSE 3: one gun VADENCOURT CHATEAU: one gun MARREVAL COPSE: one gun O.G. Line: one gun R16 G 22 for aircraft: two guns at R16 G22 in reserve: two guns at VERMAND for aircraft work.	
	12.4.17		Sub-section A relieved sub-section 104 MGCo in MAISSEMY. Two guns from R16 G22 withdrawn to VERMAND Guns in MAISSEMY – one gun near [illegible] M13 b09: one gun M19 a 06	
	14.4.17		Inter-company relief took place. One gun moved from COPSE 3 to NEW COPSE (R5d.) A barrage was carried out by four guns on M13G88 to M7d 81 in conjunction with an attack carried out by the Bde on our right – 14th Bde. 16000 rounds fired. Two guns from vicinity of MARREVAL COPSE "[illegible]" area E of PONTRUET – 6000 rounds fired. Co. HQ. moved for operation to MAISSEMY where close touch was kept with attacking infantry and guns in action. Duration of operation – one hour 4 am to 5 AM	
	16.4.17		Barrage fired by eight guns on to STE. HELENE in conjunction with a raid by WEST YORKS. It was observed that direction of fire corresponded with the bursting shells from our artillery. The ground was bad and weather wet. Barrage ably carried out under Lt H.S. LEE. Other indirect fire carried out during day and night. Total rounds expended 24000.	

A5834 Wt. W4973 M687 750,000 8/16 D. D. & L. Ltd. Forms/C.2118/13.

Instructions regarding War Diaries and Intelligence Summaries are contained in F. S. Regs., Part II. and the Staff Manual respectively. Title pages will be prepared in manuscript.

WAR DIARY
or
~~INTELLIGENCE SUMMARY.~~
(Erase heading not required.)

Army Form C. 2118.

Place	Date	Hour	Summary of Events and Information	Remarks and references to Appendices
VERMAND	17.4.17		Indirect night firing on to STE HELENE – 1000 rounds expended.	Map
	18.4.17		Indirect night firing on to PONTRUET – 2000 rounds expended.	62 B SW
			One gun moved to BERTHAUCOURT	
			Indirect night firing on to STE HELENE – 1000 rounds expended.	62 C SE
	19.4.17		Inter-company relief. Sub-section D relieved sub-section A near MAISSEMY – one gun River Bank – 1 gun BERTHAUCOURT. Gun at BERTHAUCOURT dispersed a hostile working party at STE HELENE during the day.	62 B NW
			B section relieved C section. One gun COPSE 3; one gun NEW COPSE; one gun O.G.L.; one gun MAREVAL COPSE	1/20000
	20.4.17		1800 rounds fired by night on STE HELENE – movement during daytime much reduced here.	
VILLEVEQUE	22.4.17 to 27.4.17		106 M.G. Co relieved by 104 M G Co. Rest at VILLEVEQUE	
	28.4.17		Reconnoitred GRICOURT and FRESNOY areas.	
	29.4.17		Relieved 105 M.G.Co – four guns GRICOURT; one gun ANC. MIN.; one gun copse at M15 b 7 3. Ten guns in readiness for BROWN LINE	
			Operation orders for month attached.	
			Map ref. 62 B SW 1/20000 62 C SE 1/20000 62 B NW 1/20000	

[signature] Capt
Comdg No 106
M G Co

COPY NO. 8

OPERATION ORDER No. 50

THE COMPANY WILL PROCEED TO BILLETS AT ATHIES on the 5-4-17.

WORKING PARTY WILL MARCH to ATHIES via FALVY AND ENNEMAIN ON COMPLETION OF TASK. TOOLS TO BE DUMPED AT PARGNY BRIDGE.

"D" SECTION WILL MARCH TO ATHIES BY ROUTE AT DISCRETION OF SECTION OFFICER ON COMPLETION OF TRAINING SCHEME.

TRANSPORT HDQRS AND DETAILS WILL PARADE AT 9.45 A.M. and WILL MOVE OFF AT 10.00 A.M.

ROUTE LICOURT, PARGNY, FALVY, ENNEMAIN

EXTRA KIT, ~~AS PER~~ NOT ON SCHEDULE, UNDER CHARGE OF C.S.M. WILL BE LEFT AT LICOURT and will be brought to NEW BILLETS UNDER ARRANGEMENTS TO be made by LT. H.E. Talbot.

Vehicles TO BE PACKED by 9.00 A.M.

Loads for VEHICLES WILL BE AS PER schedule issued herewith.

[signature]

COPY No. SECRET. 8

OPERATION ORDER No. 51

MAP REF. SHEET 62C.

1 MOVE. THE Co. WILL MOVE FROM ATHIES TO MERAUCOURT.

2 PARADE. THE Co. WILL PARADE AT 130 P.M.

3 STARTING POINT. HEAD OF THE COLUMN WILL PASS THE STARTING POINT — ROAD JUNCTION V7c 9.6 — AT 1.45 P.M.

4 ROUTE FOURQUES, DEVISE, MONTECOURT TO DESTINATION.

5 ORDER of MARCH. PEACE FORMATIONS B.C.D.A. HD.QRS. BATTLE WAGGONS SAME ORDER, No. 3's WATERCART AND COOKS CART.

6 BAGGAGE ALL KITS AND LIMBERS WILL BE PACKED BY 1·00 P.M. PACKS TO BE CARRIED ON BATTLE WAGGONS AND BLANKETS ON No. 3's.

7 DINNERS DINNERS WILL BE SERVED AT 12·15 P.M. DINNERS FOR WORKING PARTY ON RETURNING TO BILLETS.

ISSUED AT 10·30 A.M.
9-4-17

[signature]

Copy No. 1 SECTION OFFICER.
2 .. ..
3 .. ..
4 .. ..
5 WAR DIARY
6 FILE
7 BRIGADE
8 WAR DIARY.

SECRET

COPY No. 8

OPERATION ORDER No. 51A

1. MOVE. The 106th M.G. Co will relieve 184 M.G.C. in the VADENCOURT Sector on the afternoon of 10th April 1917

2. PARADE. B will parade at 12 noon. Starting point W.1.a.9.3 to be passed by 12.15 pm.

3. ROUTE. TERTRY, CAULAINCOURT [illegible] 30 a 3 to VERMAND

4. ORDER OF MARCH. [illegible] C. B. D. Headquarters. Battle formation. 100 yards interval between H and C. 250 yards interval between C and B, 100 yards between remainder

5. GUIDES. One guide will meet B. at VERMAND at 2 p.m. Guides from gun teams will relieving gun team at VADENCOURT to guide them to positions at 3 pm

6. DRESS. Fighting order. Greatcoat carried rolled on Belt. Waterproof sheet under flap of Haversack

RATIONS. If possible 2 days Rations will be carried by Gun teams

TRANSPORT. On completion of duty Transport will return to place as directed by C.O. to T.O.

9. RELIEF. Completion of relief will be reported to B. Hdqrs. at VERMAND by outgoing teams with a message from Section Officers by word "FINIS"

If weather conditions are unfavourable relief will be postponed until dusk.

10. DISPOSITIONS. B and D Sects will relieve left and right Sects respectively in line and A and C in Vermand.

Issued at 3am
April 10th 1917

Copy No. 1 Section Officer
2 " "
3 " "
4 " "
5 War Diary
6 File
7 Brigade
8 War Diary
9 O.C. 184 M.G.C.
10 Transport Off.

[illegible] Capt
O.C. 106 Co

SECRET

COPY NO 8

OPERATION ORDER NO 52

MOVES. The following GUN POSITIONS will be changed ON RECEIPT OF THESE ORDERS.

"B" SECTION. TWO GUNS AT SECTION H.Q WILL MOVE TO COPSE 3.
1 Gun 20yds from N CORNER JUST inside the WOOD.
LINES OF FIRE (a) To PONTRU
(b) To TUMULUS Road
1 Gun 20 yds from S. CORNER JUST inside the wood
Lines of FIRE (a) ASCENSION FARM.
(b) TUMULUS ROAD.
The GUN OCCUPYING THE SHELL HOLE WILL WITHDRAW TO SECTION H.Q. AS SOON AS THE MOVE IS completed.
AT 7AM this GUN will relieve "D" Section GUN AT MAREVAL COPSE.
GUN And SPARE-PARTS only TO BE TAKEN.

DISPOSITIONS. 1 GUN MAREVAL COPSE.
1 GUN FRONT LINE.
2 GUN COPSE III

Moves to be REPORTED TO H.Q. by RUNNER by WORD "COMPLIS".

D SECTION. On completion of MOVE of 2 GUNS of "B" Section to COPSE 3. The GUN in SHELL HOLE will WITHDRAW to COPSE R16 b 2.2 (POSITION of RESERVE GUN)
Gun at Section H.Q. will MOVE to N.E. of VADENCOURT CHATEAU.
Lines of fire (a) Along River bank to PONTRU
(b) To QUARRY & Ridge.
Gun at MAREVAL copse on Relief will move to COPSE R 16 b 2.2.

Anti-AIRCRAFT WORK. ONE GUN AT COPSE R 16 b 2.2 will be mounted for Anti-AIRCRAFT WORK from dawn TILL dusk.

DISPOSITIONS. 1 GUN N.E. of VADENCOURT CHATEAU
1 GUN Anti-AIRCRAFT WORK.
2 GUNS RESERVE. R 16 b 2.2

completion of Moves of D Section to be Reported by word BY RUNNER - "COMPLIS."

Anti-AIRCRAFT WORK. RESERVE SECTION. - 2 Guns will be mounted from dawn to dusk
one at R 26 B 5.4.
one at R 32 a 5.7.

11-4-17

COPY NO 1 Section Officer
2 " "
3 " "
4 " "
5 WAR DIARY
6 File
7 BRIGADE
8 WAR DIARY

[signature] Capt
Comdg

SECRET

COPY No. 8.

OPERATION ORDER No. 53

A SUB-SECTION OF "A" 106th Machine Gun Co will relieve A SUB-SECTION OF 104th MACHINE GUN Co.

PARADE. AT 2.00 P.M.

GUIDES. Guides will meet incoming teams AT MAISSEMY AT 3.30 P.M.

ROUTE. VIA VILLECHOLLES.

RELIEF Completion of RELIEF WILL BE REPORTED BY RUNNER BY WORD "PARTIAL"

DRESS. Fighting ORDER. Greatcoats and waterproof sheets TO BE CARRIED.

WITHDRAWAL. 2 Guns of "D" Section under 2nd LT. J. BEDDOM will withdraw TO VERMAND from R. 16 b 22. Transport will meet them AT 12. noon

12 - 4 - 17

Issued AT 10.30 A.M.

Copy No 1 Section Officer
2 " "
3 " "
4 Transport "
5 WAR DIARY
6 FILE
7 BRIGADE
8 WAR DIARY
9 O.C. 104th M.G. Co.

SECRET

COPY No. 8

OPERATION ORDER No. 54.

"C" Section under LT. S.W. KINIRED and 1 Sub-section of 'D' under 2/Lt. J. Seddon will Relieve B Section and a Sub-section of D Section Respectively during the afternoon and evening of the 14th

DISPOSITIONS. "C" Section MG.5, MG6, MG7, MG8.
'D' Section MG 3 and MG.4

PARADE. 4.00 P.M.

RELIEF. Relief of MG3, MG4, MG7 and MG8 will be carried out on arrival at Dump R16 b 2.2. M.G5 and M.G6 will not leave the Dump until 4.00 P.M.

Guides. One guide per gun team will be at the Dump R 16 b 2.2 at 5.00 P.M.

DRESS. Fighting order. Greatcoats & waterproof sheets to be carried.

COMPLETION OF RELIEF - will be reported by runner by word "COMIC."

MOVE. At 7.30 P.M. O.C NAP. LEFT will guide Right gun at COPSE 3 (MG7) to a position in copse in R 5 d previously reconnoitred.
All moves to be completed by 8.30 P.M.

RETURN TO BILLET. Sections will return to H.Q. on completion of relief bringing handing over certificates - / Sub sections moving at 200 yards interval.

Issued at. 12.30 A.M.
14-4-17.

C.W. Menerson Capt
Comdg Napier

COPY No 1 Section Officer
2 "
3 "
4 "
5 WAR DIARY
6 FILE
7 BRIGADE
8 WAR DIARY.

SECRET COPY No. 8.

OPERATION ORDER No. 58

OPERATION 106th M.G.C. will co-operate in the attack on [illegible] on the night 14/15th April by [illegible] an enfilade barrage on southern portion of [illegible] M 9 d & M 10 c and by placing "Blocks" from road junction M 10 c 2 9 to cross roads [illegible] M 5 d [illegible].

GUNS IN ACTION
One Sub-section "D" and 1 Sub-section "A" under 2/Lt. [illegible], will carry out the enfilade barrage from M 17 c 8 6 to M 4 d 8 1 as under.

GUN	RANGE YDS	ELEVATION	MAG. BEARING	SEARCH	TRAVERSE
Left Gun No 1	1925	4° 2'	90°	10' up and down	2° right
No 2	2300	5° 22'	88°		
No 3	2340	6° 20'	86°		
Right Gun No 4	2500	7° 47'	85°		

One Sub-section "B" under E. H. J. Lee at R 11 b will "B.B." from M 10 c 3 9 to M 3 b 6 2 as under

Bearings	Angle of Elevation
85	11° 15'
89	11° 30'
93	12°
97	12° 15'

HOUR OF READINESS Zero minus 1
DURATION OF FIRE Zero to Zero plus 60
ZERO HOUR Zero hour will be notified later
RATE OF FIRE "Blocking" 1 belt per gun for 5 minutes.
BARRAGE. 1 belt per gun for 4 minutes.
PARADE Section for barrage fire will leave H.Q. at 11.00 P.M.
WITHDRAWAL Sub-section of B and Sub-section of D will withdraw at Zero plus 60 to H.Q.
COMMAND Sub-section of "A" will come under command of O.C. A Section & will remain until O.C. A Section is [illegible]
DISPOSITIONS One gun will withdraw at Zero plus 60 to Sunken Road R 17 a. One gun will occupy [illegible].
LINES OF FIRE O.C. "A" Section will arrange that two guns on river will arrange to have S.O.S. lines of fire as under:-

GUN	BEARING	RANGE
LEFT GUN	92	2500
RIGHT GUN	77	2400

REPORTS O.C. 106th M.G.C. H.Qrs. will be established at MAISSEMY at R 23 b 4 2 at Zero minus 90.

Issued at [illegible]

[illegible]

14/4/17 Copy No 1 Section Officer
2 " "
3 " "
4 " "
5 War Diary
6 File
7 Brigade
8 War Diary

SECRET. COPY No. 8

OPERATION ORDER No 56

OPERATION. 106th M.G.Co. will co-operate in a minor enterprise to be carried out by 17th Batt West Yorks on the night of 16/17th April.

GUNS IN ACTION. One Gun under 2/Lt. H.N. Fisher will fire indirect from the I.F.P. on 15 hostile trench M. 3 b 2.2 and M 3 d 3.8 from 9 P.M. to 11.00 P.M. 2000 rounds to be expended. From 12 midnight 12.45 A.M. this Gun will "blob" Eastern outskirts of Pontruet M. 10 a M 10 b - 1500 rounds will be expended.

An oblique barrage under Lt. H. J. Lee will be carried out as under –

"B" Section under Lt. H. J. Lee, one sub-section of "D" and one sub-section of "A" under 2/Lt. R. Skevington. The Gun of "A" Section now at M. 17 d will be lent to "D" Section for the operation. A and D on left, B on right

From 11.45 P.M. to 12 midnight as under

Guns	Range	Elevation	Magnetic Bearing.
LEFT RIGHT	2450 2400	7° 44' 7° 22'	59° 59°
From 12 midnight to 12.5 AM as under			
LEFT RIGHT	2600 2550	8° 56' 8° 31'	63° 58°
From 12.5 A.M to 12.45 A.M. as under			
LEFT RIGHT	2600 2500	8° 20' 7° 30'	66° 66°

HOUR OF READINESS 11.15 P.M.

RATE OF FIRE. 11.45 P.M. to 12 midnight 1 Belt per Gun
12 midnight to 12.5 A.M. 2 Belts per Gun
12.5 AM to 12.45 A.M. 2 Belts per 5 mins.

WITHDRAWAL. On completion of firing B & D Sections will return to Headquarters.

RELIEF. Subsections of "A" will relieve subsection of A now in line and relieved sub-section will return to Headquarters.

REPORTS. A Report centre will be established at advanced Co. Hd Qrs R 23 b 4 3 at 11.00 P.M.

Issued at 6.30 P.M. 16-4-17

Copy No 1 Section Officer
2 " "
3 " "
4 " "
5 War Diary
6 File
7 Brigade
8 War Diary.

[illegible] Capt
Cmdg No 106 Mg Co

SECRET

COPY NO. 8

OPERATION ORDER NO. 57

A subsection of D Section under 2/Lt R. Skevington will relieve subsection of "A" in the line in the right sector on the night of 19th April.

DISPOSITIONS 1 Gun River Bank
1 Gun Berthaucourt.

PARADE 6.00 P.M.

GUIDES. One guide per gun team will be at sector H.Q.s at 7.00 P.M.

DRESS. Fighting order. Greatcoats and waterproof sheets to be carried.

COMPLETION OF RELIEF. Completion of relief to be reported by runner by word "TROUPE"

ADVANCE PARTY. 2nd Lt R. Skevington & the N.C.O. detailed for the forward gun will report at Section H.Q. Qrs at 5.00 P.M. to take over the positions.

Issued at 8.00 A.M.
19-4-17

[illegible] Capt
[illegible]

Copy No 1 Section Officer
2 " "
3 " "
4 " "
5 War Diary
6 File
7 Brigade
8 War Diary

Secret [illegible] Copy No 8

OPERATION ORDER No 58

1. [illegible] Section under Lt H. J. LEE will relieve [illegible] Section in the left Sector on the Evening of [illegible] April.

Dispositions 1 Gun [illegible] Copse
1 " Copse N of [illegible] Road.
1 " O.G.L.
1 " Copse III

Parade 6 30 p.m.

Guides. 1 Guide per gun team to be at Sect H.Q at 7.00 p.m.

Dress. Fighting order. Greatcoats and waterproof sheets to be carried.

Completion of relief. Completion of relief will be reported by runner [illegible] Will

Return to Billets. [illegible] Section will return to H.Q. by sub-sections at 200 yards interval.

Issued at 6.00 p.m.

13.4.17

[illegible]
Lt.

Copy No. 1 Section Officer
2 "
3 "
4 "
5 War Diary
6 File
7 Brigade
8 War Diary

SECRET — Copy No. 8

OPERATION ORDER No. 59

THE 106TH MACHINE GUN Co. WILL BE RELIEVED BY 104TH M.G. Co. IN THE LINE ON NIGHT OF 22/23 APRIL 1917.

DISPOSITIONS. THE FOLLOWING DISPOSITIONS WILL BE HANDED OVER:—

2 GUNS SOUTH BANK OF RIVER OMIGNON
1 GUN MAREVAL COPSE.
1 GUN NEW COPSE
1 GUN O.G.L.
1 GUN COPSE 3
1 GUN VADENCOURT CHATEAU.
1 GUN BERTHAUCOURT.

GUIDES. RIGHT SECTOR.

1 GUIDE PER GUN TEAM WILL BE AT SECTION H.D. QRS. BY 6.30 P.M.

CENTRE SECTOR

1 GUIDE PER GUN TEAM WILL BE AT SECTION H.D. QRS. AT 2.30 P.M.

LEFT SECTOR

1 GUIDE FOR GUN. COPSE 3. 1 GUIDE FOR GUN O.G.L. AT SECTION H.D. QRS. AT 2.30 PM.

1 GUIDE FOR GUN AT MAREVAL COPSE

1 GUIDE FOR GUN AT NEW COPSE AT SECTION H.D. QRS. AT 6-30 P.M.

EQUIPMENT. 10 BELT BOXES AT M.G. I WILL BE HANDED OVER TO INCOMING TEAM ALL OTHER EQUIPMENT WILL BE WITHDRAWN FROM LINE EXCEPT BOMBS AND BOXES S.A.A.

RELIEF. RELIEF WILL BE REPORTED CORRECT BY WORD 'SING'

WITHDRAWAL ON RELIEF ALL SUBSECTIONS WILL WITHDRAW TO VERMAND WHERE THEY WILL RECEIVE A HOT MEAL. AT GUIDES WILL MEET THEM ~~[illegible]~~ VERMAND TO TAKE THEM TO THEIR NEW BILLETS.

ADVANCE PARTY 'C' AND 'A' SECTIONS (LESS WORKING PARTIES) UNDER 2/Lt. F.N. FISHER WILL PROCEED AT 2000 TO NEW DESTINATION TO TAKE OVER BILLETS FROM 2ND IN COMMAND 106TH M.G. Co.

TRANSPORT REMAIDER OF TRANSPORT WILL MOVE TO NEW LINES UNDER MUTUAL ARRANGEMENTS OF TRANSPORT OFFICERS AND C.S.M.s OF 104TH M.G. Co AND 106TH M.G. Co.

ISSUED AT 7 AM.

Copy No. 1. SECTION OFFICER
2 " "
3 " "
4 " "
5 WAR DIARY
6 FILE
7 BRIGADE
8 WAR DIARY
9 TRANSPORT OFFICER.
10 [illegible]

[illegible] M.G. Co.

22-4-17

SECRET.

OPERATION ORDER No. 60.

The 106 M.G. Co. will relieve the 153rd M.G. Co on night of 29/30th April 1917.

Parade. Section will parade under section arrangements and will move off at the following times:—

A Section 6·30 P.M. C Section 6·35 P.M.
B Section 6·40 P.M. D " 6·45 P.M.
Headquarters 6·00 P.M. Transport 7·00 P.M.

Headquarters MARTEVILLE to VILLECHOLLES

Route A & B ~~Headquarters~~ MARTEVILLE B11 c2·97 road junction R34 b 23 head of valley to LONE TREE

C & D Sections MARTEVILLE VILLECHOLLES MAISSEMY - MAISSEMY CHURCH thence by sunken road to Section Hdqrs.

Guides. C Section 1 guide will meet C Section at MAISSEMY CHURCH at 8·30 P.M. 1 Guide per gun will meet Section at Section Hdqrs. at 9·00 P.M. to guide detachments to gun positions.

D Section 1 guide will meet D Section at MAISSEMY CHURCH at 9·00 P.M.
1 Guide per gun will be at Section headquarters at 9·30 P.M. to guide one representative per detachment to S.O.S. positions on the Brown line.

A Section. 1 Guide will meet section at LONE TREE at 8·30 P.M.
1 Guide will meet section at Headquarters of Right Reserve Section
1 Guide per gun team will be at W end of copse M22A and M22C at 9·00 P.M. to guide detachments to gun positions.

B Section 1 Guide will meet section at LONE TREE at 9·00 P.M.
1 Guide per gun will be at Section Hdqrs. at 9·30 P.M. to guide 1 representative per detachment to S.O.S. positions in Brown line.

Section Officers will assure themselves that they do not arrive at the positions of their first guns before the times stated.

OPERATION ORDER
SHEET 2.

Dress. Fighting order, greatcoats rolled on belts, waterproof sheets under flap of haversacks.

Handing Over. All S.A.A. in boxes, and all trench stores, emplacements will be taken over by incoming sections.

A Section will take over belt boxes from outgoing section.

The two forward guns of C will take over belt boxes from outgoing section.

A Section will hand over to the representative of the 105th M.G. Co. 30 web & 2 metal belts and boxes at VIILEVEQUE.
C Section will hand over to the representative of the 105th M.G. Co. 18 web & 1 metal belts with boxes at VILLEVEQUE.

Transport. On completion of duty it will return to Transport lines at VILLECHOLLES.

Relief. Completion of relief will be reported at Hdqrs. at VILLECHOLLES by the outgoing section officers with a message from relieving officers by the word 'Bing'.

Dispositions.

A SECTION. GRICOURT.
C " HILL 120.
B " RIGHT RESERVE.
D " LEFT RESERVE.

1 Section Officers
2 "
3 "
4 "
5 War Diary
6 File
7 Brigade
8 War Diary
9 Transport Off.
10 105 M.G. Co.

29/4/1917

Instructions regarding War Diaries and Intelligence Summaries are contained in F. S. Regs., Part II. and the Staff Manual respectively. Title pages will be prepared in manuscript.

WAR DIARY

~~or~~

~~INTELLIGENCE SUMMARY.~~

(Erase heading not required.)

Army Form C. 2118.

106 M.G. Coy

106 M G Coy

Vol 13

Place	Date	Hour	Summary of Events and Information	Remarks and references to Appendices
Field	1.5.17		Sunken Road M.26c and M.26d. and Copse M.26d. shelled between 5.15 P.M. & 5.45 P.M. FRESNOY also shelled.	
	2.5.17		Indirect Fire carried out from M.21b.6.6 on road N and S. of MON IDEE about 2000 rounds expended.	
	3.5.17		Indirect Fire carried out from M.21.b.6.6. on new trenches M.24a and M.24c. between 9.30 P.M. & 1 A.M. 3000 rds. expended.	
	4.5.17		Indirect Fire carried out onto MON IDEE and Coulter M.24.d from 10 P.M. to 12.30 A.M. 750 rounds expended.	
	5/6.5.17		An M.G. barrage placed on M.24.b. by 6 guns from M.22a & c. Also 4 guns fired indirect – 2 from M.21b.6.6. & 2 from GRICOURT on to M.18.C. 80.95 & M.30b. 35750 rounds expended. 1 Sub Section D relieved 1 sub section A.	
	6.5.17		Sub Section D relieved Sub Section A at GRICOURT. I.F. carried out.	
	7.5.17		Indirect Fire took place on to M.18 Central, M.11.d. and M.24b. from 10PM to 2.30 AM 7500 rounds expended.	
	8.5.17		Indirect Fire carried out 1000 rounds.	
	9/10.5.17		Company relieved by 105 M.G. Coy. On relief marched to billets at VILLEVEQUE	
	10.5.17 to 14.5.17		In Rest.	
	14/15.5.17		3 detachments A section relieved 3 detachments of 104 M.G. Coy 2 on river – 1 Berthaucourt. They came under command of O.C. 105.	
	19.5.17		Company (less 1 sub section) marched from VILLEVEQUE to PERONNE.	
	20.5.17		Sub section A joined Coy at PERONNE.	

A5834 Wt. W4973 M687 750,000 8/16 D. D. & L. Ltd. Forms/C.2118/13.

Instructions regarding War Diaries and Intelligence Summaries are contained in F. S. Regs., Part II. and the Staff Manual respectively. Title pages will be prepared in manuscript.

WAR DIARY

~~or~~

~~INTELLIGENCE SUMMARY.~~

(Erase heading not required.)

Army Form C. 2118.

Place	Date	Hour	Summary of Events and Information	Remarks and references to Appendices
PERONNE	21.5.17		Company moved from PERONNE to camp at SOREL-LE-GRAND.	
Field	22/23.5.17		2 section relieved 2 sections of 121 M.G. Coy in the line. 8 guns front line system.	
	23/24.5.17		2 Sections of Coy relieved 2 sections of 121 M.G. Coy in the line, 1 section Green line - 1 section Brown line.	
	24.5.17 to 29.5.17		Coy in the line on HONNECOURT SECTOR. A section relieved B and D section relieved C.	
	29/30.5.17		Indirect fire from X10c13 on Cross Road at HONNECOURT (S8a28) and Bridge at S7b5.9 from 12.45 A.M to 2.15 A.M. 2000 rounds expended.	
	30/31.5.17		Indirect fire from X10c1.3. from 11.45 A.M till 2 A.M. on to Road and bridge S7b47 to S.7 b6.9. and Road at LES TRANCHÉES. 3000 rounds expended.	
	31.5.17 1.6.17		1 Detachment 104 M.G. Coy relieved 1 Detachment D Section in the line.	

B.W. Menson Capt
Comdg No 106 MG Co

A5834 Wt. W4973/M687 750,000 8/16 D. D. & L. Ltd. Forms/C.2118/13.

SECRET.

Copy No. 5

OPERATION ORDER No 61.

THE 106 M.G. Coy WILL COOPERATE IN AN ATTACK TO BE CARRIED OUT ON THE NIGHT OF THE 5th/6th MAY. 1917.

GUNS IN ACTION.

AN OBLIQUE BARRAGE WILL BE CARRIED OUT UNDER THE COMMAND OF LT. S.W. KINDRED

SUB-SECTION OF C.

" " OF D. UNDER 2/LT. R. SKEVINGTON

" " OF 105 M.G.Co. UNDER OFFICER DETAILED BY O.C. 105 M.G.Co.

FROM FORWARD EDGE OF COPSE M22a & M22c ONTO M17d 23 TO M24 b.0.9. GUNS 25 YDS INTERVAL AS UNDER.

GUNS NUMBERED FROM RIGHT	RANGE YARDS.	BEARING MAGNETIC	ELEVATION.
1	2300	90	6°14'
2	2150	89	5°21'
3	2050	87	4°58'
4	1900	86	4°24'
5	1800	83	4°11
6	1700	82	4° 0'

B SECTION UNDER LT. H.J. LEE FROM WEST SIDE OF COPSE M21 b 66 WILL 'BLOB' M18 c 8095 WITH TWO GUNS AND M17d 98 WITH TWO GUNS.

ONE SUB-SECTION OF A UNDER 2/LT. H.N. FISHER, FROM 28 b WILL 'BLOB' ROAD JUNCTION M 30a 74. M 30a 48, HOSTILE TRENCH M24 c 91. M30 b 28 AND CRATER M24 d 36

HOUR OF READINESS. 12 MIDNIGHT.

DURATION OF FIRE. FOR LT S.W. KINDRED. OBLIQUE BARRAGE 12-30 A.M. 1-30 A.M. BLOBBING 1·30 A.M. - 2-15 A.M.
FOR LT. H.J. LEE. 12-30 AM - 1·30 A.M.
FOR 2/LT. H.N. FISHER 12-30 AM - 1·45 A.M.

RATE OF FIRE. FOR LT S.W. KINDRED
OBLIQUE BARRAGE — 1 BELT PER GUN PER 4 MINS.
BLOBBING - 1 BELT PER GUN PER 5 MINS.

1 GUN AT A TIME.

FOR LT. H.J. LEE — 1 BELT PER GUN PER 5 MINS.
FOR 2/LT. H.N. FISHER 1 BELT PER GUN PER 5 MINS

RELIEF. ONE SUB-SECTION OF D UNDER 2/LT. J. SEDDON WILL RELIEVE A SUB-SECTION OF A AND WILL MOVE UNDER ORDERS FROM 2/LT. H.N. FISHER TO TRENCH M29 a 88 APPROX. AS A POSITION OF READINESS.

SIX GUNS OF 105 M.G.Co. WILL RELIEVE B & D. SECTIONS. FOR THE DEFENCE

OF THE BROWN LINE DURING THE OPERATION.

LIMBERS. BATTLE LIMBERS WILL REPORT AT 10AM AS UNDER.

D SECTION WITH 8 BELT BOXES AT SECT H.Q.
C. SECTION WITH 20 " " " H.Q.
A. " " 30 " " " H.Q.
B. TWO EACH WITH 16 " " " D.B.

THESE WILL BE UNDER THE ORDERS OF LT. F. LISMORE FOR THE OPERATION.

ARRIVAL AND DISPOSITIONS,

THREE GUNS 105 M.G.Co. WILL ARRIVE AT LEFT RESERVE SECTION HD.QRS. AT 9.30 P.M. DISPOSITIONS FOR S.O.S. M.G. 11. M14. 7.G.12

THREE GUNS 105 M.G.Co. WILL ARRIVE AT RIGHT RESERVE SECTION HEADQUARTERS AT 9.00 P.M.

DISPOSITIONS FOR S.O.S. M.G. 7. M.G. 8 M.G. 9 POSITIONS.

ONE SUBSECTION FOR BARRAGE FIRE WITH 32 BELTS, WILL REPORT LEFT RESERVE SECTION HD.QRS. AT 9.15 P.M.

WITHDRAWAL THE GUN of THE 105 M.G.Co. WILL WITHDRAW AT 3A.M.

ONE SUB SECTION OF 105 M.G.Co. WILL WITHDRAW AT 2A.M. FROM BARRAGE FIRE POINT.

ONE SUBSECTION of B WILL WITHDRAW TO ORIGINAL DISPOSITIONS AT 1-30 A.M. THE OTHER BATTLE LIMBER of B WILL WITHDRAW AT THIS HOUR. THE REMAINING SUB SECTION of B WILL WITHDRAW MAN HANDLING JUST BEFORE DAWN.

LIMBERS WITH SPARE EQUIPMENT of A AND C WILL WITHDRAW AT 2-15 A.M. THESE SUB SECTIONS WILL MAN HANDLE BACK TO ORIGINAL DISPOSITIONS JUST BEFORE DAWN.

SUB SECTION of A ON COMPLETION of FIRING WILL WITHDRAW TO QUARRY AND WILL COME UNDER ORDERS of O.C. D. SECT.

ONE SUB SECTION of D UNDER [illegible] WILL JUST BEFORE DAWN TAKE OVER THE ORIGINAL DISPOSITIONS VACATED BY SUBSECTION of A AND WILL COME UNDER ORDERS of O.C. A. SECTION.

REPORTS

ADVANCED COMPANY HD.QRS. WILL OPEN AT QUARRY AT 10.30 P.M. TO THIS POINT ALL REPORTS WILL BE SENT.

5-5-17

Clemenson Capt
[illegible] no 10[illegible]

SECRET

COPY No 5

OPERATION ORDER No 62.

SUB SECTION of 'D' UNDER 2/LT. R. SKEVINGTON WILL RELIEVE THE REMAINING SUB SECTION of 'A' AT GRICOURT.

'C' SECTION WILL COMPLETE ITS OWN INTERNAL RELIEF TO NIGHT UNDER ARRANGEMENTS TO BE MADE BY O.C. 'C' SECTION.

DISPOSITIONS 'D' SECTION – M.G. 1. M.G. 2. M.G. 3. M.G. 4
'A' " M.G. 11. M.G. 12. M.G. 13. M.G. 14

GUIDES. & PARADE WILL BE ARRANGED BY SECTION OFFICERS CONCERNED.

COMMAND. SUB SECTION of 'D' [under 2/Lt. Seddon] WILL COME UNDER COMMAND of O.C. 'D' SECTION.

TRANSPORT. ONE LIMBER WILL BE AT LEFT RESERVE SECTION HD. QRS. AT 9·30 P.M. TO CARRY UP FOR RELIEVING SECTION AND TO BRING BACK THAT RELIEVED.

RATIONS ALL RATIONS FOR 'A' SECTION WILL BE DUMPED AT LEFT RESERVE SECTION HD. QRS.

ALL THOSE FOR 'D' SECTION WILL BE CARRIED UP ON THE LIMBER WHICH IS PROVIDED FOR CARRYING EQUIPMENT.

RELIEF COMPLETION of RELIEF WILL BE REPORTED BY RUNNERS BY WORD 'BOYS'

Copy No. 1 SECTION OFFICER
2 " "
3 " "
4 " "
5 WAR DIARY
6 FILE
7 BRIGADE
8 WAR DIARY
9 ~~A.A.F.L.~~

ISSUED AT 4·30 PM.

6-5-17

Clemency

[illegible] MACHINE GUN CO.

Copy No. 1 Section Officers
2 " "
3 " "
4 " "
5 War Diary
6 File
7 Brigade
8 War Diary
9 A/Adj.
10 Rt. Batt.
11 Lt. Batt.
12 OC. 105 M.G. Co
13 Section Officers
14 " "
15 " "

OPERATION ORDER No. 63 — COPY No. 5

THE 106 MACHINE GUN Co. WILL BE RELIEVED IN THE LINE BY THE 105 MACHINE GUN Co. ON NIGHT OF 9/10th MAY 1917.

POSITIONS. DISPOSITIONS WILL BE HANDED OVER AS TAKEN OVER.
ALL ANTI AIRCRAFT POSITIONS & ALL I.F.Ps WILL BE HANDED OVER TO INCOMING SECTION OFFICERS.

GUIDES. 1 GUIDE PER DETACHMENT FOR THE TWO FORWARD GUNS OF "C" SECTION WILL PARADE AT SECTION HD.QRS AT 9.45 P.M.
1 GUIDE PER DETACHMENT FOR GUNS IN [illegible] WILL BE AT COPSE M 22 c & C AT 9.30 P.M.

ARRIVAL. THE INCOMING SECTIONS FOR RIGHT RESERVE, LEFT RESERVE AND LEFT FRONT LINE SECTIONS WILL ARRIVE AT THE RESPECTIVE HD.QRS AT 9.4[illegible]

EQUIPMENT. NINE FILLED BELT BOXES WILL BE HANDED OVER AT GUN POSITIONS MG 1, MG 2, MG 3 AND EIGHT AT GUN POSITIONS MG 4, MG 5 AND MG 6.
ALL S.A.A. TRENCH MOUNTINGS AND PETROL TINS WILL BE HANDED OVER.
RECEIPTS WILL BE OBTAINED.

RELIEF. RELIEF WILL BE REPORTED TO CO. H.Q AT VILLECHOLLES BY WORD "ARE"

WITHDRAWAL. ON RELIEF SECTIONS WILL WITHDRAW BY ROUTE AT DISCRETION OF SECTION COMMANDERS TO BILLETS AT VILLEVEQUE FORMERLY OCCUPIED.

TRANSPORT. BATTLE LIMBERS ARRIVE AS UNDER.
"B" SECTION H.Q 9.45 P.M.
"A" SECTION HD.QRS 9.45 P.M.
"C" SECTION Hd.QRS 10.15 P.M.
"D" AT GAP IN WIRE 10.15 P.M.

REMAINDER OF TRANSPORT WILL WITHDRAW UNDER MUTUAL ARRANGEMENTS OF T.O's AND C.S.M's CONCERNED.

ISSUED AT 10 a.m.
9/5/1917

[illegible signature] Lt. for CAPTAIN,
O.C. 106 MACHINE GUN Co

COPY 1 } SECTION OFFICERS
2 "
3 "
4 "
5 WAR DIARY
6 FILE
7 BRIGADE
8 WAR DIARY
9 105th M.G.C.
10 TRANSP. OFFICER.

SECRET. COPY No. 5

OPERATION ORDER No 64

THREE detachments of 106th Machine Gun Co. will relieve 3 detachments of 104th M.G.Co on the night of 14/15th May 1917.

1. DISPOSITIONS. 1 Gun BERTHAUCOURT, 1 Gun RIVER BANK, 1 Gun EAST of MAISSEMY.
2. PARADE. "A" Section, (less 1 detachment) under 2/Lt. A.H. FISHER PARADE AT 7.15 P.M.
3. ROUTE. MARTEVILLE, VILLECHOLLES, SECTION Hd. QRS MAISSEMY R 23 d 4.3
4. GUIDES. 1 Guide per detachment will be at Section H.Q MAISSEMY At 8.30 P.M.
5. DRESS. FIGHTING ORDER. GREAT-COATS ROLLED ON BELT, WATERPROOF SHEETS UNDER FLAP OF HAVERSACK.
6. HANDING OVER. ALL S.A.A. IN BOXES, ALL AREA STORES AND ALL COVERS-TRENCH WILL BE TAKEN OVER.

   10 BELT BOXES FILLED WILL BE TAKEN OVER AT BERTHAUCOURT.

   Section Officers will EXCHANGE RECEIPTS and will RENDER RETURN OF ALL TAKEN OVER.

   10 BELTS WILL BE HANDED OVER TO 104th M.G.Co. AT VILLEVEQUE UNDER ARRANGEMENTS TO BE MADE BY Second-in-Command and Adjutants concerned.
7. Command. One detachment of "A" Section will come under command of "B" Section.

   "A" Section (LESS 1 detachment) will come under TACTICAL CONTROL OF G.O.C. 105th Brigade.
8. TRANSPORT. On completion of duty TRANSPORT WILL RETURN TO VILLEVEQUE.
9. RELIEF. Completion of Relief will be REPORTED TO Hd.QRS 106th M.G.Co. And Hd.QRS. 105th M.G.Co. MARTEVILLE by WORD "HERE"
10. HEADQUARTERS. Hd. QRS of 106th M.G.Co. will remain established at VILLEVEQUE.

MAY 13th 1917.

Issued at 9 pm

Copy No. 1 Section Officer
" 2 " "
" 3 " "
" 4 " "
" 5 War Diary
" 6 File
" 7 Brigade
" 8 War Diary
" 9 104th M.G.Co
" 10 105th M.G.Co.
" 11 105th Brigade.

COPY No. 5

SECRET

OPERATION ORDER No 65

REFCE. O.O. No 64.

1. Command "A" Section (LESS 1 detachment) will come under the orders of O.C 105th M.G.Co. on completion of Relief for discipline & Tactics.

2 Reports. DAILY TACTICAL PROGRESS REPORTS WILL BE RENDERED TO O.C. 105th M.G.Co. And all other Tactical messages after Relief has been reported complete as in O.O No. 64 PARA 7.

3 Rations & Ammunition. Rations & Ammunition will be supplied by O.C 106th M.G.Co.

4. Casualties. Casualties will be reported to both 105th & 106th M.G.Co. Hd QRS.

Issued at: 14-5-17

COPY No. 1 Section Officer
2 " "
3 " "
4 " "
5 WAR DIARY
6 FILE
7 BRIGADE
8 WAR DIARY

[illegible] Capt
Comdg no 106
M.G.Co

SECRET

COPY No. 8

OPERATION ORDER No. 66

The Co. (Less 1 Sub-section) will move from VILLEVEQUE to PERONNE on the 19th MAY 1917 by Route March.

STARTING POINT. The starting point cross roads TERTRY W2 c 3 9 at 7.22 A.M.

PARADE. Co will parade ready to march off at 5.45am. Marching off at 5.52 am.

ORDER OF MARCH. Signallers C.D.B. Subsection of A and Headquarters. Peace formations Limbers. Battle wagons C.D.B.A. Nos 3 CDBA Hd.Qrs limber water cart & cooks cart.

POINT OF ASSEMBLY.
Head of transport will be assembled at road junction VILLEVEQUE W 12 d 8.9 at 5.40 A.M

ROUTE. TREFCON TERTRY thence to PERONNE by the main TERTRY-DOINGT-PERONNE Road.

HOUR OF ARRIVAL. Probable hour of arrival 11.00 A.M.

RATIONS. The unconsumed portions of the days rations will be carried on the man. All horses will carry feeds.

DIXCIES. All Dixcies will be placed on the wagons by 5.30 A.M.

RELIEF. Sub-section of 'A' now in the line will be relieved on the night of 19/20th under orders of 105 M.G. Co. They will march from VILLEVEQUE to PERONNE on the 20th. Probable hour of starting — noon. Route as above.

TRANSPORT FOR 'A' SECTION. 1 limber 4 mules and 1 officers horse will proceed to the Transport Lines of 105th M.G. Co where they will dump 2 mules rear portion of limber & the officers charger. The fore portion of the limber with 2 mules will carry rations to the section to-night. They will return on completion of duty to the Transport Lines of 105 M.G. Co. The whole will come under orders of 105 M.G. Co.

Issued at 18—5—17

[signature] Lt for
O.C. 106 M.G. Coy

Copy No. 1 Section Officer
2 " "
3 " "
4 " "
5 War Diary
6 File
7 Brigade
8 War Diary
9 105 M.G. Co.
10 Transport Officer
11 2nd-in-Command.

SECRET. Copy No: 5

OPERATION ORDER No. 67.

The Company will move from PERONNE to camp near SOREL-LE-GRAND W 19 d. on 21-5-17.

STARTING POINT. Cross roads east of PERONNE I 22 d 6 7 at 7.25 AM.

PARADE. Coy will parade at 7.15 A.M. marching off at 7.25 A.M.

ORDER OF MARCH.

Signallers Headquarters D.B.A.C. Traffic formations 200 yards interval between sections. Nos 2 D.B.A.C. HdQrs Water cart Cooks cart.

1 man B. 1 Man C Section. Rearguard of 1 N.C.O. of D

POINT OF ASSEMBLY.

Transport will be assembled at H.Q.rs at 6.45 A.M. facing east.

ROUTE. BUSSU LONGAVESNES, LIERAMONT to camp near SOREL-LE-GRAND.

HOUR OF ARRIVAL. Probable hour of arrival 12 noon

RATIONS. The unconsumed portion of the days rations will be carried on the man.

DIXCIES. All Dixcies to be placed on wagons by 7.00 A.M.

20-5-17

[signature]

Copy No. 1 Section Officer
2 " "
3 " "
4 " "
5 WAR DIARY
6 FILE
7 BRIGADE
8 WAR DIARY.

COPY No 5

SECRET

OPERATION ORDER No 68

106 Machine Gun Co will Relieve 121 M. G. Co in the line on the night 22/23 and 23/24

B & C Sections on night 22/23

D & A " " " 23/24

1 DISPOSITIONS. B Sect 4 Guns front line system on Right
C " 4 " " " " " LEFT.
D " 4 " " " " " GREEN LINE
A " 4 " " " " " BROWN "

2 PARADE. "B" and C Sections will Parade at 7.30 P.M.

3 ROUTE. SOREL-LE-GRAND, HEUDICOURT, RAILTON VAUCELETTE FARM to Co. HQ.RS AT VILLERS.

4 GUIDES. 1 Guide for Section will be at Co. H.Q.RS at 8.30 P.M.
1 Guide for Gun Team at Sect. HQ.RS at 9.15 PM
1 Guide for S.A.A. and AREA STORES TRENCH COVERS and

5 HANDING OVER. All S.A.A. and AREA STORES [illegible] will be taken over
All Belt boxes will be taken over
Section Officers will exchange Receipts and Render a Return to this office of all taken over.
80 Belt Boxes will be handed over by [illegible] at Co. HdQRS to-night.
Transport Officer at Co. HdQRS [illegible]

6 TRANSPORT On completion of Duty Transport will Return to Camp [illegible]

7 PARADE A D Section will parade at 6.00 P.M. on the 23rd inst.
" " " 7.30 P.M. on the 23rd inst

8 ROUTE D Section. As per Order No. 3
A " Above Order to VAUCELETTE FARM.

9 GUIDES A Sect. 1 Guide per Gun Team Co. Hd.QRS 9.30 PM
D Sect. 1 " " " " at Crossing X 13 a 3.1
A Sect. 1 " " " at 7.30 P.M.

10 HANDING OVER. All S.A.A. Area Stores & Trench Covers will be taken over. 10 Belt Boxes per Gun will be taken into line.
Receipts to be Rendered to Hd. QRS.

11 TRANSPORT. On completion of Duty Transport will Return to Transport Lines HEUDICOURT.
Transport Remaining at Camp will move to HEUDICOURT under arrangements made by Transport Officers.

12 DRESS. Fighting Order. Greatcoats Rolled on Belts [illegible] Waterproof Sheets under flap of Haversack.

13 RELIEF. Completion of Relief for Half Co. in FORWARD AREA Reported by word "YAAKA" by Runner
Half Co. in Back Area by word by Runner "HULA

14 COMMAND O.C. 121 M.G. Co. will Remain in Command of Sector until completion of Second Relief. Hd QRS will be temporarily established in VILLERS X 18 d. 9.7 on completion of Double Relief.

Issued at 1 P.M. 22-5-17

[illegible] Capt
O.C. 106 M. G. Coy.

Copy No. 1 Section Officer
2 " "
3 " "
4 " "
5 WAR DIARY
6 FILE
7 BRIGADE
8 WAR DIARY
9 O.C. 121 M.G. Co.

SECRET COPY No 5

OPERATION ORDER No 69

An inter Co. Relief will take place on the night of 29/30th May 1917 as under.

"A" Section will relieve "B" Section
"D" " " " "C" "

Time "A" Section will commence Relieving at 12 midnight
"D" Section will commence Relieving at 9.30 P.M.

Dispositions
"A" Section M.G. 1, 2, 3 and 4
"B" " M.G.s 1, 2, 3 and 4
"C" " M.G.S 1, 2, 3 and 4
"D" " M.G. 5, 6, 7 and 8.

Guides.
Guides will be arranged by Section Officers.

TRANSPORT.
1 Limber will report to each of "A" and "D" Section Headquarters fifteen minutes before the times for commencement of Reliefs to assist in carrying.

Ammunition. All Belt boxes will be handed over

Reliefs. Completion of Relief will be reported to Co H.Q. by runner by word "HICKY".

Issued at 7 P.M. 28/5/17

A H [illegible] Lt for
O.C. SPY

Copy No. 1 Section Officer
2 " "
3 " "
4 " "
5 War Diary
6 File
7 Brigade
8 War Diary

SECRET. COPY No. 5

OPERATION ORDER No. 70

One detachment of 106th M.G.Co. at M.G. 8 will be Relieved by one detachment of 104th M.G. Co. on the night 31-5-17/1-6-17.

1 TIME. The Relieving detachment will proceed to "D" Section H.Q. with Ration Limber leaving Cross Roads W.16 d 9.0 at 9.30 P.M.

2 DISPOSITIONS. "D" Section M.G. 5, 6, 7. Relieved detachment at Section H.Q.

3 GUIDES. A Guide will meet incoming detachment at Section H.Q.

4 AMMUNITION. S.A.A. and Trench Stores only will be handed over for which signed Receipts will be obtained.

5. RELIEF. Completion of Relief will be Reported by word "DULA"

Issued at 1.30PM 31/5/17

[signature] Lt. for
CAPTAIN,
O.C. 106 MACHINE GUN Co

Copy No. 1 Section Officer
2 "
3 "
4 "
5 WAR DIARY
6 FILE
7 BRIGADE
8 WAR DIARY
9 104th M.G.Co.

Instructions regarding War Diaries and Intelligence Summaries are contained in F. S. Regs., Part II. and the Staff Manual respectively. Title pages will be prepared in manuscript.

WAR DIARY
or
INTELLIGENCE SUMMARY.
(*Erase heading not required.*)

Army Form C. 2118.

106th M.G.Co.

Vol 14

Place	Date	Hour	Summary of Events and Information	Remarks and references to Appendices
In the Field	1/6/17	–	The Coy was relieved by 105th M.G.C. & marched to reserve billets at AIZECOURT LE BAS.	57C
AIZECOURT LE BAS	2/6/17		Arrived at Camp	
-do	2-9/6/17		Rest at AIZECOURT LE BAS.	
In the Field	9/6/17		Coy relieved 104th M.G.Co. in the GAUCHE WOOD Sector. Dispositions B Sec. 4 guns FRONT LINE SYSTEM. A " 4 " GREEN LINE D " 1 " BROWN LINE 3 " Indirect Fire. C " 4 " HEUDICOURT.	
	13/6/17		Inter Coy Relief A Sec relieved B Sec D " " A " C " " D " B to rest at HEUDICOURT.	
	17/6/17		Inter Coy Relief. D Sec relieved A Sec C " " D " B " " C " A " at rest	
	18/6/17		a 5th gun was sent up to FRONT LINE SYSTEM.	

A5834 Wt. W4973 M687 750,000 8/16 D. D. & L. Ltd. Forms/C.2118/13.

Instructions regarding War Diaries and Intelligence Summaries are contained in F. S. Regs., Part II. and the Staff Manual respectively. Title pages will be prepared in manuscript.

WAR DIARY
or
INTELLIGENCE SUMMARY.
(Erase heading not required.)

Army Form C. 2118.

Place	Date	Hour	Summary of Events and Information	Remarks and references to Appendices
In the Field	19/6/17		Indirect fire was carried out on to BANTEUX 2000 rds fired	57
	20/6/17		Indirect fire again took place BANTEUX fired on. 3000 rds fired.	
	21/6/17		Inter Coy Relief A Sec BROWN LINE B " GREEN LINE C " FRONT LINE SYSTEM. D " at Rest Indirect fire took place 2000 rds were fired on to BANTEUX	
	22/6/17		BANTEUX & BANTOUZELLE were fired on 4000 rds expended.	
	23/6/17		In conjunction with a Brigade Entrenching Operation 1 gun fired on to BANTEUX 1800 rds between 11pm & 1am 23/6/17-24/6/17. 2 guns were standing by	
	25/6/17		The digging of the trench again continued 1500 rds were again fired on BANTEUX The Coy was relieved by 105th M.G.Co.	
	26/6/17		March to AIZECOURT LE BAS to rest billets.	

Ammerson Capt
Comdg No 106 M.G.Co.

A5834 Wt. W4973 M687 750,000 8/16 D. D. & L. Ltd. Forms/C.2118/13.

SECRET

COPY No. 5

OPERATION ORDER No. 11

The 106th M.G.Co. will be relieved in the line by the 105th M.G.Co. on the night of 1/2nd JUNE 1917.

1 DISPOSITIONS. All positions will be handed over including A.A.Ps and I.F.Ps.

2 GUIDES. 1 Guide per DETACHMENT will be at SECTION H.Q as under.

"A" SECTION 10 P.M.
"B" " 8 P.M.
"C" " 11.30 P.M.
"D" " 10.00 P.M.

In addition "A" SECTION will have 1 guide at VAUCELETTE FARM at 9.30 p.m. to guide "A" SECTION LIMBER to SECTION H.Q.

3 EQUIPMENT. S.A.A. & Trench stores only will be handed over.
PETROL TINS WILL NOT BE handed over.

4. RELIEF. SECTIONS WILL REPORT COMPLETION OF RELIEF TO THIS Office by WORD "BLACK"

5 WITHDRAWAL. On RELIEF SECTIONS WILL WITHDRAW TO CAMP AT AISECOURT-LE-BAS. Guides will be met at the QR.MR. STORES.

6 TRANSPORT. Battle limbers will REPORT AT SECTION H.Q AS FOLLOWS.

"A" SECTION AT 11.15 P.M.
"B" " " 8.30 P.M.
"C" " " 12.15 AM
"D" " " 11.00 P.M.

Remainder of TRANSPORT WILL WITHDRAW UNDER MUTUAL ARRANGEMENTS OF T.O. And C.S.M's concerned.

ISSUED AT 10.PM 31/5/17

106 M.G.Co.

Copy No. 1 Section Officer ✓
2 " " ✓
3 " " ✓
4 " " ✓
5 WAR DIARY
6 FILE
7 BRIGADE ✓
8 WAR DIARY
9 T.O. ✓
10 O.C. 105 M.G.Co. ✓

SECRET. COPY No. 5

OPERATION ORDER No 72.

The 106th M. G. Co. will relieve 104th M. G. Co. in the LINE on the night of 9/10th June 1917

1. **DISPOSITIONS.**

"A" Section 4 Guns GREEN LINE
"B" " 4 " FRONT LINE SYSTEM
"C" " 4 " HEUDICOURT.
"D" " {1 Gun BROWN LINE
{3 Guns Adv Co. Hd. QRS.

2. **GUIDES.**

"A" SECTION will meet 1 Guide per detachment AT 9.15PM AT SECTION H.Q. W16d60.15
"B" SECTION will meet Guide AT HEUDICOURT AT 8.30P.M. for KITCHEN CRATER Guides AT KITCHEN CRATER AT 10P.M.
"D" SECTION WILL MEET 1 GUIDE AT BROWN LINE (W11a 75.20) for DETACHMENT IN BROWN LINE.

3 **PARADE**

A Section move off at 7.00P.M.
B " " " 7.15 P.M.
C " " " 5.45 P.M.
D " " " 7.00 P.M
Hd. QRS. " " 5.45 P.M

DRESS. FIGHTING ORDER.

4 **EQUIPMENT** S.A.A and Trench Stores only WILL BE TAKEN OVER

5. **RELIEF** Completion of Relief will be REPORTED TO THIS Office by word "BOYS"

6 **TRANSPORT.** Transport Officer & C.Q.M.S WILL MAKE their own ARRANGEMENTS.

ISSUED AT 9.30P.M 8-6-17

J Seddon 2/Lt. CAPTAIN,
O.C. 106 MACHINE GUN CO.

Copy No 1 Section Officer
2 "
3 "
4 "
5 WAR DIARY
6 FILE
7 BRIGADE
8 WAR DIARY
9 T. O.
10 O.C. 104th MG Co.

SECRET. COPY No 5

OPERATION ORDER No 73

AN INTER COMPANY RELIEF WILL TAKE PLACE ON THE NIGHT 13/14th JUNE 1917.

1 DISPOSITIONS

"A" SECTION 4 GUNS FRONT LINE SYSTEM
"C" " 1 GUN BROWN LINE, 3 GUNS ADVANCED Co. H.Q.
"D" " 4 GUNS GREEN LINE.
"B" " RESERVE BILLETS HEUDICOURT.

2 GUIDES will be ARRANGED Between Section OFFICERS concerned.

3 EQUIPMENT. Guns TRIPODS & SPARE PARTS only will be TAKEN.

4 TIME. "C" Section will commence Relief at 9.30 P.M. "D" Section on being Relieved by "C" will Relieve "A" Sect.
"A" Section on Relief will Relieve "B" Sect.
"B" Section on Relief will proceed to HEUDICOURT BY ROUTE at discretion of SECTION Officer.

5 RELIEF Completion of relief will be Reported to this office by WORD "YACKEL"

6 TRANSPORT.

TRANSPORT OFFICER will MAKE ARRANGEMENTS for necessary LIMBERS.

ISSUED AT 7.30 P.M 12-6-17

J Seddon 2/Lt for O.C. Coy.

Copy No. 1 SECTION OFFICER
2 " "
3 " "
4 " "
5 WAR DIARY
6 FILE
7 BRIGADE
8 WAR DIARY

SECRET

COPY No. 5

OPERATION ORDER No. 74

An INTER COMPANY RELIEF will take place on the night 17/18th June 1917

1 DISPOSITIONS "A" Section Rest Billets HEUDICOURT
"B" SECTION 1 Gun Front line SYSTEM.
1 " BROWN LINE
2 GUNS Advanced C Hd QRS
"C" SECTION 4 Guns Green LINE.
"D" SECTION 4 Guns Front line System.

2. TIME. "B" SECTION commence relief at 9.30 P.M.
"C" SECTION on being Relieved By "B" will Relieve "D" SECTION
"D" SECTION on relief will relieve "A" Section
"A" Section on relief will Proceed to HEUDICOURT By ROUTE AT Discretion of SECTION Officer.

3 GUIDES will BE ARRANGED between Section Officers concerned.

4 EQUIPMENT.
GUNS, TRIPODS and SPARE PARTS only WILL BE TAKEN.

5 TRANSPORT.
NECESSARY TRANSPORT WILL BE ARRANGED BY TRANSPORT OFFICER.

6. RELIEF.
COMPLETION of relief WILL BE REPORTED BY WORD "HACKI"

Issued at 8.30 P.M. 16/6/17.

J Heddon 2/Lt for O.C. Coy.

Copy No. 1 Section Officer
2 " "
3 " "
4 " "
5 WAR DIARY
6 FILE
7 BRIGADE
8 WAR DIARY
9 TRANSPORT Officer

SECRET

Copy No 5

OPERATION ORDER No 75

DISPOSITIONS. No 4 Gun Position. Front line system (R 33 d 7.7) This position will be manned by a detachment with Gun from "B" Section and will come under the orders of O.C "D" Section

18 - 6 - 17

Copy No 1 Section Officer
2 " "
3 " "
4 " "
5 War Diary
6 File
7 Brigade.
8 War Diary

SECRET

COPY No. 5

OPERATION ORDER No. 76

An inter Company Relief will take place on the night 21/22nd June 1917

1. DISPOSITIONS

"A" Section 1 Gun Brown line, 3 Guns Adv. Co. H.Qrs.
"B" " 4 Guns GREEN LINE.
"C" " 4 Guns Front line System.
"D" " Rest Billets HEUDICOURT

2. TIME.

"A" Section will commence Relief of Brown line Gun at 9.00 P.M.
"B" Section on being Relieved by "A" will Relieve "C" Section
"C" Section on Relief will Relieve "D" Section

3. GUIDES.

"B" Section will have a guide for Brown Line Gun at Junction of ROAD and TRACK (W11 a 8.2) by 9.00 P.M.
OTHER GUIDES WILL BE ARRANGED BY SECTION OFFICERS CONCERNED.

4. WITHDRAWAL.

"D" Section on Relief will proceed to HEUDICOURT by ROUTE at Discretion of SECTION Officer.

5 EQUIPMENT

Guns, TRIPODS and SPARE PARTS only will be taken.

6 TRANSPORT.

Necessary Transport will be arranged by TRANSPORT Officer.

7 RELIEF

Completion of Relief will be Reported by WORD "WICKI"

ISSUED at 8.50 P.M. 20/6/17

Copy No. 1. Section Officer
2 " "
3 " "
4 " "
5 War Diary
6 File
7 Brigade
8 War Diary
9 T. O.

SECRET. COPY No. 5

OPERATION ORDER No. 77

The following Machine Gun Operations & Preparations are to be carried out in conjunction with a large working party during the night 23/24th June 1917.

GUN IN ACTION. One Gun "A" Section under Lt. H.N. Fisher will fire on BANTEUX from X 4 a 8.9

GUNS IN READINESS. One Gun "A" Section under 2/Lt. E.A. Hawkes will be in readiness at R 33 c 10.75 to fire on R. 28 d. 7.6 Range 1650x to 1800x Mag. Bearings 70° Height of Gun 300 Height of Target 390

One Gun "A" Section under 2/Lt J. Seddon will be in readiness at X 3 b 6.3 to fire on R29 d 55.45 and R. 29 d 2.9 Range 2500x Mag Bear. 56° to 65° Hgt. of Gun 366 Height of Target 360 & 345.

HOUR OF READINESS. 10.45 P.M.

COMMENCEMENT OF OPERATIONS. Gun under Lt/ H.N. Fisher will commence to fire at 11.00 p.m. and continue firing until 1.00 A.M.

Guns under 2/Lts. E.A. Hawkes & J. Seddon will open fire on Artillery firing one round

RATE OF FIRE. Lt. H.N. Fisher - 1 Belt per Gun per 20 minutes (1500 rounds in all)

2/Lts. Hawkes & Seddon - Rapid for 20 Seconds between 1st & 2nd Rounds of the Artillery

S.O.S. SIGNAL. On S.O.S. Signal going up the three T.P. Guns will fire 1000 Rounds Rapid on their targets.

TRANSPORT. Limbers will be up at Front Line System H.Q. at 10.15 P.M.

WITHDRAWAL. The Guns will withdraw at 3.00 pm. under arrangements of officers unless previously advised

S.O.S. GUNS. The following S.O.S. lines will be laid out as under. —

	RANGE	MAG. BEARING.
L 1.	2250x	51° to 63°
L 2.	1700x	57° to 71°
L 4.	1700x	80° to 86°

These Guns will open fire on the S.O.S going up. Expenditure of Ammunition 1,000 Rounds.

COMPANY HD. QRS. Co. Hd. Qrs will be established "A" Section H.Q. GLASS STREET, to where all reports will be sent.

Issued at 6.15 PM. 23/6/17

Copy No 1 Section Officer
2 " "
3 " "
4 " "
5 War Diary
6 File
7 Brigade
8 War Diary
9 O.C. D.V.
10 O.C. J.G.
11 O.C. Q1
12 O.C. E.P.

[signature] Capt.
Comdg C H

SECRET.

COPY No. 5

OPERATION ORDER No. 78

The 106th Machine Gun Co. will be relieved by the 105th M.G. Co. in the line on the night of 25/26th June 1917.

1 DISPOSITIONS. All positions handed over including A.A.P's and I.F.P's.

2. GUIDES. 1 Guide at Heudicourt for Front line Section H.Qrs. at 9.15 P.M.

1 Guide at HEUDICOURT for Adv. Co. Hd. Qrs at 9.15 P.M.

1 Guide for Brown line Gun will be at point where Track crosses Road (W 11 a 8.2) at 9.20 P.M.

1 Guide per detachment for

"B" Section at Adv. Co. HQ at 9.30 P.M.

"C" " " Section HQ at 10.30 P.M.

A Section will have a Guide at Adv. Co. H.Q. to show incoming detachment to their Billets.

C.H. Smith will be at Adv. Co. Hd. Qrs to show the Relieving Officer round the I.F.P's.

3 EQUIPMENT. S.A.A. and Trench Stores only will be handed over.

4 RELIEF. Completion of Relief to be reported to Co. Office by word "WACKI"

5. WITHDRAWAL. Sections on being relieved will withdraw to rest Billets at AIZECOURT-LE-BAS.

The 3 Guns of "A" Section employed for indirect fire will withdraw on completion of the Minor Operation in accordance with O.O. No. 79

6 TRANSPORT. Limbers to report as follows:—

"B" Section to report at Adv Co. H.Q. at 10.00 P.M.

"C" " " " "C" Sect HQ at 10.30 P.M.

"A" " " " Adv. Co. H.Q. at 10.00 P.M.

Remainder of Transport will withdraw under mutual arrangements of T.O's and C.S.M's concerned.

Issued at 11.00 A.M. 25/6/17

[signature illegible]

Copy No. 1 Section Officer
2 " "
3 " "
4 " "
5 War Diary
6 File
7. Brigade
8 War Diary
9 T.O.
10 O.C. 105th M.G.C.

SECRET. COPY No. 5

OPERATION ORDER No. 79

The following Machine Gun Operations & Preparations are to be carried out in conjunction with a large working party during the night 25/26th June 1917.

GUN IN ACTION. One Gun "A" Section under Lt H.N. Fisher will fire on BANTEUX from X4a 8.9

GUNS IN READINESS. One Gun "A" Section under ~~2/Lt E.A.~~ Lt P. H. Cooper ~~Hawes~~ will be in readiness at R 33 d 10.75 to fire on R 28 d 7.6
Range 1650x to 1800x Mag Bearing 70°
Height of Gun 300' Height of Target 390'
One Gun "A" Section under Lt H.E. Talbot will be in readiness at X 3 b 6.3 to fire on R29 d 55.45 and R29 d 2.9
Range 2500x Mag. Bearing 56° to 65° Height of Gun 366' Height of Target 360' & 345'

HOUR OF READINESS 10.45 P.M.

COMMENCEMENT OF OPERATIONS. Gun under Lt/H.N. Fisher will commence to fire at 11.00 P.M. & continue firing until 1.00 AM. Guns under ~~2/Lts E.A. Hawes~~ Lt. P. H Cooper and Lt H.E. Talbot will open fire on Artillery firing one round.

RATE OF FIRE. Lt H.N Fisher - 1 Belt per Gun per 20 minutes (1500 Rounds in all)
Lts. Cooper & Talbot - Rapid for 20 seconds between 1st & 2nd Rounds of the Artillery.

S.O.S. SIGNAL. On S.O.S. Signal going up the three I.F. Guns will fire 1,000 Rounds rapid on their targets.

TRANSPORT. 1 Limber of "A" Section to be at Advanced Co. Hd. QRS at 9.30 A.M.

WITHDRAWAL. The Guns will withdraw at 3.00 A.M. under arrangements of Officers unless previously advised.

COMPANY Hd. QRS Co. Hd. QRS will be established at Section H Q GLASS STREET to where all reports will be sent.

25/6/17

Copy No 1 Section Officer
2 " "
3 " "
4 " "
5 War Diary
6 File
7 Brigade
8 War Diary
9 OC D.V.
10 " J G
11 " Q. 1
12 " E.P.

[signature] Capt.
Comdg C H

Copy No 5

Operation Order No 101

The following inter-company relief will take place on the night of 30/31st August 1917

<u>Relief</u> The personnel of A Section under [illegible] will relieve the personnel of B Section. The personnel of C Sect. on relief will relieve the personnel of D Sect. in the front line posts

<u>Dispositions</u> B Section CAT Post
TUNCAN "
DOLEFUL "
A Section EGO "
I Group at BASSE BOULOGNE
C " H " to LEMPIRE [illegible]

<u>Guides</u> 1 Guide per detachment will be at BASSE BOULOGNE S. at 8 p.m.

<u>Command</u> 2/Lt J Seddon will take over command of "C" Section, 2/Lt E. A. Hawkes returning to H.Q.

<u>Withdrawal</u> D Section under 2/Lt R. SKEVINGTON will withdraw to H.Q. on Completion of Relief.

<u>Completion of Relief</u> will be reported by wire by word "EMERGETIC"

30/8/17

Copy No 1 Section Officer
2 "
3 "
4/5 War [illegible]
6 File
7 Brigade
8 War Diary

C W Merrison [illegible]

Army Form C. 2118.

Instructions regarding War Diaries and Intelligence Summaries are contained in F. S. Regs., Part II. and the Staff Manual respectively. Title pages will be prepared in manuscript.

106th Machine Gun Company
WAR DIARY
or
~~INTELLIGENCE SUMMARY.~~
(Erase heading not required.)

(July 1917)

No 15

Place	Date	Hour	Summary of Events and Information	Remarks and references to Appendices
Field	July 1		The Company cooperated in a raid which was carried out by a battalion of 104 Inf. Bde. 8 guns of this Coy. and 2 guns of 104 M.G Coy. placed a frontal barrage on HONNECOURT WOOD; duration of firing - 5 mins. Rounds expended 7750 (see O.O. No 80). It was stated by a prisoner that this barrage was very effective and that the success of the raid was due to it. That the fire was very accurate and many casualties inflicted. Had high banks not existed in the wood the enemies losses would have been very heavy. See 35th Div, 3rd Corps, and 3rd Army summaries.	
	2nd		Co. moved from AIZECOURT-LE-BAS to LONGAVESNES.	
	5th		Co. moved to ST. EMILIE to take over the line from 4th Cavalry M.G. Squadron. 12 guns front line - 4 guns KEN. HQ at ST EMILIE.	
	5th/6th		Relieved the 4th M.G. Squadron	
	7th		Dispositions altered to be as follows - 1 gun F post - 2 guns E post, 2 guns C post 1 gun D post, - 2 guns at H.Q - 4 guns at KEN.	
	8/9		2 guns withdrawn. 1 gun from E post - 1 gun from C post. Intermediate line taken up. 1 gun TOINE post - ORCHARD post, 2 guns BASSÉ BOULOGNES, 1 gun LEMPIRE C., LEMPIRE E., 2 guns YAK post. Indirect fire carried out onto MALAKOFF and QUENNEMENT farms. Time 10 P.M. - 12 M.N. 4000 rounds expended	
	9th/10th		Inter Coy Relief B Sec - front line - C & D Secs Intermediate line - A Sec. at H.Q. Indirect Fire carried out onto QUENNET COPSE and QUENNEMENT FARM - Time 12 M.N. - 2 A.M. 3000 rounds expended. Aircraft engaged.	

B. Wimerson Capt

A5834 Wt. W4973 M687 750,000 8/16 D. D. & L. Ltd. Forms/C.2118/13.

Army Form C. 2118.

Instructions regarding War Diaries and Intelligence Summaries are contained in F. S. Regs., Part II. and the Staff Manual respectively. Title pages will be prepared in manuscript.

WAR DIARY
or
INTELLIGENCE SUMMARY.
(Erase heading not required.)

Place	Date	Hour	Summary of Events and Information	Remarks and references to Appendices
	JULY 11th		Indirect fire carried out onto new hostile work on new hostile work at F.6. - A.1. and S 25. from 10 30 P.M to 1 A.M. New work on TOMBOIS trench was fired on from 1 A.M. to 2 A.M. 6000 rounds expended.	
	12/13		In answer to S.O.S. guns at TOMBOIS farm - E post and D post opened fire on their S.O.S. lines. Guns at Yak post and LEMPIRE E (intermediate line) also opened fire. 7750 rounds fired. L/Cpl PRENDERGAST recommended for D.C.M. for good work. Indirect fire carried out on MALAKOFF farm & QENNET COPSE. Time 10.30 P.M - 2 A.M. 4000 rounds expended. Enemy aircraft engaged during daylight. 500 rounds expended.	
	13th		Guns at BASSE BOULOGNES opened fire on S.O.S. lines and reported to be very effective. (hitting hostile wire ~~in enfilade~~) Time 2-15 A.M.	
	13/14		Inter-Coy relief carried out without incident. A Sec. relieved D Sec. D Sec relieved C sec. relieved B Sec. B sec. to H.Q. Indirect fire was carried out on BONY and cross roads A 14 d 9.2 and A 15 c 4.6. Time 12 MN - 12.45 A.M. 4000 rounds expended.	
	15th		Indirect fire carried out on QUENNEMENT farm and QUENNET COPSE. also M.G. position near LONETREE.	
	17th		Indirect fire carried out to harass a hostile relief. Points selected A 14 c & d, and A 20 a. Time 10 P.M. - 11.30 P.M. 8000 rounds expended	
	18th		Inter Coy relief carried out without incident (see O.O.) Indirect fire again carried out to harass enemy relief on D 14 c and A 20 a. 11 PM - 1 AM. 9250 rounds expended	
	19th		In answer to S.O.S. Cats post gun fired 500 rounds. E post 1500 rounds 4 guns in S portion of intermediate line fired 10000 rounds. Indirect fire carried out on to A 14 c & d and A 20 a to harass hostile relief. Time 10.30 P.M. - 12 MN. 4800 rounds expended.	G W [illegible]

A5834 Wt. W4973 M687 750,000 8/16 D. D. & L. Ltd. Forms/C.2118/13.

Instructions regarding War Diaries and Intelligence Summaries are contained in F. S. Regs., Part II. and the Staff Manual respectively. Title pages will be prepared in manuscript.

WAR DIARY
or
INTELLIGENCE SUMMARY.
(*Erase heading not required.*)

Army Form C. 2118.

Place	Date	Hour	Summary of Events and Information	Remarks and references to Appendices
	19th contd.		A Sunken Road from A.20d 2.6 to A20a 7.0. was heavily fired on from 10.15 P.M. to 1 P.M. 3500 rounds expended.	
	21st		Indirect Fire carried out on QENNEMENT farm between 10 45 P.M. and 12.30 A.M. also ration dump at A.7.08.1. was searched from 9.45 P.M. to 11 P.M. 4000 rounds expended	
	22nd		Several hostile aircraft engaged 2000 rounds expended.	
	22nd/23rd		Co. relieved in the line by 105 M.G. Coy. On relief proceeded to rest billets at AIZECOURT-LE-BAS. (see O.O. No 88)	
	23rd TO 31st		Co. in rest at AIZECOURT-LE-BAS.	
			Lc. Cpl. PRENDERGAST awarded the Military Medal for gallantry and devotion to duty on the night 12/13 July.	
			WORK Barrage practice and cooperation with infantry in field training, and Company training	

106 MACHINE GUN CO.
Date
ORDERLY

C W Mennon Capt
Comdg No 106 MG Co

A5834 Wt. W4973 M687 750,000 8/16 D. D. & L. Ltd. Forms/C.2118/13.

SECRET COPY No. 5

OPERATION ORDER No 81

MOVE. The company will move from AIZECOURT-LE-BAS to LONGAVESNES passing the starting point – ROAD JUNCTION D 23 b 5.8 – at 10.5 A.M. 2/7/17

HOUR. Company will parade at 9.45 A.M. and move off at 10 A.M.

ORDER OF MARCH. Signallers B.C.D.A. and Hd. Qrs.
PEACE FORMATIONS, IN THREES.
Battle wagons B.C.D.A, No. 3's B.C.D.A. Hd. Qrs wagon, water cart & Mess cart.

HOUR OF ARRIVAL. Probable hour of arrival, 10.45 A.M.

TRANSPORT.
Transport will be drawn up on road West of Hd. Qrs., – head of column facing AIZECOURT-LE-BAS – by 9.45 A.M.
All limbers will be packed by 9.30 A.M.

Issued at 7 p.m. 1/7/17

Copy No 1 Section Officer
2 " "
3 " "
4 " "
5 War Diary
6 File
7 Brigade
8 War Diary
9 Transport Officer.

[illegible] Capt.
Comdg No 101 M.G. Coy

SECRET.

COPY No 5

OPERATION ORDER No 82.

106th Machine Gun Co. will Relieve 4th M. G. Sqd. in "C" Sector on the Night 5/6th July 1917

1. DISPOSITIONS. "C" Section on the right.

2 Guns "A" Post.
2 " "B" "

"A" Section, Centre.

2 Guns "C" Post.
1 Gun "D" "
1 " Guillemont Farm.

"B" Section on the Left.

2 Guns E. Post
2 " "F" "

"D" Section in Reserve at KEN

2 Guides. "A" Section. One Guide per detachment "D" Post Guillemont Fm. will be at Brock at 10.15 P.M. one Guide per detachment for "C" Post will be at KEN at 10.00 P.M.
"B" Section. one Guide per detachment will be at Brock at 10.00 P.M.
"C" Section. One Guide per detachment will be at KEN at 10.00 P.M.
"D" Section one Guide will be at ST. Emilie at 6.30 P.M.

3. Parade. The Co. will Parade at 4.15 P.M. Dress:- Fighting order.

4. ORDER OF MARCH. D Sect. A Sect. B Sect. C Sect.

5. ROUTE. Villers-Faucon to St Emilie 100 yds. interval between sections after leaving Villers-Faucon.

6. MARCH TO LINE. The personnel of D Section will move off from St. Emilie at 6.30 P.M. remaining sections will move off when it is dark enough to proceed.

7. TRANSPORT. will be ready to move off about 8.00 P.M. to take their place in the column of wagons in the following order:—
2 Limbers of "A" Section
2 " " "C" " as near the head of the column as possible.
2 Limbers of B Sect & 2 Limbers of "D" Sect near the end of the column. The guide of these limbers will be the limbers of the 4th M.G. Sqdrn.

8 HOT MEALS. Hot Tea will be provided at St Emilie about 6.00 P.M. Cooks Dixies and necessary transport will proceed under instructions of C.Q.M.S.

9 EQUIPMENT. All S.A.A. & Trench Stores only will be taken over.

10 RELIEF. Completion of relief will be reported to this office by word "MAID"

11 TRANSPORT LINES. T.O. and C.Q.M.S. will make their own arrangements. The transport which is not wanted at St. Emilie will leave the column at Villers-Faucon & go straight to transport lines.

12 CLEARANCE OF CAMP. The Camp at Longavesnes will be cleared by 4.30 P.M.

Issued at 3 P.M.
5/7/17.

Copy No 1 Section Officer
2 " "
3 " "
4 "
5 War Diary
6 File
7 Brigade
8 War Diary
9 T.O.
10 No 4 M.G. Sqdrn.

J. [signature] for
CAPTAIN.
O.C. 106 MACHINE GUN CO.

SECRET. COPY No. 5

OPERATION ORDER No 83.

The following movements will take place on the night of 6/7th July 1917

1 DISPOSITIONS CHANGED. CH 1 SECTION

1 Gun at GUILLEMONT FM. will be relieved by Lewis Gun of E.P.

CH 3 Section The Gun in A & B POSTS will be relieved by Lewis Guns of J.G.

CH 2 SECTION. F. 1 Gun will withdraw

2. WITHDRAWAL Sub section of CH 3 at A Post under Senior N.C.O will withdraw to ST EMILIE on Completion of Relief

Sub section of CH 3 at B post on relief will move to BROCK.

The Gun from GUILLEMONT FM. when relieved will proceed to BROCK

One Gun from F Post will withdraw to BROCK

3 ACCOMMODATION. O.C. CH2 at BROCK will find accommodation in LEMPIRE EAST and LEMPIRE WEST and YAK POSTS.

4 COMMAND. The Gun of CH 2 and the Gun of CH 1 will come under the tactical control of O.C. CH 3 but remain under their respective Commanders for Rations and discipline.

5 DEFENCE. Guns under O C CH 3 and O.C. CH 4 are for defence of the intermediate line

6. TRANSPORT. One limber of CH 3 will be at KEN to draw the Gun to ST EMILIE.

7 COMPLETION OF MOVE will be reported to this Office by wire by the word "OF"

Issued at 1 p.m. 6/7/17

J Seddon 2/Lt for Capt
OC. CH.

Copy no 1 Section Officer
2 " "
3 " "
4 " "
5 War Diary
6 File
7 Brigade
8 War Diary
9 T.O.
10 Div. M.G.O.

Copy No 5

Operation Order No. 85

The following reliefs and moves will take place on the night 8/9th July 1917

1) **Disposition.** 1 Gun of B Sect will be relieved by a Lewis Gun of the H.L.I.

1 Gun of "A" Section C1 will be relieved by a Lewis Gun of the [illegible]

These guns after relief will move to BROCK [illegible]

The following gun positions will be occupied in the intermediate line as under:–

D Section 1 Gun from KEN will relieve the Lewis Gun in TOMBE [illegible] will fire left, the Lewis Gun will occupy the position 20 yards to its right to fire [illegible]

1 Gun from KEN [illegible] Post to fire left.

1 S/Section from KEN to BASSE BOULOGNE with 1 Gun firing right and 1 firing left.

B Section. 1 S/Sect of B Section will occupy the position south of [illegible] Central – 1 firing left and 1 firing right.

A Section. 1 S/Section of "A" Section from Brock Post will occupy two positions at YAK, 1 firing to its front and 1 firing to its right.

2) **Withdrawal.** At 11 pm. 1 S/Section of "C" Section under 2/Lt T.A. Hankes will withdraw to ST EMILIE

3) **Reconnaissance.** During the morning O.C. "C" Sect. will reconnoitre & hand over the position [illegible] portion of intermediate line to O.C. "B" Section

4) **Command.** Sub section "C" YAK POST will come under the command of O.C. "F" Section.

5) **Lines of fire.** Lines of fire for defence of the [illegible] and the intervening ground between front and intermediate line will be [illegible]

6) Completion of [illegible] will be reported to the [illegible] by [illegible] "THE"

Issued at 11.30pm 7/7/17

J. [illegible] 2/Lieut
Capt O.C.
[illegible] M. G. Co.

Copy No 1 Section Officer
2 "
3 "
4 "
5 War Diary
6 File
7 Brigade
8 War Diary
9 Transp. Off.
10 Div. M.G.O.

SECRET

COPY No 5

OPERATION ORDER No 55

THE FOLLOWING RELIEFS AND MOVES WILL TAKE PLACE ON THE NIGHT 9/10th JULY 1917.

1. DISPOSITIONS. "C" SECTION. 1 SUB SECTION OF "C" [illegible] RELIEVE 1 SUB-SECTION OF "B" SECT. IN SOUTH OF LEMPIRE CENTRAL.
1 SUB-SECTION OF "C" SECTION WILL RELIEVE 1 SUB-SECTION OF "A" AT YAK POST
"B" SECTION. 1 GUN OF "B" SECTION FROM SOUTH OF LEMPIRE CENTRAL ON RELIEF WILL RELIEVE 1 GUN OF "A" SECT. AT "C" POST.
1 GUN OF "B" SECTION FROM SOUTH OF LEMPIRE CENTRAL ON RELIEF WILL RELIEVE 1 GUN OF "A" SECTION AT D POST.

2. WITHDRAWAL. "A" SECTION ON RELIEF WILL WITHDRAW UNDER LT. H.M. FISHER TO ST. [illegible]

3. GUIDES. "B" SECTION WILL SEND 1 GUIDE FOR DETACHMENT TO BROCK AT 10 P.M.
"B" SECT. WILL HAVE 1 GUIDE FOR DETACHMENT FOR YAK POST.

4. PARADE. "C" SECTION WILL PARADE AT 9.30 P.M. DRESS. FIGHTING ORDER.

5. TRANSPORT. LIMBERS OF "A" & "C" WILL BE READY TO MOVE OFF AT 9.30 P.M.
1 LIMBER OF "A" WILL BE AT LEMPIRE CENTRAL TO TAKE GUNS TO QUENNEMONT WOOD AND WILL THEN WITHDRAW GUNS OF "A"

6. EQUIPMENT. ALL S.A.A. AND TRENCH STORES WILL BE HANDED OVER.

7. RELIEF. COMPLETION OF RELIEF WILL BE REPORTED BY THE WORD "[illegible]"

ISSUED AT 11 P.M. 8/7/17

J. Beddon [illegible]
for Capt. Cdg. [illegible]

COPY No. 1 SECTION OFFICER
2 " "
3 " "
4 " "
5 WAR DIARY
6 FILE
7 BRIGADE
8 WAR DIARY
9 [illegible]
10 SPARE

SECRET. COPY No. 5

OPERATION ORDER No. 86

THE FOLLOWING RELIEFS WILL TAKE PLACE ON THE NIGHT 13/14th JULY 1917

1 DISPOSITIONS. "A" SECTION WILL RELIEVE "D" SECTION
1 DETACHMENT TOINE POST.
1 " SOUTH OF ORCHARD POST
1 SUB-SECTION [illegible] BOULOGNE SOUTH.
"D" SECTION WILL RELIEVE "C" SECTION
1 DETACHMENT AT SOUTH OF LEMPIRE [illegible]
1 " " LEMPIRE EAST.
1 SUB-SECTION " YAK POST.
"C" SECTION WILL RELIEVE "B" SECTION.
1 DETACHMENT "C" POST
1 " "D" "
1 " "E" "
1 " "F" "

2. WITHDRAWAL. "B" SECTION ON RELIEF WILL WITHDRAW TO ST. EMILIE.

3 GUIDES. "D" SECTION WILL HAVE 1 GUIDE PER DETACHMENT AT [illegible] [illegible] P.M.
"C" SECTION WILL HAVE 1 GUIDE PER DETACHMENT AT [illegible] AT [illegible] P.M.
"B" SECTION WILL HAVE ONE GUIDE PER DETACHMENT AT [illegible] [illegible] AT 11.30 P.M.

4. PARADE. "A" SECTION WILL PARADE AT 9.30 P.M. [illegible] [illegible] OFFICER.

5. TRANSPORT. LIMBERS OF "A" SECTION WILL [illegible] WITH GUNS TO [illegible] AT [illegible] 9.30 P.M. THESE LIMBERS WILL [illegible] BE USED [illegible] "D" SECTION.
LIMBERS OF "D" SECTION WILL REPORT AT BROOK [illegible] 10.30 P.M. AND WILL BE USED TO BRING THE GUNS OF "B" SECTION TO ST. EMILIE.

6. EQUIPMENT. ALL S.A.A. & [illegible] [illegible] STORES WILL BE HANDED OVER.

7 RELIEF. COMPLETION OF RELIEF WILL BE REPORTED BY [illegible] THE CODE WORD "[illegible]" BY THE

8 COMMAND ON COMPLETION OF RELIEF [illegible] WILL BE AS UNDER:
"C" SECTION. LT. [illegible] FRONT LINE.
"D" " 2/LT [illegible] SOUTHERN HALF OF INTERMEDIATE LINE
"A" SECTION LT. [illegible] FISHER, NORTHERN HALF OF INTERMEDIATE LINE.

ISSUED AT 6am. 13th JULY 1917

COPY No 1 SECTION OFFICER
2 " "
3 " "
4 " "
5 WAR DIARY
6 FILE
7 BRIGADE
8 WAR DIARY
9 [illegible]
10 D.M.G.O.

J Seddon 2/Lt for
O.C. C.H.

Copy No. 5

Secret

Operation Order No 87

The following reliefs will take place on the night 17/18th July 1917

Dispositions

'B' Section will relieve 'D' Section
1 detachment at South of Lempire Central
1 " " Lempire East
1 Subsection at YAK post
'D' Section will relieve 'C' Section
1 detachment at C Post
1 " " A "
1 " " E "
1 " " F "

Withdrawal

'C' Section on relief will withdraw to ST EMILIE

Guides

'D' Section will have 1 guide per detm at BROCK at 10 PM
'C' Section will have 1 guide per detm at BROCK at 10 30 PM

Parade

'B' Section will parade at 9 30 pm
Dress. Fighting Order.

Transport

Limbers of 'B' Section & half limber of 'D' Sec will be ready to move off at 9.30 pm
'B' Section limber will be used to withdraw the guns of 'C' Section to ST EMILIE from 'D' 'E' & 'F' posts. The half limber of 'D' Section will be used to withdraw the gun from 'C' post on relief.

Equipment

All SAA, tripods, & trench stores will be handed over.

Relief

Completion of relief will be reported to this office by the word "CHIN"

Command

On completion of relief will be as under

C Section [illegible]
B " [illegible]
D " 2/Lt EA [illegible]

Issued at 8.30PM 17/7/17.

Copy No 1 Section Officer
[illegible]

[illegible signature]

Appx 5

Order No 88

[illegible] M. G. C. will be relieved in C1 Sector in the line by the [illegible] M. G. C. on the night 22/23rd July 1917

Dispositions. All positions will be handed over as follows:—

1 Gun C Post; 1 Gun D Post; 1 Gun [illegible] [illegible] 1 [illegible] [illegible]; 1 [illegible] Tome post; 1 [illegible] Orchard post; [illegible] gun [illegible] Buildings; 1 gun [illegible] [illegible] [illegible] [illegible] [illegible]

[illegible] Central [illegible] Bar [illegible] [illegible]

[illegible] [illegible] Word and Sgt [illegible] and 2 Cpls

Guides. 1 Guide from B Sec. will be at HQ. to guide 1 Section & 3 detachments to BRICK at 8.30 pm.

1 Gun from "A" Sect. will be at HQ to guide 1 Sect and 1 Detachment to KEH at 8.30 pm.

A Sect. 1 Guide per detachment will be at KEH at 9.30 pm.

B Sect. 1 Guide per detachment will be at BRICK at 9.30 pm.

D Sect. Guides for D E & F posts will be at BRICK at 9.30 pm.

1 Guide for "C" post will be at KEH at 9.30 pm.

Equipment. S.A.A. Sketch maps & Trench Stores will be handed over and receipts obtained.

Relief. Sections will report completion of relief by word "C[illegible]W".

The detachment from [illegible] post will report to O.C. A Sect on completion of relief.

Withdrawal. On relief A Sect (with 1 detachment of D Section), B Section & D Sect (less 1 detachment) will withdraw to ST EMILIE.

Section in Reserve. C Section – [illegible] under Sgt [illegible] will parade 8.00 am. to proceed to [illegible]-LE-BAS.

1 Section under Sgt [illegible] will leave [illegible]COURT-LE-BAS after [illegible] & proceed to T[illegible] to take over [illegible] [illegible] from a Sect. of 145 M.G.C.

Transport. Battle limbers of "C" Section will report at to H.Q. at 7.30 [illegible].

Battle limbers of A [illegible] & D which will act as guides to relieving Company's transport will be in the column for ST EMILIE by 9.15 pm arriving at HQ at 8 pm.

Remainder of Transport will withdraw to [illegible]-le-bas under arrangement of T.O.

C.Q.M.S. Sec. and Sgt. [illegible] will be ready for occupation by 8.30 pm.

Issued at 12.30 pm [illegible]/7/17

Copy no 1 Section Officer
2 "
3 "
4 "
5 War Diary
6 File
7 Brigade
8 [illegible] Diary
9 [illegible]
10 105 M.G.C.

[illegible] Capt
Comdg No 106 [illegible] M.G. Co.

SECRET

COPY No. 5

OPERATION ORDER No 89.

The Sub-section of "C" on Anti-aircraft work at TINCOURT will be relieved on the 29th inst. by a sub-section of 241 M. G. Co.

DISPOSITIONS. The two A.A.P's. near HAMEL copse will be handed over.

GUIDE. The 241 M. G. Co. will be met at the crossroads (E 25 d 5.9) LONGAVESNES at 3.00 P.M. by Lt. R. Skevington and guided to TINCOURT.

EQUIPMENT. S.A.A. sketches, fixtures, aeroplane sights (on loan) will be handed over and receipts obtained.

WITHDRAWAL. On relief the sub-section will withdraw to AIZECOURT-LE-BAS.

TRANSPORT. Battle limbers of "C" Sect. will report to sub-section Sergt. at TINCOURT at 2.45 P.M.

ISSUED AT 6.00 P.M. 28-7-17

J Seddon 2/Lt for

Copy No. 1 Section Officer Seddon 2/Lt for
2 O. C. 241 M.G.Co.
3 Transport Officer
4 Div. M. G. Co.
5 War Diary
6 File.
7 Brigade
" War Diary.

Instructions regarding War Diaries and Intelligence Summaries are contained in F. S. Regs., Part II. and the Staff Manual respectively. Title pages will be prepared in manuscript.

WAR DIARY
or
~~INTELLIGENCE SUMMARY.~~
(Erase heading not required.)

Army Form C. 2118.

106th M.G. COY.

Vol 16

Place	Date	Hour	Summary of Events and Information	Remarks and references to Appendices
In the Field	1-8-17		B. Section relieved one Section of 104th M.G. Coy. Dispositions 1 Gun EAGLE QUARRY, 3 Guns at GRAFTON POST.	
	2-8-17		The remainder of the COMPANY relieved 105th M.G. Coy. A. Section. 1 Gun CAT POST, 1 Gun LEMPIRE-CENTRAL 1 Gun LEMPIRE EAST, 1 Gun BASSE BOULOGNE SOUTH, C. Sect. 1 Gun EGO POST, 1 Gun FLEECAL POST, 1 Gun YAK POST, 1 Gun BROCK. D. Section rest.	
	3-8-17		Indirect fire was carried out onto VENDHUILE from 10-15 pm to 11-30pm. 1,500 rounds fired.	
	4-8-17		Indirect fire again carried out onto VENDHUILE. " 9-45pm to 11-30pm 2,000 "	
	6-8-17		Indirect fire as above carried out. 1,500 rounds. Inter:sect: relief carried out D Sect relieved B. Sect.	
	7-8-17		Ration tracks in F23.a. A14.c. and A20.a. were fired on with Indirect fire between 9+10-30pm 2,500 rounds expended. OPERATION ORDER No. 93. was not carried out.	
	8-8-17		Indirect fire carried out on to Tracks A.1.c. from 11pm till 12-3am 2,500 rounds expended.	
	9-8-17		Tracks in A.14.c. fired on with Indirect fire from 9-45pm till 11pm 4,000 rounds expended.	
	10-8-17		The Company relieved by 241 M.G. Coy.	
	11-8-17 to 14-8-17		At St. EMILIE, preparing + rehearsing for barrage onto GUILLEMONT FARM. No. 12. M.G. Squadron Joined us + 1 Sub Section 241. M.G. Coy.	
	15-8-17 16-8-17 17-8-17		Making barrage positions. Guns + Ammunition move up.	

A5834 Wt. W4973 M687 750,000 8/16 D. D. & L. Ltd. Forms/C.2118/13.

Instructions regarding War Diaries and Intelligence Summaries are contained in F. S. Regs., Part II. and the Staff Manual respectively. Title pages will be prepared in manuscript.

WAR DIARY
or
INTELLIGENCE SUMMARY.
(Erase heading not required.)

Army Form C. 2118.

106th M. G. Coy.

Place	Date	Hour	Summary of Events and Information	Remarks and references to Appendices
In the Field	18-8-17		Moved up to barrage positions.	
	19-8-17		Barrage fired in conjunction with an attack on GUILLEMONT FARM.	
			PROGRAMME OF EVENTS as under; — O. O. No 95.	
			4am Barrage commenced.	
			5-30am " ceased.	
			5-35am Groups informed of capture + consolidation of position.	
			5-53am A Gun for A. A work left D. Group + mounted at LEMPIRE. CENTRAL. 6.10am.	
			6-11am C. Section as mobile guns move forward.	
			6-12am No. of Prisoners + Booty captured reported to Groups.	
			6-30am A. A. Gun mounted at BASSÉ BOULOGNE. SOUTH.	
			7-10am New Gun for F. Group wired for.	
			9-am Mobile Guns in position	
			10-20am Intermittent bursts of fire by G. Group + Right Battery F. Group	
			11-15am Ceased fire	
			11-17am Bursts of 100 rounds per gun every 3 minutes opened.	
			11-30am All Groups answer S.O.S. signal.	
			12-1pm Ceased fire.	

A5834 Wt. W4973 M687 750,000 8/16 D. D. & L. Ltd. Forms/C.2118/13.

Army Form C. 2118.

WAR DIARY
or
~~INTELLIGENCE SUMMARY.~~

(*Erase heading not required.*)

Instructions regarding War Diaries and Intelligence Summaries are contained in F. S. Regs., Part II. and the Staff Manual respectively. Title pages will be prepared in manuscript.

106th M. G. Coy.

Place	Date	Hour	Summary of Events and Information	Remarks and references to Appendices
			PROGRAMME OF M.G. ~~EVENTS~~ Contd	
In the field.	19-8-17.	7-30 pm	6 Guns commenced night firing especially on CLAYMORE VALLEY + Tracks in rear of GUILLEMONT CRESENT Trench. 1 belt per gun every ¼ hour.	
		8-45 pm	S.O.S. sent up from between KNOLL + GUILLEMONT FARM	
		8-48 pm	D. Group opened fire to form a block	
		8-49 pm	All Groups warned to stand by	
		9-15 pm	D Group S.O.S fire ceased.	
		10-30 pm	New gun arrived for F. Group.	
	20-8-17.	4-42 am	Two of the mobile guns (BLUNTNOSE + DOG Trench) fired 2,500 rounds in answer to S.O.S. Gun at DUNCAN fired 1,500 rounds + Gun at DOLEFUL 1,750 rounds. Both emplacements at GUILLEMONT were hit but only one man wounded. (doing duty)	
		4-45 am	D. Group answered S.O.S.	
		5. am	Night firing on sensitive points ceased.	
		5.10 am	F + G. Groups opened up answering S.O.S.	
		5.48 am	All Groups rate of fire reduced to half.	
		6.0 am	One gun of D. Group mounted for A.A. work at LEMPIRE CENTRAL.	
		6.27 am	Fire ceased except occassional bursts on to sensitive points.	

A5834 Wt. W4973 M687 750,000 8/16 D. D. & L. Ltd. Forms/C.2118/13.

Army Form C. 2118.

Instructions regarding War Diaries and Intelligence Summaries are contained in F. S. Regs., Part II. and the Staff Manual respectively. Title pages will be prepared in manuscript.

WAR DIARY
or
~~INTELLIGENCE SUMMARY.~~
(Erase heading not required.)

106th M.G. Coy.

Place	Date	Hour	Summary of Events and Information	Remarks and references to Appendices
In the field	20-8-17		PROGRAMME OF M.G. EVENTS Contd.	
	"	7-20 am.	Gun at CAT POST out of action. 1 Gun sent up from BASSE BOULOGNE SOUTH.	
		5-45 AM.	Fire on all sensitive points which had been going on all day, ceased.	
		6-pm.	Rt battery of F. Group + G Group opened S.O.S. barrage at the rate of 2 minute bursts every 20 minutes.	
		7-25 pm.	Rate of fire reduced to bursts of 1 minute every half hour.	
		7-30 pm.	D. Group commenced fire as previous night except the gun on GUILLEMONT ROAD firing 3 belts every ½ hour.	
		7-55 pm	all Groups answered S.O.S.	
		8-2 pm	D. Group + left Battery (G Group) continued S.O.S. Rt Battery (F Group) + G Group reduced to ¼ rate of fire	
		8-20 pm	Barrage ceased. G Group + Right Battery F Group continued firing 1 min bursts every ½ hour.	
		8-25 pm	D Group continued as at 7-30 pm.	
		10-5 pm	S.O.S fire ceased. all Groups commenced night firing on sensitive points.	
		10-30 pm	Spare parts wired for.	
	21-8-17	2-15 Am	" " arrived.	

A5834 Wt. W4973 M687 750,000 8/16 D. D. & L. Ltd. Forms/C.2118/13.

Instructions regarding War Diaries and Intelligence Summaries are contained in F. S. Regs., Part II. and the Staff Manual respectively. Title pages will be prepared in manuscript.

WAR DIARY
or
~~INTELLIGENCE~~ SUMMARY.
(Erase heading not required.)

Army Form C. 2118.

106th M.G. Coy.

Place	Date	Hour	Summary of Events and Information	Remarks and references to Appendices
			PROGRAMME. OF. M.G. EVENTS contd.	
In the field	21-8-17		3-50am All Groups opened to S.O.S. signal seen ½ way between GUILLEMONT FARM + the KNOLL.	
			4-18am Fire ceased.	
			5-30am Gun mounted at LEMPIRE CENTRAL for AA work.	
			5-45am All fire on sensitive points ceased.	
			5-30am Guns of D Group + G. Group ready for amended scheme caused by the withdrawal of No. 12. M. G. Squadron.	
			8-20am Cavalry squadron withdrew.	
			10. am F. Group as per Appendix F (New barrage) ~~ready~~ ready for action	
			11-47am Hostile aeroplane brought down near TOMBOIS FARM by our Vickers at LEMPIRE CENTRAL by Pte Lacey. One man was seen to fall out.	
			5-30pm Personnel of the detachments of the mobile guns relieved	
			6-15pm An F.A. turned.	
			9-38pm All Groups warned to be alert for Gas Shells.	
			9-40pm D Group opened rapid fire on GUILLEMONT Road + Communication Trench at A.8.c.1.4. CLAYMORE VALLEY was also fired on.	[initials]

A5834 Wt. W4973 M687 750,000 8/16 D. D. & L. Ltd. Forms/C.2118/13.

Instructions regarding War Diaries and Intelligence Summaries are contained in F. S. Regs., Part II. and the Staff Manual respectively. Title pages will be prepared in manuscript.

WAR DIARY
or
~~INTELLIGENCE~~ SUMMARY.
(Erase heading not required.)

Army Form C. 2118.

106th M.G. Coy.

Place	Date	Hour	Summary of Events and Information	Remarks and references to Appendices
			PROGRAMME of M.G. EVENTS Contd.	
In the field	21-8-17	10-10pm	Fire of above reduced to 1 belt every ¼ hour.	
		11.45pm	Gas shells reported to be falling near LEMPIRE. EAST POST.	
	22-8-17	3.48 am	Night firing on sensitive points ceased.	
		3-48am	Barrages put down by F+G Groups as it was called for	
		4-17am	F+G ceased fire + stood to.	
		5-55am	F. Group opened for ½ minute (registration)	
		11-55am	BLUNTNOSE detachment challenged a man who stated he was a Sherwood Forester who had been out in No Mans land 3 nights, Sentry considering circumstances suspicious handed over to the nearest Coy HQ at GUILLEMONT FARM for the necessary interrogation. This man reported our M G barrage to be very accurate + well placed.	
		8-10pm	All Groups warned to stand to	
		9 pm	2 Guns of G Group commenced fire on CLAYMORE VALLEY	
		9-15pm	All Groups ordered to add 15' elevation for wear + tear of guns	
		10.46pm	D. Group position lightly shelled, no damage done.	
	23-8-17	1-30am	A few shells fell in the vicinity of G, Group.	
	–	2-am	G. Group ceased fire on CLAYMORE VALLEY.	

A5834 Wt. W4973 M687 750,000 8/16 D. D. & L. Ltd. Forms/C.2118/13.

Instructions regarding War Diaries and Intelligence Summaries are contained in F. S. Regs., Part II. and the Staff Manual respectively. Title pages will be prepared in manuscript.

WAR DIARY
or
~~INTELLIGENCE SUMMARY.~~
(*Erase heading not required.*)

Army Form C. 2118.

106th M G Coy.

Place	Date	Hour	Summary of Events and Information	Remarks and references to Appendices
			PROGRAMME OF M G EVENTS contd.	
In the Field	23-8-17	2am to 6am	BLUNTNOSE shelled off + on.	
		10.45am	Few shells fell in the vicinity of Coy H.Q. at LEMPIRE ~~[illegible]~~ WEST.	
		11.45am	BLUNTNOSE Position found to be untenable.	
		9 pm	G. Group opened night firing on to CLAYMORE VALLEY.	
		11. 20pm	Registration of new barrage at G. Group carried out with success.	
	24-8-17	5 am	2 Guns of G. Group ceased night firing	
		7-25am	RONNSOY + vicinity Coy H.Q. lightly shelled	
		7.45am to 8-30am	Sunken road from A Dump towards BASSE BOULOGNE heavily shelled. Two shelters belonging to this Unit blown in, no casualties inflicted	
		7-30pm	7-30pm Fire opened on to pensitive points.	
	25-8-17	3-30am	2 Guns of G. Group firing on A 14.a. 80.85 ceased.	
		3-35am	Same guns searched + traversed CLAYMORE VALLEY.	
		4-30am	Both Groups opened to S.O.S. from GUILLEMONT FARM.	
		5-40am	D. Group informed of situation wire to G Group cut.	
		6 am	Gun in BLUNTNOSE put out of action. Two men wounded (L/Cpl Willis + Pte Lee).	

A5834 Wt. W4973 M687 750,000 8/16 D. D. & L. Ltd. Forms/C.2118/13.

Instructions regarding War Diaries and Intelligence Summaries are contained in F. S. Regs., Part II. and the Staff Manual respectively. Title pages will be prepared in manuscript.

WAR DIARY
or
~~INTELLIGENCE SUMMARY.~~
(*Erase heading not required.*)

Army Form C. 2118.

106th M.G. Coy.

Place	Date	Hour	Summary of Events and Information	Remarks and references to Appendices
			PROGRAMME OF M G. EVENTS Contd	
In the field	25-8-17	6-10am	G. Group ceased fire owing to being heavily shelled.	
		6-18am	D. Group ceased fire	
		6-30am	G. Group ordered to move + occupy F. Group position	
		7-40am	Situation reported verbally to Brigade by 'phone	
		4-20pm	Groups at F in position ready to fire new barrage.	
		7-30pm	F + D Groups + guns in posts put down a barrage in conjunction with an attack by the 19th D.L.I. to regain lost ground in accordance with O.O. 98.	
		8-18pm	All guns ceased fire + stood by for eventualities.	
		8-45pm	Situation reported to Groups.	
		9-28pm	S.O.S. received by both Groups from GUILLEMONT FARM. Both Groups + forward guns opened fire	
		10 pm	Fire reduced to ½ rate. Guns, barrels + spare parts wired for.	
		10.28pm	Fire ceased + groups ordered to stand by for eventualities	
	26-8-17	8am	Message received from D.L.I to stand to. D + F. Groups warned to do this.	
		8-30am	M G fire asked for. D + F. Groups ordered to fire for 3 minutes	
		8-32am	E.A flying low dropped Red + White lights in front of D Group, no action followed. E.A. turned by our Vickers	
		11-12am	Groups ordered to fire 1 minute bursts every ½ hour by half Groups.	[illegible]

A5834 Wt. W4973 M687 750,000 8/16 D. D. & L. Ltd. Forms/C.2118/13.

Instructions regarding War Diaries and Intelligence Summaries are contained in F. S. Regs., Part II. and the Staff Manual respectively. Title pages will be prepared in manuscript.

WAR DIARY
or
INTELLIGENCE SUMMARY.
(Erase heading not required.)

Army Form C. 2118.

106th M.G. Coy.

Place	Date	Hour	Summary of Events and Information	Remarks and references to Appendices
			PROGRAMME OF M G Events Contd.	
In the Field	26-8-17	4 pm	F Group ceased fire.	
		5-45 pm	E.A's flew over our lines & were fired at by our A.A. Vickers which caused them to return to own lines	
		8-16 pm	D. Group ceased fire.	
		8-53 pm	Orders received to open on to CLAYMORE VALLEY with 6 guns.	
		9 pm	Fire opened on CLAYMORE VALLEY	
		9-5 pm	Fire ceased as situation became quiet	
		10-55 pm	Guns opened fire on to sensitive points.	
	27-8-17	2 am	Relief of forward guns completed by 3 detachments of F. Group.	
		4 am	Night firing on sensitive points ceased.	
		11 pm	D. Group moved to LEMPIRE CENTRAL & become H Group F. Group moved to BASSÉ BOULOGNE & become I Group. A Sect & 1 sub sect 241 M G Coy withdrawn to HQ. 1 Detachment 241 M. G. Coy Joins C Group.	
	31-8-17	4-54 am	Guns in all forward Pos's opened fire, guns kept firing throughout heavy bombardment.	
		4-55 am	S.O.S. signal received by phone re GUILLEMONT FARM (D.L.I.)	
		4-56 am	H & I Group firing on GUILLEMONT FARM S.O.S. lines. Cpl. T. SEDDON reports S.O.S. from KNOLL.	

A5834 Wt. W4973 M687 750,000 8/16 D. D. & L. Ltd. Forms/C.2118/13.

Instructions regarding War Diaries and Intelligence Summaries are contained in F. S. Regs., Part II. and the Staff Manual respectively. Title pages will be prepared in manuscript.

WAR DIARY
or
INTELLIGENCE SUMMARY.
(Erase heading not required.)

Army Form C. 2118.

106th M. G. Coy

Place	Date	Hour	Summary of Events and Information	Remarks and references to Appendices
In the Field	31-8-17		PROGRAMME OF M. G. EVENTS. contd.	
		5.15 am	Detachment in DUNCAN POST knocked out. 3 Killed (Ptes Garrity, Vaughan & Tudge) 2 Wounded (L/cpl Byrne & Pte Taylor). 1 wounded in CAT POST. (Pte McFarlane)	
		5-45 am	I Group reduced fire to occasional bursts.	
		6-6 am	Orders received from Brigade Major to turn fire on to the KNOLL	
		6-7 am	Message from D. L. I. all clear GUILLEMONT FARM.	
		6-10 am	H. Group firing on KNOLL S.O.S. lines.	
		6-11 am	I. Group ceased fire.	
		6-38 am	Orders received to reduce to occasional bursts of fire on KNOLL S.O.S. lines.	
		11-59 am	H Group still firing	
		1-48 pm	Instructions received to open fire on TOMBOIS & KNOLL Trenches.	
		2-10 pm	Fire opened by H Group	
		3-30 pm	H Group ceased fire owing to reconnaissance made from FLEECALL POST.	
		4-15 pm	Occasional bursts of fire opened by H & I Groups on KNOLL S.O.S. lines.	
		6-50 pm	An E.A. flew over towards H Group & dropped Red & White lights S. E. of H Group. This was followed by shelling on the same spot.	

A5834 Wt. W4973 M687 750,000 8/16 D. D. & L. Ltd. Forms/C.2118/13.

Instructions regarding War Diaries and Intelligence Summaries are contained in F. S. Regs., Part II. and the Staff Manual respectively. Title pages will be prepared in manuscript.

WAR DIARY
or
~~INTELLIGENCE SUMMARY.~~
(Erase heading not required.)

106th M.G. Coy

Army Form C. 2118.

Place	Date	Hour	Summary of Events and Information	Remarks and references to Appendices
In the field	31-8-17		10 pm. 1 Gun from each Group received instructions to search + traverse ground area of S. O.S. line 11 pm Remaining guns of H. Group were instructed to search the reverse slope of the KNOLL. AMMUNITION expended during the operation since Zero on 19th inst until 12pm 31st - 1st 764,000 rounds.	

[illegible] Capt
Comdg 106th M.G. [illegible]

SECRET

COPY No 5

OPERATION ORDER No 90

"B" SECTION OF 106th M.G. COY WILL RELIEVE A SECTION OF 104 M.G. Co. IN THE LINE ON THE NIGHT OF 1/2nd AUGUST 1917.

1 DISPOSITIONS. 1 GUN M.G.T.5 1 GUN. M.G.R 14
1 " M.G.R.15 1 " M.G.R.16

2 GUIDES. GUIDES will be MET AT BROCK AT 10.00 P.M.

3 PARADE. "B" SECTION WILL PARADE AT 7.15 P.M. AND WILL MOVE OFF AT 7.30 P.M.

4 ROUTE. LONGAVESNES – VILLERS FAUCON – ST. EMILIE – RONSSOY – BROCK.

5 TRANSPORT. ON COMPLETION OF DUTY TRANSPORT WILL RETURN TO LINES AT AIZECOURT-LE-BAS.

6 EQUIPMENT. S.A.A. & TRENCH STORES WILL BE TAKEN OVER.
AEROPLANE PHOTOGRAPHS & MAPS WILL BE TAKEN OVER FROM O.C. COY.

7 COMMAND. SECTION WILL COME UNDER COMMAND OF O.C. 104 M.G.Co. UNTIL 10.00 A.M. 2-8-17 AND O.C. 105 M.G.Co. FROM 10.00 A.M. 2-8-17 UNTIL 106th M.G.Co. RELIEVE 105 M.G.Co.

8 RELIEF. COMPLETION OF RELIEF WILL BE REPORTED BY WIRE BY WORD "HELLO"

1/8/17

Copy No 1 Section Officer
2 " "
3 " "
4 " "
5 WAR DIARY
6 FILE
7 BRIGADE
8 WAR DIARY
9 D.M.G.O.
10 104 M.G.C.
11 105 M.G.C.

Secret Copy No 5

OPERATION ORDER [illegible]

106th M.G. Coy less 1 Section will [illegible] 105 M.G.C. in the line on the night [illegible]

1 DISPOSITIONS "A" Sect. 1 Det. "C" Post 1 Det. [illegible] Boulogne S.
1 Det. Lempire Cent. 1 Det. Lempire East
"C" Sect. 1 Det. "E" Post 1 Det. "F" Post
1 " Yak Post 1 " Brock.
"D" Sect. in rest at St. Emilie.

2. GUIDES "A" Section. 1 Guide per detachment will be at [illegible] for [illegible] Post & [illegible] Boulogne South at 10.30 P.M.
1 Guide per detachment at Brock for Lempire East and Lempire Central at 10.00 P.M.
"C" Section. 1 Guide per detachment for "E" "F" and Yak Posts will be at Brock at 10.00 P.M.

3 PARADE. The Company (less "B" Sect.) will parade at 6.30 P.M. Dress. Fighting order

4 ORDER OF MARCH. "A" Sect. "C" Sect. & "D" Sect.

5 ROUTE. [illegible] — Villers Faucon — St. Emilie
100 yds interval between sections after leaving Villers Faucon.

6 TRANSPORT. Transport not required will leave the column for transport lines at Villers Faucon but the limbers necessary for relief will be in the column at St Emilie by 9.00 P.M. "C" at the head & "A" in rear of the column

7 HOT MEAL. Tea will be provided on arrival at St Emilie.
Cooks, dixies etc. will proceed under C.Q.M.S.' orders.

8 MOVE FROM ST. EMILIE. "A" & "C" Sections will be ready to move off at 9.30 P.M.

9 EQUIPMENT. All S.A.A., trench stores & petrol tins (5 at [illegible], 5 at Brock) & at Q. H.Q.) will be taken over

10 RELIEF. Completion of relief will be reported to this office by word "MY"

11 ACKNOWLEDGE.

ISSUED AT 9 AM 2/8/17

[signature] Lt. for
O.C. 106 M.G. Coy

Copy No 1 Section Officer
2 " "
3 " "
4 " "
5 War Diary
6 File
7 Brigade
8 War Diary
9 D.M.G.O.
10 105 M.G.C.
11 T.O.

Secret

Operation Order No 92

Copy No 5

[illegible] Relief [illegible] Section [illegible]

1 Distribution 1 Gun MGS 5 [illegible]
1 " MGR 15 [illegible]

2 Guides will be arranged [illegible]
[illegible] concerned [illegible]
Transport Officer [illegible]
a driver & guide [illegible]

3 Parade "D" Section [illegible]
[illegible]

4 Transport No 1 and 2 [illegible] Section will
be [illegible] and [illegible]
will [illegible]
1 [illegible] mule [illegible]
[illegible] of [illegible]

5 Equipment S.A.A. [illegible] Belt
Boxes will [illegible]

6. Relief Completion of Relief will be
reported by [illegible]

Issued at 10. 20 a.m.
6/8/17

[illegible] Lieut
[illegible] 106 M.G.C.

Copy No 1 Section Officer
2 " "
3 " "
4 " "
5 War Diary
6 File
7 Engineer
8 War [illegible]
9 [illegible]
10 T. O.

[illegible] 5

93

OPERATION ORDERS [illegible]

"B" Section, 1 detachment of "C" Sect. and 1 detachment of "D" Sect. [illegible] [illegible] in a feint attack to be carried [illegible] [illegible] evening of 7-8-17.

GUNS IN ACTION. "B" Section under Lt. [illegible] will fire from X 28 c 2.5 to X 28 c 5.8

1 Gun "C" under Lt. S. W. KINGED from [illegible] F 4 d 2.6

1 Gun "D" Section under Lt. [illegible] from X 28 a 15.30

TARGETS. "B" Section will place a frontal creeping barrage from [illegible] [illegible] and X 30 a 1.3 to [illegible] 24 c 5.0 and X 30 a 7.4.

TIME 7.30 P.M. to 7.35 P.M.

Then will search & traverse tracks X 30 a X 24 c, S 25 d, S 19 d

TIME 7.35 P.M. to 7.50 P.M.

1 DETACHT "C" will traverse Bela trench from X 30 c 15 [illegible] to X 30 a 5.1

TIME 7.30 P.M. to 7.50 P.M.

1 DETACHT "D" will traverse HAWK trench from X 30 a 5.5 to X 30 a 2.9

TIME 7.30 P.M. to 7.50 P.M.

RATE OF FIRE "B" Section. BARRAGE – 1 belt per gun per 3 mins.

TRACKS – 1 Belt per gun per 5 mins.

"C" Sect. } 1 Belt per gun per 5 mins.
"D" " }

HOUR OF READINESS – 6.30 P.M.

PARADE. "B" Sect. will parade under Section Officers arrangements.

TRANSPORT. Equipment & ammunition will be conveyed by Pack Mules.

WITHDRAWAL. "B" Section will withdraw at 7.50 P.M. to H.Q.

Detachments of C and D to resume normal at 8.00 p.m.

WATCHES – SYNCHRONIZATION OF. Watches will be synchronised at Left Section H.Q. at 6.15 p.m.

REPORTS. From 5 pm to 8 pm. all reports will be sent to Left Sect H.Q. (F 4 d 1.3)

[illegible] Lieut
for O.C.
106 M.G. Co

Copy No 1 Section Officer
2 " "
3 " "
4 " "
5 War Diary
6 File
7 Brigade
8 War Diary
9 DMGO
10 T.O.

10/11th

10

TOMBOIS

MGR
MGR

CUTTING

COPY No 5.

SECRET

OPERATION ORDER No 95

[illegible] Machine Gun Co; 12 M.G. Sqn; 1 Sub-section of 241 M.G.C. will co-operate in an attack on Gillemont Farm by the 18th H.L.I. on the morning of 19th August 1917

1. **CO-OPERATION OF FORCE.** "D" Group. "B" Section & 1 sub-section of "D" 106th M.G.C.
"F" " 12th M.G. Sqn.
"G" " A Sec; "C" Sec; 1 sub-section of "D" 106th M.G.C. and 1 sub-section 241 M.G.C.

2. **BARRAGE & TARGETS.** Barrage & targets will be as laid down in Appendix "A"

3. **SCHEDULE OF FIRE.** Fire will be carried out as in Appendix "B"

4. **BAROMETER & THERMOMETER, WIND &c** These will be notified later by Appendix "C"

5. **ZERO HOUR** will be notified later.

6. **HOUR OF READINESS.** Guns will be laid by 8 P.M. 18/8/17. Hour of readiness. Zero – ½ hrs.

7. **RATE OF FIRE.** Creeping barrages – intense. Standing barrages – 1 belt per gun per 5 mins.

8. **DURATION OF FIRE.** Zero to Zero + 90 mins.

9. **AMMUNITION** 6,000 rounds per gun.
Reserve to fill belts 6,000 " per gun
" at position in S.A.A. boxes – 5,000 per gun.
" at St. Emilie 5,000 per gun.

10. **PARADE.** Units will parade at 4.15 P.M. and will move off by gun teams ¼ mile intervals.

11. **ROUTE.** Route to positions is left to the discretion of group commanders

12. **WATCHES, SYNCHRONIZATION OF**
Representative an officer will report Bde H.Q. at 5.15 P.M. on the 18th. One officer from H.Q. one officer from each of D.E and F Groups will report at Batt H.Q. Ken Lane at 10.00 P.M. to synchronise. Further synchronization will take place at M.G. HQ F 16 c 4.8 at Zero – 2½ hours.

13. **WORKING PARTY.** The following working parties will be met at Batt H.Q. at F.15 d 65.75. at 9 P.M. on the 18th. 1 N.C.O. & 12 men for "G" Group. 4 N.C.Os and 16 men for "C" Section. These will be returned on the night of 19th.

14. **MOBILE GUNS.** "C" Section under Lt. S.W. [illegible] on completion of barrage & at an hour to be notified later will advance to forward positions as under
1 gun Blunt Nose, 1 gun Dog Trench,
1 " Duncan Post, 1 " Doleful Post.
Ammunition & water as previously arranged. Carrying party for belt boxes as in para. 12. For roles & schedule vide Appendix "D".

15. **AIRCRAFT.** The following guns will be mounted for A.A. work at Zero + 2 hours:–
1 gun Basse Boulogne South. 1 gun Lempire Central

16. **RATIONS** will be delivered as under at 10.15 P.M. on the 18th
"D" Group at F 11 c 2.0. F Group at F 16 c 55.05
G " " F 22 b 45.25
2 days rations will be issued to "C" Section.

17. **REPULSION OF COUNTER-ATTACK.** Barrages for repulsion of counter attack will be laid down as in Appendix "A".

18. **DISPOSITIONS BY 241 M.G.C.** Gun in E Post under Lt Boyle will move from the centre of the post to emplacement south end of sap F 12 c 05.40 so that it can command the valley towards the Knoll. S.O.S. line. M.B. 112° Range 950x. Move to be completed by 8 P.M. 18th inst.
Gun at "C" Post under Lt Bown will have an S.O.S. line 66° Mag. Range 1400x

19. **SIGNALS.** The following signal will be used. S.O.S. signal – [illegible] bursting into 2 red & 2 white lights. [illegible] range – [illegible] Very lights. This signal refers to [illegible] fire only.

2

20 CONTACT AEROPLANES. 2 CONTACT AEROPLANES WILL FLY OVER THE AREA OF ATTACK FROM ZERO TO ZERO PLUS 30 MINS. AFTER THAT 1 PLANE. INFANTRY WILL LIGHT FLARES ON REACHING THEIR OBJECTIVES.

21 MEDICAL ARRANGEMENTS.
ADVANCED DRESSING STATION LEMPIRE [illegible] C.T. WITH AID POST 1 AT JUNCTION GILLEMONT C.T. WITH DUNCAN POST.
2. IN SUNKEN ROAD behind F POST. EACH GROUP IS PROVIDED WITH 1 STRETCHER.
WOUNDED WILL BE CARRIED TO THE NEAREST DRESSING STN. BY PERSONNEL OF THE GROUP.

22 REPORTS. H.Q. OF 106 M.G.C. & UNITS CO-OPERATING WITH 106 M.G.CO. WILL BE ESTABLISHED AT F 16 c 4.8

ISSUED AT - - - 18/8/17

E W [illegible] Capt
Comdg 106 M G Co

COPY No 1 C.O.
2 D GROUP COMMANDER
3 F " "
4 G " "
5 WAR DIARY
6 FILE
7 BRIGADE
8 WAR DIARY
9 Lt [illegible] Comm "F" GROUP
10 Lt " " G "
11 Lt " " F "
12 Lt " " F "
13 Lt R. SKEVINGTON
14 " S.W. KINRED.
15 2/Lt E A HAWKES.
16 Lt BOYLE 241 M.G.C
17 " BOWN "
18 H.L.I.
19 D.M.G.O
20 Royal Scots
21 West Yorks
22 D.L.I.
23 Transport Officer
24 C.Q.M.S.
25 R A Group Commander
26 OC 241 M.G.Co
27 " " 105 M.G.C
28 Signals
29 [illegible] M.C
30

APPENDIX B

[illegible]	No of Gun	Range	M.B.	Q. E.	Clearance	Kind of Fire
F.	12	2350	87½	6° 58'	400'	Standing barrage
	11	2350	85½	7° [illegible]	[illegible]	
	10	2350	83	7° 13'	400'	
	9	2350	80	7° 16'	400'	
	8	2450	81	7° 23'	400'	
	7	2450	82	7° 32'	400'	
	6	2450	93	7° 32'	400'	
	5	2450	85½	7° 14'	400'	
	4	2450	84	6° 34'	400'	
	3	2300	84	6° 39'	400'	
	2	2300	88	6° 47'	300'	
	1	2300	85	6° 34'	276'	
G	12	2300 to 2800	65	6° 16' to 10° 10'	Good	Creeping Barrage
	11		"	"	"	
	10		"		"	
	9		"	6° 7' to 10° 1'	"	
	8	DITTO.	"	6° [illegible] to 10° [illegible]		
	7		"			
	6		"	5° 44' to 9° 30'		
	5			"		
	4					
	3		"	"		
	2		"	5° 28' to 9° 58'	"	
	1			"		
G [illegible] battery	12	2425	70	6° 56'	GOOD	Standing Barrage
	11	2350	69½	6° 15'	"	
	10	2275	68½	5° 44'	"	
	9	2200	68	5° 14'	"	
	8	2125	67	4° 45'	"	
	7	2050	66	4° 30'	"	
	6 to 1	1600 to 2200	116	3° to 5°	24' to 96'	Creeping Barrage
D	6	1600	109	2° 15'	18'	Standing Barrage
	5	1700	108	2° 45'	33'	
	4	1800	106	3° 15'	45'	
	3	1600	108	2° 30'	24'	
	2	1700	107	3° –	33'	
	1	1800	106	3° 15'	45'	
C	6	1575	116	2° 45'	15'	Standing defensive barrage
	5	1650	115	3° –	24'	
	4	1725	114	3° 30'	33'	
	3	1800	113	3° 45'	45'	
	2	1875	112	4° –	57'	
	1	1950	111	4° 15'	65'	

Appendix C

Right. D. Group. nil
E. Group. nil
G. Group. [illegible]

Wind + light.
will be notified later

Thermometer D. Group + 21 } need
E. Group + 26 } not be
G. Group + 30 } used

Barometer D. Group − 17 } need
F. Group − 21 } not be
G. Group − 23 } used

Appendix D

Role of Mobile Guns.

C-Sect under H. S. W. KINRED move forward when the position has been captured for the purpose of facilitating the repulsion of counter attacks. By doing this direct observation can be obtained. The SOS lines of the 2 forward guns must be determined by them on a gaining information as to the position of the Right and Left Standing Patrol.

S.O.S. Lines. DOLEFUL
Mg. Br. 772 QE 1° 45' Range 1400

DUNCAN
Mg Br 97? QE [illegible]' Range 1050

Secret   Copy No 5

Operation Order No 96

The personnel of 1 sub-section of B Sect. under Lt [illegible] will relieve the personnel of a sub section of "C" on the afternoon of 21-8-17

DISPOSITION One Gun DUNCAN POST
ELLIOTT'S SE
Two DUNCAN POST

GUIDE One guide will be at F Group barrage position at [illegible] pm.

EQUIPMENT. All Guns, tripods, spare parts, ammunition etc will be handed over on relief.

WITHDRAWAL The sub-section of C under 2/Lt E. A. HAWKES will replace the sub-section of B in D group.

RELIEF Completion of Relief to be reported by wire by word BONCOCK

21/8/17 Copy No 1 Section office.
2 " "
3 " "
4 " "
5 War Diary
6 File
7 Brigade
8 War Diary
9 T.O.
10 C.Q.M.S.

[illegible] Lt

Operation Orders No 97. Copy No 5

The following moves & reliefs will take place afternoon 23rd & night 23rd & 24th.

Moves. The personnel of 1 Sub Section C will relieve personnel of 1 Sub Sect. D. at D group. On relief 1 Sub Section D will move to G group to relieve 1 Sub Section A. On relief 1 Sub Section A will move to F group.
Moves to commence as soon as possible.

Relief. 1 Sub Section A. at F group will move at 9 pm. to relieve 1 Sub Section 221 M. G. Coy.
1 Gun at CAT Post.
1 Gun at EGO Post.
1 Sub Section A will move at 10.30 pm to relieve 1 Sub Section B. at DUNCAN and BLUNTNOSE.

Guards. Sufficient men will be left at the F group to be able to fire the guns until relieved by A. Sect: these then proceeding to D group.
Men of D. Sect: will man the remainder of A Section Guns until detachment of B Section relieve them.

Command. 2/Lt J Seddon will command A Sect. in the forward Posts.
D. Group. Lieut. P.H.COOPER.
G. Group Lieut. F.M.FISHER.

Equipment. All guns etc. will be taken by F. Group to relieve 221. Sub Section. Remainder will not move anything. Receipts for the former to be taken.

Relief. Reliefs & moves will be reported by phone, by word BALLSUP.

Issued at 1 pm.

1. S.C.	5. W.D.	9. Q.E.
2. S.C.	6. FILE.	10. D.M.G.O.
3. S.C.	7. BDE.	11. 221.
4. S.C.	8. W.D.	12. T.O.
		13. C.Q.M.S. & 14 Spare.

Cameron
Capt

23/8/17

SECRET

Copy No 5

Operation Order No 48

The following [illegible] [illegible] [illegible] [illegible] place in conjunction with [illegible] [illegible] the 11th R. [illegible] [illegible] on the afternoon of 25/9/17

Guns in Action. D Group: C Section, 1 Sub Section "B" under Lt [illegible] COOPER.

F Group: 1 Sub Section of B, 3 Detachments of D and 3 Detachments of 241 M.G.C. under Lt [illegible] [illegible]

Forward Guns: 3 Detachments of [illegible] Section & 1 Detachment of D [illegible]

Barrages & Lines of Fire. Barrages and lines of fire will be as laid down in Appendices [illegible]

Time. Zero to zero + 45

Rate of Fire. Rapid

Move. 1 Detachment of D Section will move from F Group to [illegible] [illegible] [illegible] with the [illegible] [illegible] [illegible] [illegible] [illegible] [illegible] in Belt.

Cooperation. C Group consisting of [illegible] guns of 241 M.G.C. will cooperate by barraging [illegible] [illegible]

Zero Hour will be notified later by the following names:

1	[illegible]	7	[illegible]
2	Bessie	8	Helen
3	Caroline	9	[illegible]
4	[illegible]	10	[illegible]
5	Emma	11	[illegible]
6	Frances	12	[illegible]

[illegible] [illegible] ¼ hours [illegible] [illegible] shown as follows:–

5.15 4 Emmas

5.30 2 Emmas

5.45 3 Emmas

Receipt of Zero hour will be notified by word "GIRLIE"

Issued at 4.50 pm.

[illegible]

Copy No 1 D Group
2 F
3 [illegible] Section
4 [illegible]
5 [illegible]
6 File
7 Brigade
8 [illegible]
9 [illegible]
10 [illegible] M.G.O.
11 241 M.G. Coy

Copy no 5.

SECRET

Operation Order no 9[illegible]

The following inter company relief will take place on the night 26/27th Aug 1917

RELIEF The [illegible] personnel on the [illegible] detachments of [illegible] will relieve [illegible] of A in the following posts [illegible]
CAT [illegible] DUNCAN [illegible] POST

TIME Relieving [illegible] will move off at 9 pm.

GUIDES [illegible] be arranged between [illegible] [illegible] concerned.

[illegible] [illegible] of men to [illegible] [illegible] and 2 H M [illegible] [illegible]

COMMAND [illegible] will [illegible] under Lieut R. [illegible] [illegible] will be [illegible] at DOLEFUL POST

RATIONS Rations will be dumped [illegible] [illegible] 10.15 p.m. [illegible] BROCK [illegible] [illegible] BOULEVARD NORTH.

COMPLETION OF RELIEF will be reported by [illegible]

Issued at 6.30 p.m. 26/8/17

[illegible]

Copy no [illegible]
[illegible]
[illegible]
[illegible]
4 [illegible]
5 [illegible]
6 [illegible]
7 [illegible]
8 [illegible]
9 [illegible]
10 [illegible]
11 [illegible]

SECRET

Copy No. 5

OPERATION ORDER No. 100

The following moves will take place on the night of 27/28th Aug 1917

MOVES. One sub section of B will move from D Group to I Group.
One sub section of B will move from F Group to I Group.
'C' Section will move from D Group to H Group.

POSITION OF GROUPS. H Group LEMPIRE CENTRAL
I " BASSE BOULOGNE SOUTH.

COMPOSITION & COMMANDERS OF GROUPS. H Group under 2/Lt E.A. HAWKES.
'C' Section 106th M.G. Co. & 1 detachment of 241 M.G. Co

I Group under Lt. P.H. COOPER
B Section 106th M.G. Co.

WITHDRAWAL. 'A' Section under Lt. H.H. FISHER & 1 Sub-section of 241 M.G. Co. will withdraw to St EMILIE on completion of moves.

COMPLETION OF MOVES. Completion of move will be reported by Code word by wire "PYGMALION"

Copy 1 H Group
2 I "
3 O.C. D Sect.
4 D.V.
5 War Diary
6 File
7 Brigade
8 War Diary
9 Transp Sgt.

G Wemerson [?] Capt

27/8/17

Instructions regarding War Diaries and Intelligence Summaries are contained in F. S. Regs., Part II. and the Staff Manual respectively. Title pages will be prepared in manuscript.

Secret

WAR DIARY
or
INTELLIGENCE SUMMARY.
(Erase heading not required.)

Army Form C. 2118.

106 M G COY

Vol 17

Place	Date	Hour	Summary of Events and Information	Remarks and references to Appendices
Sept	2.9.17		D Section relieved C Section at H Group	
			C Section relieved B Section in the front line	
	5.9.17		The Company was relieved in the line on the night 5/6 Sept by the 241 Machine Gun Coy. On completion of relief the Coy withdrew to HQ at St EMILIE.	
	7.9.17		The Coy relieved the 104 M G COY in the left Sector on the night 7/8 Sept	
			D Section Front line	
			B " Green line	
			A " VILLERS GUISLAIN SECTOR	
			C " Advanced Coy H.Q. Reserve	
	10.9.17		Inter Coy relief C Section relieved D Section in the front line	
			D Section relieved B Section in the Green line B Section to Advanced Coy H.Q.	
	13.9.17		B Section relieved A Section in the VILLERS GUISLAIN Sector	
	13.9.17		A Section & 1 detachment of D Section co-operated in an artillery concentration on the night of 13/14 Sept. firing on the ST QUENTIN CANAL Crossings & Ration tracks.	

A5834 Wt. W4973 M687 750,000 8/16 D. D. & L. Ltd. Forms/C.2118/13.

Instructions regarding War Diaries and Intelligence Summaries are contained in F. S. Regs., Part II. and the Staff Manual respectively. Title pages will be prepared in manuscript.

WAR DIARY
or
INTELLIGENCE SUMMARY.
(Erase heading not required.)

Army Form C. 2118.

106 M G COY

Place	Date	Hour	Summary of Events and Information	Remarks and references to Appendices
	13/14 [illegible]		9 Guns of the Front Line Opened fire at midnight in answer to an S.O.S. sent up from the BIRDCAGE. The attempted Raid was driven off and normal was resumed at 12 20 AM. Rounds fired 8,000.	
	14 [illegible]		D Section relieved C Section in the Front Line.	
	15/16 [illegible]		A Section 3 Detachments of C Section and 1 Detachment of B Section Co-operated in a Raid carried out by the 17th Royal Scots. The guns were divided into 2 Groups of 4. A Group consisting of 3 guns C Section & 1 gun B Section put up a Frontal Creeping Barrage from X 18c 05 30 and X 18c 00 50 TO X 18c 90 50 and X 18c 85 70 Time Zero - 5 to Zero. They then placed an Oblique Standing Barrage from X 18c 45 55 to S 24d 00 50 Time Zero + 1 to Zero + 20	MAP REF 62c

A5834 Wt. W4973 M687 750,000 8/16 D. D. & L. Ltd. Forms/C.2118/13.

Instructions regarding War Diaries and Intelligence Summaries are contained in F. S. Regs., Part II. and the Staff Manual respectively. Title pages will be prepared in manuscript.

WAR DIARY
or
INTELLIGENCE SUMMARY.

(*Erase heading not required.*)

Army Form C. 2118.

106 M.G. Coy

Place	Date	Hour	Summary of Events and Information	Remarks and references to Appendices
	17/8/17		B Group fired a frontal creeping Barrage from X11d 2 7 and X11d 00 95 to X11b 70 and X11b 55 40 time Zero-5 to Zero. They then placed an Oblique Standing Barrage from X11b 70 to X11b 55 40 Time Zero to Zero+10. The Raiding Party were very satisfied with the manner in which the Barrage was put down. Rounds expended 7500	
	17.8.17		A Section and 3 detachments of C Section fired a machine gun concentration on the CATELET ROAD, eastern end of CANAL WOOD and Ration tracks. Times 9pm 10.30pm & 11.35pm 1 Belt per gun. Rounds expended 5250	

A5834 Wt. W4973 M687 750,000 8/16 D. D. & L. Ltd. Forms/C.2118/13.

Instructions regarding War Diaries and Intelligence Summaries are contained in F. S. Regs., Part II. and the Staff Manual respectively. Title pages will be prepared in manuscript.

WAR DIARY
or
INTELLIGENCE SUMMARY.
(Erase heading not required.)

Army Form C. 2118.

106 M G COY

Place	Date	Hour	Summary of Events and Information	Remarks and references to Appendices
	19/9/17		The Coy were relieved in the line on the night of 19/20 Sept by the 105 M G Coy and withdrew to rest billets at AIZECOURT-LE-BAS	
	20/9/17		Reorganization & rest	
	21/9/17		The Coy relieved the 104 M G COY in the LEMPIRE SECTOR A Section Front Line B Section Right Support C " Left Support D " Reserve ST EMILIE	
	30.9.17		1 Gun of B Section at LEMPIRE CENTRAL and 1 Gun of C Section at A Group position fired bursts throughout the night on to a Gap cut in the enemy wire at junction of GRUB LANE and WILLOW TRENCH. Rounds expended 5000	

R S Kewington Lieut
for CAPTAIN
O.C. 106 MACHINE GUN COY

A5834 Wt. W4973 M687 750,000 8/16 D. D. & L. Ltd. Forms/C.2118/13.

SECRET

COPY No 5

OPERATION ORDER No 102

THE FOLLOWING INTER-COMPANY RELIEF WILL TAKE PLACE ON THE NIGHT 2/3rd SEPT 1917

1. RELIEF THE PERSONNEL OF D SECTION UNDER LT R. SKEVINGTON WILL RELIEVE THE PERSONNEL OF "C" SECTION. THE PERSONNEL OF "C" SECTION UNDER LT. S.W. KIMRED ON RELIEF WILL RELIEVE THE PERSONNEL OF "B" SECTION IN THE FRONT LINE POSTS.

2. DISPOSITIONS.

D SECTION "H" GROUP AT LEMPIRE CENTRAL
A " I " " BASSE BOULOGNE. S
C " CAT POST
DUNCAN "
DOLEFUL "
E 40 "

3. GUIDES will be arranged between Section officers concerned.

4. COMMAND. LT. H.M. FISHER WILL COMMAND THE GROUPS FROM ADVANCED H.Q.
2/LT. J. SEDDON WILL TAKE OVER COMMAND OF "A" SECTION AT BASSE BOULOGNE SOUTH
"C" SECTION UNDER LT S.W. KIMRED IN THE FRONT LINE POSTS.

5. WITHDRAWAL. THE PERSONNEL OF "B" SECTION UNDER LT. F.H. COOPER WILL WITHDRAW TO H.Q. ON COMPLETION OF RELIEF.

6. RATIONS FOR THE FRONT LINE POSTS WILL BE DUMPED AT DUNCAN POST AT 10.15 P.M.

7. COMPLETION OF RELIEF WILL BE REPORTED BY WORD BY WIRE "SPEARMINT".

Issued at 3.00 p.m. 2/9/17

Copy No: 1 Section officer
2 " "
3 " "
4 " "
5 WAR DIARY
6 FILE
7 BRIGADE
8 WAR DIARY
9 D.M.G.O.

H.E. Talbot [illegible]
[illegible]

SECRET Copy No. 5

OPERATION ORDER No. 103

[illegible] 2nd [illegible] on the night of 5th Sept 1917

1. DISPOSITIONS. [illegible] 2 guns [illegible] STREET

[illegible]

2. GUIDES. Guide [illegible] BRICK [illegible] will [illegible]

Guide [illegible]

3. HANDING OVER. [illegible]

[illegible] ELEMPIRE CENTRAL [illegible]

4. EQUIPMENT.

All S.A.A. [illegible]

[illegible] be handed over [illegible]

[illegible] left at [illegible]

5. TRANSPORT. 1 [illegible] C [illegible] will be at BRICK [illegible] p.m.

[illegible] C [illegible] BULLCOMB S. at 10 p.m.

[illegible] BULLCOMB S. at 9.3[illegible]

[illegible] LEMPIRE CENTRAL at 9.30 p.m.

[illegible] at 9.30 p.m.

6. WITHDRAWAL. 1 gun of D Sect from 4 Group & [illegible] Sect from 5 Group will withdraw [illegible] on [illegible] ST. EMILIE.

7. COMPLETION OF RELIEF will be reported by all [illegible] "NAPOO".

Issued at 10.45 pm 4/9/17

H. E. Talbot Lieut

for O.C. 106 M.G. Coy

Copy No. 1 [illegible]

2 [illegible]

3 "

4 [illegible]

5 [illegible]

6 War Diary

7 File

8 Brigade (106)

9 War Diary

10 105 M.G.C.

11 241 "

12 [illegible]

105 [illegible]

SECRET Copy No 5

Operation Order No 104

106th M.G.C. will relieve 104 M.G.Co. in D Sector on the night of 7/8th Sept 1917

1 DISPOSITIONS A Sect 3 Guns front line [illegible] Section
1 Gun GREEN LINE

D Section 1 Gun EAGLES NEST
2 Guns OSSUS 1.
1 Gun PIGEON QUARRY.

B Section. GREEN LINE.
2 Guns MORCH.
1 Gun LIMERICK.
1 " NEAR KILDARE POST

4 Guns in Reserve at adv Q.H.Q.

2 GUIDES. A SECTION –
1 Guide will be at MUNNER HOUSE (X 8 a 3.1) at 9.30pm to guide Section to Sect. H.Q. where 1 guide per gun team will be at 9.45pm. to guide detachments to gun positions.

– D. SECTION –
1 Guide will meet the Section at CAUSEWAY, Corner (F 1 b 7.6) at 9pm, a guide for detachments will be at Sect. H.Q. at 9.30pm.

– B SECTION –
1 Guide at EPEHY Cross roads 8.15 pm.
1 " per detachment at fork roads F 27 a X.1 at 8.30pm.

– C SECTION –
1 Guide will meet the section at cross roads EPEHY at 8.30pm.

3 PARADE the Sections will parade and move off at the following hours
"A" Section 7.30pm. D Section 7.35pm.
"B" " 7.40pm. C " 7.45pm.

4 ROUTE. Route for A Sect:- ST. EMILIE Xroads EPEHY, fork roads PEIZIERS W 30 a 9.9 fork roads X 25 c 1.8 to MUNNER House.
Remaining Sections – ST. EMILIE, EPEHY and thence to Guides.

5 EQUIPMENT All S.A.A. and trench stores, aeroplane photographs, maps and schemes will be handed over.
O.C. D Sect. at EAGLES NEST will take over 4 Belt Boxes. 4 Belt Boxes from C Sect. will be handed over at C.H.Q.

6 TRANSPORT will be under orders of [illegible] concerned. On completion of Section Officers will return to Limbers at VILLERS-FAUCON.

7 QR. MR. STORES. Quarter Master Sgt. will take over transport lines and arrange to [illegible] for the situation of the company in the line.

8 COMPLETION OF RELIEF to be reported to H.Q. by wire by word "FEDUPALL".

Issued at 5pm 7/Sept 1917

1	Sect Officer	7	Brigade
2	" "	8	War Diary
3	" "	9	D.M.G.O
4	" "	10	104 M.G.Co
5	War Diary	11	105 M.G.Co.
6	File	12	Transp. Sgt.

H.E. Talbot Lieut
for

SECRET

COPY No 5

Operation Order No 105

The following inter company relief will take place on the night 10/11th Sept 1917

1. RELIEF. The personnel of "C" section will relieve the personnel of "D" section in the front line.
The personnel of D section on relief will relieve the personnel of B section in the Green line.
B section on Relief will relieve "C" section in Reserve.
Relief to commence at 8 P.M.

2. DISPOSITIONS. "C" Sec'n F. 5,6,7 & 8
D Sections 20, 21, 22 & 24
A " F 9-10-11 & R 2-5
B " four guns in reserve.

3. GUIDES will be arranged between Section Officers concerned.

4. Completion of Relief will be reported complete by wire by word "CHOOCHIE"

Issued Sept 10th 1917 at 1pm.

Copy No 1 Section Officer
2 " "
3 " "
4 " "
5 War Diary
6 File
7 Brigade
8 War Diary
9 C.Q.M.S.
10 Transp. Sgt.

H. E. Talbot
Lieut
for O.C. C.H.

Secret.

Copy No. 5

Operation Order No. 105

The following inter-company relief will take place on the night 12/13th Sept.

1. RELIEF The personnel of B Sect. from Reserve will relieve the personnel of "A" Section in the VILLERS-GUISLAIN [illegible] advance C.H.Q. at 9.15 p.m.

2 DISPOSITIONS.
B Section F 9, 10, 11 R 15.
"A" " 4 Guns Reserve (Barrage positions)

3 GUIDES will be arranged by Section Officers concerned

4. COMPLETION OF RELIEF will be reported to Co. H.Q. by word by wire "CRICKET"

H. G. Lee. Lieut.
for
O.C. 106 M.G. Co.

Issued at 5 p.m. 12/9/17

Copy No. 1 Section Officer
2 " "
3 " "
4 "
5 War Diary
6 File
7 Brigade
8 War Diary
9 C.Q.M.S.
10

Operation Order No 107

"A" Section & 1 detachment of D will co-operate in an Artillery concentration on the night 13/14 [illegible]

1. [illegible] 1 Gun of D Section will fire on [illegible] Trench [illegible] vide Appx [illegible]
   2 Guns will diagonal search from S 25 b [illegible] to S 25 d 85.85 vide Appendix "A"
   2 Guns will concentrate fire on to Canal crossing at S 25 b 6.7 vide App. "A"

2. GUNS IN ACTION.
   A Section and 1 Gun of D Section under Lieut R. SKEVINGTON.

3. BAROMETER & THERMOMETER. As the weather is normal Barometer and Thermometer are negligible.

4. HOUR OF READINESS.
   All guns will be ready to fire at 7.15 pm.

5. RATE OF FIRE. As intense as possible

6. HOUR & DURATION OF FIRE. 7.30 pm. 11.20 pm and 4.30 am. 1 Belt per Gun per time.

7. AMMUNITION. 750 rounds per Gun

8. WITHDRAWAL. at 4.40 am "A" Section will withdraw to Reserve

9. PARADE "A" Section will parade under orders of Lt. R. SKEVINGTON.

10. WATCHES – SYNCHRONIZATION OF. Watches will be synchronised at C.H.Q. at 4.30 pm and 7.00 pm.

Issued at 11.30 am 13/9/17

Copy 1 Section Officer
2 " "
3 " "
4 " "
5 War Diary
6 File
7 Brigade
8 War Diary
9 D.M.G.O.

[illegible] Capt

APPENDIX "A"

	RANGE	QE	MAG BEARING
LEFT GUN	2300 – 2400	4°34′ – 5°21′	103°
	2300 – 2400	4°34′ – 5°21′	103°
	2300 – 2400	4°34′ – 5°21′	102°
	2200 – 2250	4°19′ – 4°41′	110° — 111°
RIGHT GUN	2250 – 2300	4°38′ – 4°54′	110° — 111°

SECRET

Copy No. 5

OPERATION ORDER No. 108

THE FOLLOWING INTER-COMPANY RELIEF WILL TAKE PLACE ON THE NIGHT 14/15th SEPT. 1917.

(1) RELIEF. THE PERSONNEL OF "D" SECTION FROM GREEN LINE WILL RELIEVE THE PERSONNEL OF "C" SECTION IN THE BIRDCAGE SECTOR.

(2) TIME. RELIEVING SECTION WILL LEAVE ADV. C. H.Q. AT 5.30 P.M.

(3) DISPOSITIONS

"C" SECTION F20, 21, 22 & 24

"D" " F5, 6, 7 and 8.

(4) GUIDES – WILL BE ARRANGED BY SECTION OFFICERS CONCERNED.

(5) COMPLETION OF RELIEF WILL BE REPORTED BY WORD BY WIRE "FOOTBALL"

ISSUED AT 11.30 a.m. 14/9/17

[illegible] Lt for
O.C. 106 M. G. Coy

Copy 1 Section Officers
2 "
3 "
4 "
5 War Diary
6 File
7 Brigade
8 War Diary
9 C.Q.M.S.

SECRET [illegible] 5

OPERATION ORDER No 10[illegible] (A)

"A" Section, 3 detachments of "[illegible]" Section & 1 detachment of "B" Section will cooperate in a [illegible] enterprise to be carried out by [illegible] Royal Scots on the night 16/17th Sept 1917.

(1) **Guns in Action** 3 [illegible] of "C", 1 [illegible] of "B" under [illegible] KINRED MEATH POST [illegible] ("A" GROUP)
"A" Section under Lt. [illegible] Talbot [illegible] A [illegible] ("B" GROUP)

(2) **BARRAGES** to be [illegible] as in Appendix "A"

(3) **TARGETS.** Fire will be [illegible] in Appendix "B"

(4) **BAROMETER & THERMOMETER** will [illegible] [illegible]

(5) **Zero Hour** will be notified later.

(6) **Hour of Readiness** [illegible] guns will be ready to [illegible] at Zero [illegible] minus 30.

(7) **Rate of Fire.** [illegible] per gun per [illegible] minutes
[illegible] barrages – [illegible]
Duration of fire. "A" Group Zero [illegible] Zero + 20
"B" " Zero [illegible] Zero + 40
Ammunition – A – 3,000 rounds per gun
B – 2,000 " " "
[illegible] rounds per gun in belt boxes must be kept at [illegible] positions

(8) **Parade & Route.** Hour of parade & route to barrage positions [illegible] arrangements to be made by [illegible].

(9) **Watches** – Synchronisation of [illegible] will be at [illegible] H.Q. at [illegible]

(10) **Transport** A limber will be at "B" group barrage position at Zero + 90 for carrying material and equipment.

(11) **Withdrawal.** Groups will withdraw & resume normal on [illegible] from [illegible]

(12) **Reports** will be sent to [illegible] H.Q. [illegible]

Issued at 12 m.n. 15/16th Sep 1917

Copy No.
1 C.O.
2 "A" Group
3 "B" Group
4 O.C. "[illegible]" Bty.
5 [illegible]
6 [illegible]
7 [illegible]
8 [illegible]
[illegible] O.C. [illegible]
10 O.C. [illegible]
11 O.C. [illegible]
12 Transport.
13 Signals.
14 [illegible]

APPENDIX "[illegible]"

[illegible] [illegible] [illegible] [illegible] FOR
[illegible] [illegible] [illegible] [illegible] [illegible]

DISTRIBUTION OF GUNS. [illegible] [illegible] [illegible] of 8 VICKERS
GUNS DIVIDED INTO TWO GROUPS OF 4 GUNS
[illegible].

COMPOSITION & POSITION OF GROUPS. "A" GROUP 3 GUNS & SECT
and [illegible] of "B" Section.
[illegible] X 21 b 6.4 to X 21 b 20 55

"B" GROUP [illegible] GUNS "A" SECTION
POSITION X 16 c 05.15 to X 15 d 55 40

POSITION OF BARRAGES.

"A" GROUP will FIRE A FRONTAL CREEPING BARRAGE AS UNDER:–

FROM X 18 a 05.[illegible] and X 18 a 00.50 } to { X 18 c 90.50 and X 18 a 55.70

TIME ZERO [illegible] [illegible] ZERO + [illegible]

then will place an OBLIQUE STANDING BARRAGE FROM X 18 c 45 55 TO S 13 d 00.50.

TIME ZERO +1 to ZERO + 20

"B" GROUP will FIRE A CREEPING FRONTAL BARRAGE FROM:–

X 11 d 2.7 AND X 11 d 00.95 } To { X 11 b 70.00 and X 11 b 55.40

TIME ZERO [illegible] to ZERO +10

THEN WILL PLACE [illegible] OBLIQUE STANDING BARRAGE FROM X 11 b 70.00 to X 11 b 55.40

TIME ZERO TO ZERO +10

APPENDIX B

GROUP A

	Gun	Range	M.E.	Q.E.	[illegible]
Creeping Barrage	1	2300 to 2350	90°	5°17 to [illegible]	[illegible]
	2				
	3				
	4				
Standing Barrage	1	2000	90°	[illegible]	
	2	2000	90°	[illegible]	200'
	3	2?00	90°	[illegible]	
	4	2800	90°	[illegible]	

GROUP B

	Gun	Range	M.E.	Q.E.	Clearance
Creeping Barrage	1	2000 to 2300	64°	[illegible]	200'
	2	2000 to 2300	64°	[illegible] to [illegible]	200'
	3	2000 to 2350	63°	[illegible] to [illegible]	200'
	4	2000 to 2350	63°	[illegible] to [illegible]	200'
Standing Barrage	1	300	64°	5°17	200'
	2	300	64°	5°4[illegible]	200'
	3	350	63°	5°4[illegible]	200'
	4	350	63°	5°4[illegible]	200'

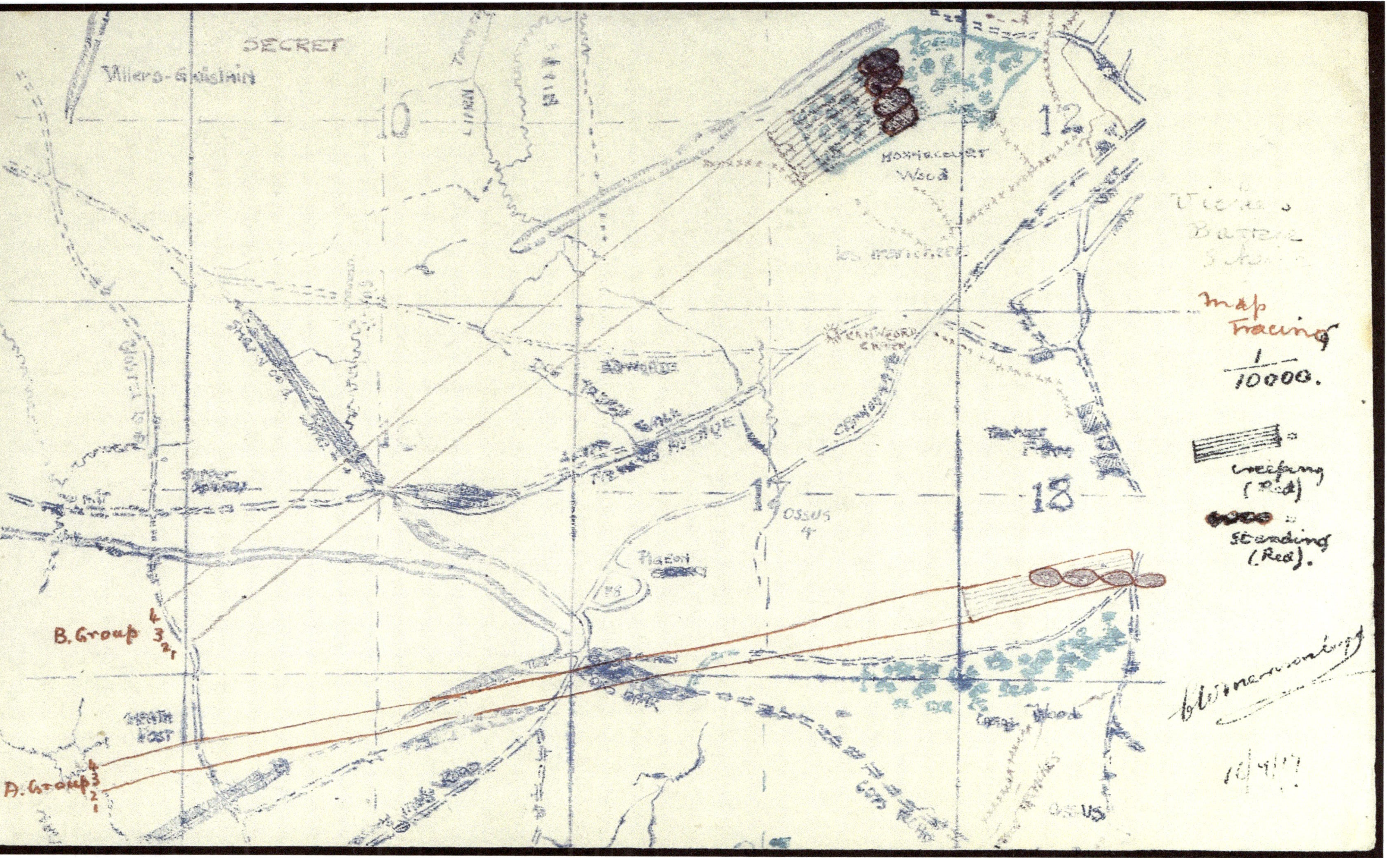
SECRET
Villers-Ghislain
10
12
17
18
Honnecourt Wood
Ossus 4
Pigeon
Map Tracing
1/10000.
creeping (Red)
standing (Red).
B. Group 4 3 2 1
A. Group 4 3 2 1
Ossus

SECRET

Copy No. 5

OPERATION ORDER No. 109

A Section & 3 detachments of C Section will fire a Machine Gun concentration on the night of 17/18th Sept 1917.

① TIME (a) 'A' Section and R21 will barrage the LE CATELET road from X23d 9.4 to X24 c 65.65
(b) 1 Subsection of A will concentrate fire on to X24 c 85.75.
(c) 'A' Section R20, R21 and R22 will Barrage eastern end of CANAL WOOD.

② GUNS IN ACTION.
A Section and 3 detachments of C Section under LT. S.W. KINRED

③ HOUR OF READINESS. All lines of fire will be laid out by 7.30 p.m.
(a) 8.50 pm.
(b) 10.20 pm.
(c) 4.20 am.

④ RATE OF FIRE — Intense.

⑤ HOUR AND DURATION OF FIRE
(a) 9.00 pm
(b) 10.30 pm.
(c) 4.30 am.
1 Belt per gun per time.

⑥ AMMUNITION 750 Rounds per gun

Issued at 11.30 am 17/9/17

Copy No
1 Lt S W Kinred
2 D.M.G.O.
3 S.O.
4 S.O.
5 War Diary
6. File
7 Brigade
8 War Diary

SECRET COPY No. 5

OPERATION ORDER No. 110

THE 106th M.G. Co. will be relieved in the line by 108th M.G. Co. on the night of 19/20th SEPT 1917.

1. DISPOSITIONS will be handed over by Sections as follows:–

"A" Section – At Guns Reserve ([illegible] position)
"B" " Positions F9, F10, F11 and R21
"C" " " R20, R22, R24 and R25
"D" " " T5, T6, T7 and T8.

A Receipt will be obtained by Section Officers that positions are handed over in a good and sanitary condition.

2. GUIDES

"A" Section – 1 Guide at [illegible] Cross Roads at 6.45 P.M.
"B" Section – 1 Guide [illegible] at MEUNIER HOUSE
Villers Guislain [illegible] at 6.00 P.M.
1 Guide per detachment at Section H.Q. at 8.15 P.M.
"C" Section – 1 Guide per detachment at Section H.Q. at 7.30 P.M.
" 1 Guide at [illegible] Cross Roads at [illegible]
"D" Section – 1 Guide per detachment at Section H.Q. at [illegible] P.M.
1 Guide at [illegible] Cross Roads at [illegible]

3. EQUIPMENT. All S.A.A. & Trench Stores will be handed over & receipts obtained. Belt Boxes will not be handed over.
Special attention will be paid to handing over [illegible] complete.

4. WITHDRAWAL
On completion of relief sections will proceed independently to camp at [illegible].

5. TRANSPORT.
[illegible] limbers for B & D will report to Section H.Q. at [illegible] P.M. and [illegible] H.Q. for A & C Sections at 6.15 P.M.

6. Q. M. STORES.
[illegible] stores & transport not required for relief will move back to camp at [illegible] under arrangement of C.Q.M.S. and Transport Sergeant.

7. COMPLETION OF RELIEF will be reported by [illegible] by wire "[illegible]"

Issued 18/9/17

[illegible] Lt.
Comdg. 106 [illegible]

Copy No. 1 [illegible]
2 " "
3 " "
4 " "
5 War Diary
6 File
7 [illegible]
8 War Diary
9 [illegible]
10 [illegible]
11 [illegible]

Instructions regarding War Diaries and Intelligence Summaries are contained in F. S. Regs., Part II. and the Staff Manual respectively. Title Pages will be prepared in manuscript.

WAR DIARY
or
~~INTELLIGENCE SUMMARY~~
(Erase heading not required.)

Army Form C. 2118.

106th M. G. Coy
35

Vol 18

October 1917

Place	Date	Hour	Summary of Events and Information	Remarks and references to Appendices
	1st/2nd .10.17		Six detachments took up positions to cooperate in a minor enterprise to be carried out at dawn (see O.O. No 112.) Operation cancelled at last moment owing to weather condition	
	2nd/3rd		Coy. relieved in the line by 165 M.G. Co. Relief carried out without incident and Co. withdrew to AIZECOURT-LE-BAS.	
	3rd		Co. moved to PERONNE by motor lorry – transport by road	
	4th		Entrained at PERONNE at 9AM to proceed to ARRAS. Transport again moved by road. On detrainment at ARRAS about 5PM the Co. marched to billets at MONTENESCOURT.	
	5th to 12th		Training at MONTENESCOURT. Special attention paid to packsaddlery in view of forthcoming operations.	
	13th		Co. marched to AUBIGNY.	
	14th		Entrained for ESQUELBECQ. and marched to billets at RUBROUCK.	
	16th		Entrained at ARNEKE for PROVEN.	
	17th		Marched to BOX Camp in Reserve.	
	19th		Relieved 104 M.G. Co in the line. 10 guns front line 6 guns support line	
	20th		Relieved in the line by 1 sec. 105 M.G. Co. and withdrew to Barrage posn	
	21st		Relieved on left by 1 Sec. 105 M.G. Co. & withdrew to barrage position.	
	22nd		Coy cooperated in an attack by 104 and 105 Infy. Bdes by firing a barrage as per O.O. 120 dated 21.10.17	

2449 Wt. W14957/M90 750,000 1/16 J.B.C. & A. Forms/C.2118/12.

Army Form C. 2118.

Instructions regarding War Diaries and Intelligence Summaries are contained in F. S. Regs., Part II. and the Staff Manual respectively. Title Pages will be prepared in manuscript.

WAR DIARY
or
~~INTELLIGENCE SUMMARY~~

(Erase heading not required.)

Place	Date	Hour	Summary of Events and Information	Remarks and references to Appendices
	23rd/10/17		Half Coy remained in barrage position - B and C groups. Remainder withdrew to Box Camp.	
	24th		Remaining half Coy relieved by 245 M.G. Co	
	25th		Withdrew to Box Camp.	
	29th		Moved to "H" Camp. Transport remained at Box Camp.	

C W Menson Capt
Comdg No 106 M G Co

106 M[illegible] GUN CO.
Nov 3rd 1917
ORDERLY ROOM.

2449 Wt. W14957/M90 750,000 1/16 J.B.C. & A. Forms/C.2118/12.

SECRET Copy No. 5.

OPERATION ORDER No. 2.

Six detachments of 106th M.G.C. will cover [illegible] of a minor enterprise to be carried out by [illegible] on the night 1/2nd Oct 1917.

1. Guns in action.
   4 Detachments 'D' Sect. under 2/Lt E.A. [illegible] in sunken road from F 16 d 55.25 to F [illegible] 75
   1 Detachment B Section under 2/Lt [illegible] at Lempire Central.
   1 Detachment 'C' Section under 2/Lt [illegible] at F 4 d 8.5
2. Barrages to be laid down as in Appendix A.
3. Zero Hour will be notified later.
4. Hour of Readiness. All guns will be ready to fire at Zero – 30 mins.
5. Rate of fire. Zero – [illegible] to Zero ... Rapid.
   Zero to Zero + 20 ... 1 belt per gun per 5 mins.

   Ammunition: – C Detachment 2,500 Rounds
   B " 2,500 "
   D Section – 2500 rds per gun.
6. Parade.
   Hour of parade & route under arrangements of officers concerned.
7. Synchronisation of watches will be at 'B' Sect Hd. Qrs. at 12 midnight.
8. Transport. Two battle limbers of 'D' Sect will report at Co. H.Q. at 7.00 P.M.
9. Withdrawal.
   D Section will withdraw to St. Emilie on completion of firing.
10. Code Word. If code word "[illegible]" is received no shooting will take place.
11. Reports will be sent to Co. H.Q. St. Emilie.

Issued at 4.00pm 1-10-17

[illegible] Lieut.
O.C. 106 M.G.C.

Copy No. 1 Adv. Off.
2 " "
3 " "
4 " "
5 War Diary
6 Bde
7 Brigade
8 War Diary
9 D.M.G.O.
10 O.C. [illegible]

APPENDIX "A"

DISTRIBUTION OF GUNS ...

'D' SECTION 4 GUNS SUNKEN ROAD FROM F 16 d 55·25 To F. 15 d 7·5
'B' DETACHMENT. LEMPIRE CENTRAL
'C' DETACHMENT. F 4 d 8·5

POSITION OF BARRAGES ...

'D' SECTION will place A FRONTAL BARRAGE ON WILLOW TRENCH FROM A 7 d 7 1 TO A 7 d 5.5.
TIME:– ZERO MINUS 5 TO ZERO AND WILL THEN LIFT ON TO LONE TREE TR UNTIL ZERO +20

TIME	GUN	RANGE	M.B.	Q.E.
ZERO – 5 TO ZERO.	4 3 2 1	2200 2200 2200 2200	74° 75° 76° 77°	271' 277' 277' 287'
ZERO TO ZERO + 20	4 3 2 1	2400 2400 2450 2450	74° 75° 76° 77°	353' 360' 384' 391'

'B' DETACHMENT will search GRUB LANE FROM ZERO – 5 TO ZERO AND will THEN LIFT ON TO MACQUINCOURT VALLEY UNTIL ZERO + 20

TIME	GUN	RANGE	M.B.	Q.E.
ZERO – 5 TO ZERO	B	2353 TO 2550x	92	365' TO 457'
ZERO TO ZERO + 20	B	2500x TO 2800x	78	408' TO 575

'C' DETACHMENT will FIRE ON JUNCTION OF GRUB LANE & WILLOW Trench FROM ZERO – 5 TO ZERO AND WILL THEN LIFT ON TO CROSS ROADS IN MACQUINCOURT VALLEY AND SEARCH

TIME	GUN	RANGE	M.B.	Q.E.
ZERO – 5 TO ZERO	C	2250	132°	328'
ZERO TO ZERO + 20	C	2000 TO 2300	121°	228' TO 335'

A H [illegible] Lieut.
O.C. 186 M.G.C.

SECRET. Copy No. 5

OPERATION ORDER No. 13.

The 106 M.G.Co will be relieved in the line by the [illegible] Machine Gun Co. on the night [illegible] 1917.

1 DISPOSITIONS will be handed over by Sections as follows.

"D" Section ... 4 guns in reserve at St. Emilie.

"A" " ... 1 gun Duncan, 1 gun Doleful, 1 " Ego, 1 " Fleeceall posts.

"B" " ... [illegible] Fag, 2 guns Basse Boulogne South, [illegible] Lempire Central.

"C" " ... 2 guns Grafton Post, 1 gun "A" Group position, 1 gun Brook.

A receipt will be obtained by Section Officers that all positions are handed over in a clean & sanitary condition.

2 GUIDES.

"A" Section ... Guides for Ego & Fleeceall posts will be at Section H.Q. at 8.15 P.M. Guides for Duncan & Doleful posts [illegible] Duncan Post at 8.15 P.M.

"B" Section ... Guides for detachment will be at Section H.Q. at 8.00 P.M.

"C" Section ... Guides for Grafton Post & "A" Group will be at Section H.Q. at 8.15 P.M. Guide for Brook at the junction of Brook & Lempire Roads at 8.00 P.M.

"D" Section ... Will provide 4 men to guide the limbers of 165 M.G.Co. to the 3 Section H.Qrs & Duncan Post.

3 EQUIPMENT.

All S.A.A., [illegible] Stores, Aeroplane Photographs and Sketch Maps will be handed over & receipts obtained. Special attention will be paid to the handing over of L.T.M.'s & A.A. [illegible]

4 WATER

All Petrol tins belonging to the Company will be brought out of the line. The reserve water at the gun emplacement will be handed over.

5 WITHDRAWAL

On completion of relief Sections will proceed independently to camp at Aizecourt-le-Bas.

6 TRANSPORT. Battle limbers for A, B & C Sects. will report at Co. H.Q. St. Emilie at 7.00 P.M. All transport not required for the relief will move under arrangements to be made by the Transport Officer.

7 COMPLETION of RELIEF will be reported by wire to Co. H.Q. St. Emilie "HICKEY"

Issued at 9.30 A.M. [illegible]

[signature] Lieut.
O.C. 106 M.G. Co.

Copy No. 1 Section Officer
2 " "
3 " "
4 " "
5 War Diary
6 File
7 Brigade
8 War Diary
9 [illegible] Off.
10 O.C. 165 M.G.C.
11 D.M.G.O.

SECRET. Copy No. 5

OPERATION ORDER No 14.

[illegible] M.G.Co. WILL MOVE IN [illegible] WITH [illegible] TO [illegible] ON OCTOBER 3RD 1917

1. MOVE. THE CO. WILL PARADE AT [illegible] AND MOVE BY MOTOR LORRY TO [illegible] [illegible] ORDER WITH BLANKET. [illegible] BE [illegible] [illegible]

2. RATIONS. [illegible]

3. BILLETING. [illegible]

VINGTON
14 Q · AT 9.30 AM

[illegible]

4. C.Q.M.S. STORES. [illegible] OF THE O.C. No. 4 Co. [illegible] TRAIN

5. TRANSPORT. [illegible] LIMBERS [illegible]

6. OFFICERS' VALISES. A LORRY WILL BE [illegible] TO CARRY OFFICERS' VALISES [illegible]

7. MARCH DISCIPLINE. [illegible]

8. BRAKESMEN. [illegible]

Issued at [illegible] P.M. [illegible]

[illegible] 106 M.G.C. [illegible]

Copy No 1 [illegible]
2 [illegible]
3 [illegible]
4 [illegible]
5 [illegible]
6 [illegible]
7 [illegible]
8 [illegible]
9 [illegible]
10 [illegible]
11 [illegible]
12 [illegible]

Copy No. 5

SECRET

OPERATION ORDER No 115.

THE UNIT WILL ENTRAIN AT PERONNE TO MOVE TO THE NEW BILLETING AREA, LEAVING PERONNE (FLAMICOURT) AT 9 AM. ON THE 4th OCT. 1917.

1. **PARADE.** Co. WILL PARADE IN FULL MARCHING ORDER (AS PER O.O. No 114) AT 7AM AND WILL MARCH TO THE STATION FOR ENTRAINMENT TO ARRIVE 1 HOUR BEFORE THE DEPARTURE OF THE TRAIN. PROBABLE HOUR OF ARRIVAL AT ARRAS - 2 PM. ON ARRIVAL AT ARRAS COMPANY WILL DE-TRAIN (PACKS & BLANKETS WILL BE CARRIED ON A MOTOR LORRY PROVIDED FOR THAT PURPOSE) AND WILL MARCH TO THE NEW BILLETS AT MONTENESCOURT. ORDER OF MARCH :- A. B. C. D AND H.Q.

2. **TRANSPORT** 1st LINE TRANSPORT LESS MESS CART WILL MOVE BY ROAD UNDER LT. ROBINSON WITH Co. DIV. TRAIN TO BAPAUME ON OCT. 4th AND FROM BAPAUME TO NEW AREA ON OCT 5th. STARTING POINT :- J 21 CENTRAL MAP 62c. TIME 6.00 AM. 106th M.G.C. TRANSPORT WILL FOLLOW DIRECTLY AFTER Bde H.Qrs TRANSPORT.

3. **OMNIBUS TRAIN.** 2/Lt. H.H. BUCKLEY, 2/Lt. W.S. WHITEHOUSE, MESS CART, 2 L.D. ANIMALS & 3 O.R. (TO BE DETAILED BY TRANSPORT OFFICER) WILL BE AT PERONNE (FLAMICOURT) STN. AT 9.30AM ON OCT 4th & WILL MOVE TO NEW AREA BY THE OMNIBUS TRAIN.

4. **OFFICERS VALISES.** THE MOTOR LORRY FOR CARRYING OFFICERS VALISES & MESS KIT WILL BE AT THE TOWN MAJOR'S OFFICE THE GRAND PLACE, AT 6.00AM. OCT 4th. A GUIDE WILL BE DETAILED TO BRING THE LORRY TO THE UNIT'S H.Q. TO COLLECT THE VALISES ETC.

5. **MARCH DISCIPLINE.** STRICTEST ATTENTION MUST BE PAID TO THE MARCH DISCIPLINE. THE USUAL CLOCK HOUR HALTS WILL BE OBSERVED. INTERVALS OF 200 YARDS WILL BE MAINTAINED BETWEEN UNITS.

ISSUED AT 3.30PM 2/10/17

Copy No 1 Section Officer
2 " "
3 " "
4 " "
5 WAR DIARY
6 FILE
7 BRIGADE
8 WAR DIARY
9 C.Q.M.S
10 TRANSP. Off.
11 W R. Skevington
12 2/Lt HAWKES.

SECRET

COPY No 5

OPERATION ORDER No 116

106th M.G. COMPANY WILL ENTRAIN AT HUBIGNY ON 14/10/17 FOR MOVE TO NEW AREA

1. PARADE. Co. WILL PARADE AT 11 P.M. ON 13-10-17 TO MARCH TO HUBIGNY FOR ENTRAINMENT
2. ORDER OF MARCH. B, C, A, D SECTIONS, H.Q. [illegible] BATTLE WAGONS - B, C, A, D; NOS 3, H.Q. [illegible] AND WATER CART, COOKS CART.
3. ROUTE. HABARCQUE - HERMAVILLE - HUBIGNY
4. TRANSPORT WILL BE DRAWN UP ON THE WARLUS - MONTENESCOURT ROAD; HEAD OF THE COLUMN 150 YARDS FROM H.Q. BILLET.
5. OMNIBUS TRAIN. No 19 PORTION 3536
6. BLANKETS. All blankets will be rolled up in bundles of 10 and clearly marked, [illegible] stacked outside H.Q. billet at 7.00 P.M. and will be loaded on lorry by men detailed by C.S.M.
   Lcpl GUMMERY will accompany this lorry.
7. BAGGAGE. All baggage will be packed by 5.30 P.M. with exception of officers' mess gear & dixies which will be packed by 10 P.M.
8. ARRIVAL. Probable hour of arrival at de-training station will be 1.30 P.M. 14/10/17.
9. ROUTE ON DETRAINMENT. ESQUELBECQ - ZEGGERS CAPPEL - L'ERKELSBRUGGE - RUBROUCK
10. ARRIVAL. Probable hour of arrival 5.30 P.M.

Issued at 10.00 AM 12/10/17

H. J. Lee Lieut for
O.C. 106 M.G. Co

Copy No
1 Section Officer
2 " "
3 " "
4 " "
5 War Diary
6 File
7 Brigade
8 War Diary
9 Transport Off.
10 C.Q.M.S.
11 2nd in Command
12 C.S.M.

SECRET COPY No 5

OPERATION ORDER No 11[illegible]

THE 106th M.G. Co. WILL ENTRAIN AT ARNEKE ON 16-10-17 TO MOVE TO PROVEN AREA

1. TRAIN. No 3 TRAIN WILL DEPART AT ZERO
2. PARADE. Co. WILL PARADE AT ZERO – 3 HOURS TO MARCH TO ARNEKE FOR ENTRAINMENT
3. ORDER OF MARCH. R.C.A.D. SECTIONS [illegible]
4. ROUTE. RUBROUCK – [illegible] – ARNEKE.
5. DRESS. FIGHTING ORDER. BLANKETS WILL BE ROLLED INSIDE WATERPROOF SHEET & CARRIED AT BACK OF BELT.
6. TRANSPORT. WILL PARADE AT 7.45 AM. TO MOVE OFF AT 8.00 AM.
7. ORDER OF MARCH. B.C.A.D. No 3 H.Q. LIMBERS WATER CART, COOKS CART.
8. STARTING POINT. X ROADS [illegible] WHICH WILL BE PASSED AT 9.40 AM.
9. DESTINATION CAMP P [illegible] PROVEN AREA
10. BAGGAGE. All Baggage will be packed on LIMBERS BY 7.15 AM.
11. ARRIVAL. PROBABLE HOUR OF ARRIVAL ZERO + 4 HOURS.
12. ZERO. ZERO HOUR will be notified later.

ISSUED AT 9.00 PM 15/10/17

[illegible]
[illegible] 106 M.G. Co.

COPY No
1 SECTION OFFICER
2 " "
3 " "
4 " "
5 WAR DIARY
6 FILE
7 BRIGADE
8 WAR D[illegible]
9 T.O.
10 C.Q.M.S.
11 2nd IN C.
12 C.S.M.

SECRET.

OPERATION ORDER [illegible]

100th Machine Gun Co. will relieve 103 M.G.Co. in the line on the night 19/20 October 1917

1. DISPOSITIONS. Royal Scots on right H.Q. [illegible] Farm. [illegible] in centre. [illegible] on left [illegible] H.Q. [illegible] Farm. [illegible] [illegible] of Wit[illegible]

2. M.G. DISPOSITIONS.

Approx. [illegible] as under.

"A" SECTION. H.Q. [illegible] FARM.

1 Gun on hill [illegible] Farm. 1 Gun [illegible] Point 29.

1 " S. of [illegible] X roads. 1 " for R.A. work [illegible]

"C" SECTION. H.Q. [illegible] FARM.

1 Gun Les 5 [illegible] south of [illegible]

1 " 300 yds east of [illegible]

1 " [illegible] of [illegible] of the [illegible]

1 " [illegible] for R.A. work [illegible]

D. SECTION H.Q. [illegible] HOUSE.

1 Gun right [illegible] north of [illegible] House

2 Guns Les 5 Chemins.

1 Gun half way between Angel Point & Aden House.

B. SECTION H.Q. PASCALL FARM

2 Guns Egypt House. 2 Guns Pascall Fm. for R.A. work.

241 M. G. Co.

4 Guns Cemetery between Hey Farm & Hey Wood.

Lt. R. Skevington will establish Adv. Co. H.Q. at Montmirail Farm.

3. PARADE. Co. will parade at 11-25 AM in the following order C.A.D.B. sections; intervals of 200 yds being maintained between sections.

4. DRESS. Fighting order. Jerkins if available rolled on belts. 2nd pair of socks being carried in haversack.

5. GUIDES.

1 Guide per section will be at Signal Fm. (Co. H.Q.) at 2 P.M.

1 " " gun team at Section H.Q. at 4 PM.

6. RATIONS.

2 days rations will be carried on the man in addition to the unconsumed portion of the days rations. No further rations will be issued until relief. 1 bottle of whale oil per gun team will be carried.

7. WATER. 9 tins per section & 4 for H.Q. will be taken up filled into the line.

8. TRANSPORT. Nos. [illegible] limbers to carry guns, tripods, spare-parts, water & rations will march with each section with 4 mules per limber. H.Q. wagon for H.Q.

Transport D.B. sections will [illegible] in vicinity of "B" H.Q. [illegible] at Wit[illegible]. Transport on completion of duty will return to present lines.

9. ROUTE

[illegible] X roads - [illegible] - [illegible] - and corduroy roads to destination

10. HANDING OVER. All belt boxes, S.A.A. trench stores, aeroplane photos, maps & schemes will be taken over receipts being taken & sent to H.Q.

[illegible] DISPOSITION REPORTS will be rendered at once to H.Q.

[illegible] COMPLETION OF RELIEF to be reported by message by word "ALICE" to be brought back by runner attached H.Q. who will come out with relieved section.

[illegible] REINFORCEMENTS under Sgt. Whitehouse will remain at Box Camp.

[illegible] [illegible]RS will close at Box Camp at 12 noon 19th inst & will re-open at Signal Farm on completion of relief.

Issued at 6 pm 18-10-17

Copy No.

1 Section Officer

2 " "

3 " "

4 " "

5 War Diary

6 [illegible]

7 Brigade

8 War Diary

9 T. O

10 D.M.G.

11 C.Q.M.S.

12

13

[illegible] Lt.

For O.C. 100 M.G. Co.

SECRET

Copy No. 5

OPERATION ORDER No. 119

20/21 Oct 1917

THE 106th M.G.Co. WILL BE RELIEVED IN THE LINE BY ONE SECTION OF 105 M.G.Co. AND 1 SECTION OF 104 M.G.Co. AND WILL WITHDRAW.

THE FOLLOWING POSITIONS WILL BE TAKEN OVER BY 105 M.G.Co.

F.1. AT U 5 c 6.2 (ROAD WEST OF FAIDHERBE ROAD AND IN FRONT OF S.P. 79)
F.2. LOUVOIS FARM ROAD - - - - - - - - - - } [illegible]
F.6. FAIDHERBE ROAD "C" SECTION
No. 3 - - - - - - - - - - - - - - "D" SECTION

BY 104 M.G.Co.

No. 2 ... ...
No. [illegible] ... ... } D SECTION.
No. 5 ... ...

THE REMAINING GUNS WILL WITHDRAW BY SECTIONS WHEN REMAINDER OF THE SECTION IS RELIEVED

"[illegible]" SECTION 2 DETACHMENTS
[illegible] 4 "
[illegible] 3 "

WITHDRAWAL

[illegible] WILL WITHDRAW & DUMP GUNS [illegible]

[illegible] LOUVOIS FARM
[illegible] PASCALL FARM
B [illegible] LOUVOIS FARM
[illegible] PASCALL FARM

DUMPS [illegible] SPLIT TO LESSEN RISK [illegible] DAMAGE BY SHELL FIRE.

SECTIONS WILL THEN REPORT TO COY. H.Q. WHERE FURTHER INSTRUCTIONS WILL BE ISSUED.

GUARDS

SUFFICIENT GUARDS WILL BE LEFT AT EACH DUMP

EQUIPMENT

All S.A.A. AND TRENCH STORES WILL BE HANDED OVER. BELT BOXES WILL NOT BE BROUGHT OUT BY DETACHMENTS RELIEVED BUT ONLY BY THOSE WITHDRAWING WITHOUT RELIEF.

GUIDES

DETACHMENTS OF 105 M.G.Co. WILL BE GUIDED TO SECT. H.Q. WHERE 1 GUIDE PER DETACHMENT WILL BE REQUIRED

GUIDES FOR 104 M.G.Co. WILL BE FURNISHED WHERE REQUIRED.

RELIEF.

COMPLETION OF RELIEF WILL BE REPORTED TO THIS OFFICE BY WORD "BEATRICE".

Issued at 8 pm 20/10/17

[signature] for 106 M.G. Co.

Copy No.
1 Section Officer
2 "
3 "
4 "
5 War Diary
6 File
7 Brigade
8 War Diary
9 Div. G.O.
10 104 M.G.Co.
11 105 M.G.Co.
12 104 Bde.

SECRET 5

OPERATION ORDER [illegible]

The 106th M.G.C. & 1 Section 104 M.G. Coy will co-operate in an attack to be carried out by [illegible] on the morning [illegible] October 1917

1 [illegible] "A" GROUP UNDER Lt. [illegible]

[illegible] BATTERY A SECTION UNDER SGT. [illegible]
[illegible] BATTERY C Do " Lt. [illegible]

"B" GROUP UNDER Lt. [illegible]

RIGHT BATTERY – B SECTION UNDER Lt. [illegible] COOPER
LEFT BATTERY – D Do " SGT. WILES.

"C" GROUP [illegible] 104 M.G.C.

UNDER [illegible]

2 BARRAGES. [illegible] APPENDIX "A"

3 SCHEDULE OF FIRE. [illegible] APPENDIX "B"

4 ZERO HOUR. WILL BE [illegible] LATER

5 HOUR OF READINESS. All guns will be READY TO FIRE AT ZERO – 3 HOURS.

6 RATE OF FIRE. 2,500 ROUNDS PER GUN PER HOUR

7 AMMUNITION. 10,000 RDS PER GUN WILL BE AT EACH BARRAGE POSITION

8 PARADE & ROUTE. HOUR OF PARADE & ROUTE TO BARRAGE POSITIONS UNDER ARRANGEMENTS OF GROUP COMMANDERS

9 WATCHES – SYNCHRONISATION OF. WATCHES WILL BE SYNCHRONISED AT BATTN. H.Q. AT FASCALL FARM FOR B & C GROUPS. [illegible] FARM FOR [illegible] GROUP AT 8·30 P.M.

10 TRANSPORT. [illegible] FOR A & B GROUPS [illegible] TO R.E. DUMP U [illegible] [illegible] EQUIPMENT, FROM THERE [illegible] BARRAGE POSITIONS.

11 DUMPS. All S.A.A. [illegible] BARRAGE POSITIONS. S.A.A. DUMPS [illegible] 10,000 RDS. will be [illegible]

U 16 b 9.0 U 21 a 2.6
U 11 a.0.5 U 21 a 7.1
U 15 d 1.0

12 COUNTER AT[illegible] [illegible] S.O.S. [illegible] GROUPS WILL [illegible] THEIR [illegible] BARRAGE LINES

13 REPORTS WILL BE SENT BY GROUP COMMANDERS [illegible]

1. PREPARATIONS COMPLETE.
2. LINES OF FIRE [illegible] OUT
3. All GUNS READY TO FIRE TO BE REPORTED AT HOUR OF READINESS.
4. AFTER [illegible] [illegible] ROUNDS FIRED [illegible]

14. H.Q. GRS WILL REMAIN [illegible] AT [illegible] FARM [illegible] REPORTS will be sent.

ISSUED AT 11·20 AM. 21/10/17

A.H. [illegible]
for O.C. 106 M.G. Co.

[illegible] SECTION OFFICER
" "
" "
" "
WAR DIARY
FILE
BRIGADE
[illegible]
9 D.M.G.O.
10 104 M.G.Co.
11 [illegible] BDE
12 T.O
13
14
15

SECRET

COPY No 5

OPERATION ORDER No 120 (A)

THE 106th M.G.Co. LESS 2 SECTIONS PLUS 1 SECTION 104 M.G.C. WILL REMAIN IN BARRAGE POSITIONS FOR THE PURPOSE OF REPELLING COUNTER ATTACK.

1. GUNS IN ACTION "B" GROUP 8 GUNS.
   RIGHT BATTERY. B SECTION UNDER LT. P.H.COOPER.
   LEFT BATTERY. D SECTION UNDER SGT WILKS.
   "C" GROUP
   1 SECTION 104 M.G.Co.
   LIEUT. R. SKEVINGTON WILL COMMAND B & C GROUPS.
2. BARRAGES. AS LAID DOWN IN APPENDIX "C"
3. SCHEDULE OF FIRE. AS LAID DOWN IN APPENDIX "D"
4. AMMUNITION. 28,000 ROUNDS WILL BE DELIVERED AT KOEKUIT R.E. DUMP DURING THE FORENOON BY PACK ANIMAL.
5. REINFORCEMENTS.
   8 MEN OF C SECTION WILL REINFORCE "B" GROUP.
6. EQUIPMENT.
   B GROUP WILL BE MADE UP TO 8 GUNS. 4 GUNS FROM H.Q. WILL BE TAKEN UP TO B GROUP WHICH WILL RETURN 4 GUNS AS SOON AS POSSIBLE FOR CLEANING.
7. WITHDRAWAL.
   A' GROUP WILL BE EVACUATED. LT. M.N. FISHER & 2/LT. J SEDDON, 1 SGT. 7 GUNNERS AND 8 ATTACHED INFANTRY WILL WITHDRAW TO BOX CAMP. 5 ATTACHED INFANTRY FROM B GROUP WILL WITHDRAW TO COY. H.Q.
8. * 25%
   THE PARTY ABOVE MENTIONED WILL SUBSTITUTE THE SAME NUMBER OF ALL RANKS FROM THE 25%
9. RELIEF
   THE PARTY OBTAINED FROM PARA* WILL RELIEVE THE CORRESPONDING NUMBER OF ALL RANKS AT B GROUP WHO WILL THEN RETURN TO BOX CAMP FOR REST. THIS PARTY WILL HOLD THEMSELVES IN READINESS FOR EMERGENCIES.
10. H.Q. HEADQUARTERS WILL REMAIN ESTABLISHED AT SIGNAL FARM.

Issued at 8pm. 23/10/17

Copy No.
1 Section Officer
2 " "
3 " "
4 " "
5 WAR DIARY
6 FILE
7 BRIGADE
8 WAR DIARY
9. TRANSP Off
10 104 M.G.Co.

SECRET

COPY No 5

OPERATION ORDER No. 121

106th M.G.C. LESS 2 SECTIONS & 1 SECTION 104th M.G.Co. WILL BE RELIEVED BY PERSONNEL OF 245 M.G.C. ON THE NIGHT 24/25th Oct. 1917.

1 DISPOSITIONS

B & C GROUP POSITION WILL BE HANDED OVER IN ACCORDANCE WITH APPENDICES C AND D

2 GUIDES

ONE GUIDE will be AT JUNCTION OF TRAPIOON AND BOESINGHE HIGH STREET AT 4 PM

2 GUIDES AT C. H.Q. AT 5.00 P.M. TO GUIDE THE PERSONNEL TO PASCALL FARM.

3 EQUIPMENT

ALL S.A.A. BELT BOXES, LINES OF FIRE & PETROL TINS WILL BE HANDED OVER & RECEIPTS OBTAINED

4 WITHDRAWAL

ON COMPLETION OF RELIEF B & D SECTIONS WILL MOVE IN SMALL PARTIES UNDER N.C.Os INDEPENDENTLY TO BOX CAMP.

SECTION OF 104 M.G.Co. UNDER ARRANGEMENTS OF O.C. 104 M.G.Co.

A & C. SECTIONS will WITHDRAW UNDER SECTION OFFICERS ARRANGEMENTS

5 TRANSPORT

ONE LIMBER WILL BE AT JUNCTION WIDJERDRIFT-ROAD - HUNTER STREET ~~AT~~ AT 9.30 P.M. TO BRING BACK GUNS & EQUIPMENT OF B & D SECTIONS.

ONE LIMBER IN VICINITY OF Co. H.Q. AT 9.00 P.M. - UNDER ARRANGEMENTS OF T.O.

6 ROUTE

PASCALL FARM - JUNCTION WIJDERDRIFT - HUNTER STREET - BOESINGHE - ELVERDINGHE - DE WIPPE X ROADS TO BOX CAMP.

7 COMPLETION OF RELIEF WILL BE REPORTED BY WORD "CAROLINE" TO Co. H.Q AT SIGNAL FARM.

8 STRENGTH. SECTION OFFICERS ON ARRIVAL AT BOX CAMP WILL REPORT STRENGTH TO Co. H.Q.

Issued at 2 pm. 24/10/17

[illegible]
O.C. 106 M.G.C.

Copy No.
1 Section Officer
2 " "
3 104 Bde Office
4 S.O. 104 M.G.C.
5 War Diary
6 File
7 Brigade
8 War Diary
9 O.C. 245 M.G.C.
10

Instructions regarding War Diaries and Intelligence Summaries are contained in F. S. Regs., Part II. and the Staff Manual respectively. Title pages will be prepared in manuscript.

WAR DIARY

~~or~~

~~INTELLIGENCE~~ SUMMARY. 35

(*Erase heading not required.*)

106 M. G. Coy. Vol 19

Army Form C. 2118.

Place	Date	Hour	Summary of Events and Information	Remarks and references to Appendices
	Nov. 1st/2nd		Coy less one section relieved by parts of 104 and 241 M.G.Co. in the HOUTHULST FOREST SECTOR. Details remained at H Camp.	
	4th		Co. relieved by 34th M.G.Co and withdrew by train to PEGWELL CAMP PROVEN. (See O.O. No 123)	
	8th		Moved Camp to POINT CAMP. (See O.O. No 124)	
	14th		Co. moved to SIEGE CAMP. Personnel by train and transport by road	
	15th		Co. + 1 sec. 241 M.G.Co moved to KEMPTON PARK (See O.O. No 126) Transport and details remained at SIEGE CAMP.	
	16th		Co. relieved No 198 M.G.Co. in the POELCAPPELLE SECTOR (See O.O. No 127) Relief complete by 7.15 P.M. 2 guns TRACAS FM. - 2 guns MEUNIER HO. - 1 gun HELLES HO. - 1 gun Nobles Fm. 1 BREWERY - 1 Sec HQ. 2-241 M.G.Co guns NORFOLK HO. & 2 at Gloster Fm.	
	18th/19th		Inter Section relief took place C relieved A and D relieved B. (See O.O. No 128)	
	19th		M.G.s cooperated in a practice ARMY BARRAGE. Time 6.30 AM to 6.45 A.M. and 7.6 AM to 7.24 AM. Usual harassing fire took place. Total rounds fired 15750. Enemy patrol tried to raid one of our posts. Our gun opened fire and killed and wounded some of the party. The Co. assisted in taking some prisoners in vicinity of TRACAS FM.	
	19/20		Two detachments proceeded to relieve two detachments of 1st M.G.Co. on right batt. front. Owing to the fact that	[illegible]

A5834 Wt. W4973 M687 750,000 8/16 D. D. & L. Ltd. Forms/C.2118/13.

Instructions regarding War Diaries and Intelligence Summaries are contained in F. S. Regs., Part II. and the Staff Manual respectively. Title pages will be prepared in manuscript.

WAR DIARY

~~or~~

~~INTELLIGENCE SUMMARY.~~

(Erase heading not required.)

Army Form C. 2118.

Place	Date	Hour	Summary of Events and Information	Remarks and references to Appendices
			that] no guides were provided it was impossible to get the guns into position. Our relieving guns waited at VACHER FARM until relieved by 104 M.G.Co.	
	20th		Three prisoners were captured in front of HEGLES and NOBLE Fm. Many letters and other documents secured. One prisoner was wounded and brought in on a stretcher.	
	20/21st		Co relieved in the line by 104 M.G.Co. and then proceeded to SUPPORT billets at SIEGE CAMP.	
	21st/28th		In support at SIEGE CAMP.	
	28th		Personnel of Co. divided into 30 detachments in order to provide relief.	
	28th/29th		Co. relieved 105 M.G.Co. in the line. 15 detachments in the line same as previously with the addition of 2 - BANFF, 1 VACHER FM. - 2 GLOSTER HO. - 2 NORFOLK HO. Relief complete by 7.10 P.M.	
	29th		1 gun blown up at V14C1.1. Usual harassing fire. CAMERON H. and WHITECHAPEL being engaged. 3000 rds fired. A.A gun turned on E.A. 1000 rounds fired by NORFOLK HO GUN.	
	30th		Inter Coy relief carried out without incident being complete by 7.10 P.M. WHITECHAPEL & CAMERON HOUSES fired on - 4000 rounds being expended.	

[illegible] Capt
Comdg [illegible] M.G. Co.

A5834 Wt. W4973 M687 750,000 8/16 D. D. & L. Ltd. Forms/C.2118/13.

SECRET

COPY No 5.

OPERATION ORDER No. 122

[illegible] M.G.C. (LESS 1 SECTION) PLUS PERSONNEL OF 1 SUB-SECTION 241 M.G.Coy WILL RELIEVE 6 DETACHMENTS OF 104 [illegible] AND 6 DETACHMENTS OF 241 M.G.C. ON THE NIGHT OF 1/2nd NOV. 1917.

1. DISPOSITIONS. "C" SECTION UNDER Lt. S.W. KIRKED, FRONT LINE SYSTEM.
   "D" GROUP POSITIONS – 1 SUB-SECTION OF "D" UNDER LIEUT J. SEDDON.
   "E" GROUP UNDER Lt. P.H. COOPER B.S. [illegible] AND 1 SUB-SECTION 241 M.G.C. UNDER [illegible] ALDERSON
   ANTI-AIRCRAFT WORK. 1 SUB-SECTION OF "D" UNDER 2/Lt. W.S. WHITEHOUSE.
   1 GUN LOUVOIS FM. 1 GUN EAST OF SUEZ FARM.
2. PARADE. THE C. LESS 1 SECTION PLUS THE PERSONNEL OF 1 SUB-SECTION OF 241 M.G.Coy PARADE AT 11.00AM.
3. DRESS. FIGHTING ORDER – JERKINS ROLLED ON BELT. THE SECOND PAIR OF SOCKS WILL BE CARRIED IN THE HAVERSACK
4. GUIDES. 1 GUIDE PER GROUP & 1 GUIDE FOR SECTION FRONT LINE SYSTEM WILL BE AT C.H.Q. SIGNAL FARM AT 4 P.M. 1 GUIDE PER DETACHMENT FOR FORWARD SECTIONS AT SECT. H.Q AT 5.30P.M.
5. RATIONS. 2 DAYS RATIONS will be CARRIED ON THE MAN IN ADDITION TO THE UNCONSUMED PORTION OF THE DAYS RATIONS. 1 BOTTLE OF WHALE OIL PER GUN DETACHMENT WILL BE [illegible].
6. WATER. WATER BOTTLES WILL BE CARRIED FULL. PETROL TINS WILL BE TAKEN UP UNDER ARRANGEMENTS OF SECTION OFFICERS CONCERNED.
7. EQUIPMENT. All BELT BOXES [illegible] A.A. & TRENCH STORES WILL BE TAKEN OVER. GUNS TRIPODS AND SPARE-PARTS WILL BE TAKEN [illegible] THE LINE.
8. ROUTE. [illegible] STATION – THENCE BY TRAIN TO BOESINGHE – CLARGES STREET TO SIGNAL FARM.
9. TRANSPORT. 1 LIMBER OF "C" SECT, 1 LIMBER OF "B" SECT 1 LIMBER OF "D" SECT AND 1 LIMBER FOR HD.QRS. WILL PARADE AT "H" CAMP AT 12 NOON & WILL MOVE OFF UNDER T.O. WHO WILL BE ACCOMPANIED BY 1 MOUNTED ORDERLY TO ESCORT LIMBERS AS NEAR TO SIGNAL FARM AS POSSIBLE, THE ORDERLY BEING SENT TO BRING DETACHMENTS TO LIMBERS.
10. [illegible] R's. will be rendered by All concerned to reach H.Q. by 8.00AM. DAILY
11. COMPLETION OF RELIEF. will be REPORTED BY THE OUTGOING SECTIONS TO SIGNAL FARM BY MESSAGE BY WORD "DORA"
12. REINFORCEMENTS. 20% AND "A" SECTION will REMAIN UNDER Lt. H.H. FISHER AT "H" CAMP.
13. BAGGAGE. All BAGGAGE of officers – BLANKETS AND PACKS OF MEN & ALL STORES WILL BE PACKED & TAKEN TO BOX CAMP UNDER ARRANGEMENTS OF C.Q.M.S.
14. HD.QRS. will close AT 11 AM. AT "H" CAMP & REOPEN AT SIGNAL FARM ON COMPLETION.

Issued at 8pm 31/10/17

Copy No 1 Section Officer
2 "
3 "
4 "
5 War Diary
6 File
7 Brigade
8 War Diary
9 D.M.G.O.
10 T.O.
11 104 M.G.C.
12 241 M.G.C.
13 Lt Alderson
14 C.Q.M.S.

SECRET — COPY NO. 5

OPERATION ORDER No. 123

106th M.G. Co. & 1 SUB-SECTION of 241 M.G. Co. WILL BE RELIEVED AND WILL WITHDRAW FROM THE LEFT DIVISIONAL FRONTAGE OF THE XIX CORPS ON THE AFTERNOON OF 4th NOV. 1917.

1. DISPOSITIONS. THE FOLLOWING DISPOSITIONS WILL BE HANDED OVER.
"C" SECTION – FRONT LINE SYSTEM.
FAIDHERBE CROSS ROADS, GUN AT U 5 d 7.4 AND GUN NEAR COLUMBO HOUSE ROAD.
"D" GROUP AND "E" GROUP.
THE FOLLOWING DISPOSITIONS WILL BE VACATED AT DUSK.
1 GUN AT ANGLE FARM N. of PANAMA HOUSE.
2 A.A. GUNS UNDER 2/Lt W.S. WHITEHOUSE.

2. GUIDES. "C" SECTION.
1 GUIDE FOR SEC. H.Q. TO BE AT Co. H.Q. AT 12 NOON.
1 GUIDE PER DETACHMENT FOR GUNS TO BE RELIEVED AT SECTION H.Q. AT 4.30 P.M.
"D" GROUP 1 GUIDE AT Co. H.Q. AT 1.30 P.M.
"E" GROUP 1 GUIDE " " " 1.30 P.M.

3. EQUIPMENT. All S.A.A. TRENCH STORES, PETROL TINS, DEFENCE SCHEMES, SKETCH MAPS (1:10,000) SCHEDULES, BELT BOXES & TRIPODS will be HANDED OVER & RECEIPTS OBTAINED. "C" SECTION. THE GUN N. of PANAMA HOUSE WILL LEAVE BELT BOXES AT GUN POSITION; TRIPOD WILL BE BROUGHT BACK TO SEC. H.Q. AND HANDED OVER.

4. WITHDRAWAL OF A.A. DETACHMENTS.
THE SUB SECTION UNDER 2/Lt W.S. WHITEHOUSE WILL WITHDRAW WITH GUNS, TRIPODS, SPARE-PARTS BOXES & BELT BOXES TO BOESINGHE STATION BY THE FOLLOWING ROUTE CLARGES STREET TO HEY WOOD THENCE BY THE LIGHT RAILWAY TRACK TO BOESINGHE. All TROOPS ON CLARGES STR. GOING IN EITHER DIRECTION HAVE PREFERENCE.

5. TIME OF DEPARTURE IS LEFT TO THE DISCRETION of SECTION OFFICERS. TIME of ARRIVAL AT BOESINGHE STATION TO BE BY 12 MN. 4th/5th.

6. ROUTES "C" SECTION – CLARGES STR: TO HEY WOOD THENCE BY LIGHT RAILWAY TRACK to BOESINGHE. All TROOPS ON CLARGES STREET HAVE PREFERENCE. [illegible] GROUPS: – HUNTER STREET BUT DETACHMENTS [illegible] MOVE AT 300x DISTANCES.

7. COMPLETION of RELIEF AND SECTIONS PASSING THE STEENBEEK ROAD WILL BE REPORTED TO THIS OFFICE BY MESSAGE "EMMA"

8. ARRIVAL. THE Co. WILL BE REPORTED PRESENT AT BOESINGHE STATION AT 12 MIDNIGHT.

9. HOT MEAL WILL BE PROVIDED AT BOESINGHE STATION.

10. TRAIN. TRAINS LEAVE BOESINGHE STATION AT 1 AM. & 4 AM. 106th M.G.Co. & 1 SUB-SECTION 241 M.G.Co. will proceed BY THE FIRST TRAIN. SHOULD ANY OF THE Above FORCE BE ABSENT AT that time [illegible] will proceed by THE SECOND TRAIN.

11. DESTINATION PROVEN STATION THENCE BY MARCH ROUTE TO PEGWELL CAMP.

12. TRANSPORT.
H.Q. – 1 LIMBER WILL REPORT AT Co. H.Q. AT 2 P.M.
B SECTION – – – – – – } 1 LIMBER AT JUNCTION OF
D " (INCLUDING A.A DETACHMENT) } WIDJENDRIFT ROAD & HUNTER
1 Sub-Sec. 241 M.G.Co. } STREET AT 4 P.M.

"C" SECTION. 1 LIMBER AT JUNCTION OF WIDJENDRIFT & THE LIGHT RAILWAY (BETWEEN HUNTER ST. AND CLARGES STREET) AT 7 P.M.

THESE LIMBERS WILL PROCEED INDEPENDENTLY TO PEGWELL CAMP.

13. DETAILS Q.M. STORES & TRANSPORT. FORCES AS PER MARGIN WILL MOVE UNDER ORDERS OF LT. [illegible] FISHER TO PEGWELL CAMP BY MARCH ROUTE ON 4-11-17

14 PARADE. TIME OF PARADE WILL BE 11·30 AM
ALL TRANSPORT Q.M. STORES & DETAILS FROM BOX CAMP TO BE AT "H" CAMP AT 11·00 AM.

15 ROUTE. INTERNATIONAL CORNER - [illegible] b0 - F12a 8.1 F11b 8.9 - COUTHOVE - TO PEGWELL CAMP.
DISTANCES OF 200^x WILL BE LEFT BETWEEN EVERY EIGHT LIMBERS.

16. DUTIES. 2/LT. H.H. BUCKLEY & 2 CYCLE ORDERLIES TO BE DETAILED BY O.C. DETAILS WILL MEET CAPTAIN EDGAR AT AREA COMMANDANTS OFFICE PROVEN AT 12 noon ON THE 4TH FOR BILLETING.

2/LT. E.A. HAWKES IS DETAILED AS O.C. SECOND TRAIN AND WILL BRING ON ALL STRAGGLERS OF THE BRIGADE. HE WILL REPORT AT BOESINGHE STATION AT 10.00 P.M.

C.Q.M.S. will detail 1 ORDERLY to BE AT BENSON FARM AT 9 AM TO GUIDE A LORRY to BOX CAMP.

Issued at 12.30 am 4/11/17

[signature] Lt. O.C. 156 M.G. Co.

Copy No.
1 O.C. B Sect.
2 O.C. D "
3 O.C. C "
4 2/Lt Whitehouse
5 War Diary
6 File
7 Brigade
8 War Diary
9 Transp Off.
10 Lt. Alderson.
11 O.C. Details
12 CQMS.
13 2/Lt Buckley
14 2/Lt Hawkes.
15 O.C. 53 M.G.C.
16 C.O.
17 [illegible] M.G.C.

SECRET. Copy No 5

OPERATION ORDER No 124

106th M.G.Co. will move from P.4 Area to P.3 Area on the morning of the 8th Nov 1917

1 **Parade.** Co. will parade at 9.15 a.m.
Dress. Fighting order.

2. **Order of March.**
A Section followed by "B" - followed by "D" - followed by "C" and H.Q. [illegible].
Battle formations. No 3, H.Q. wagon, water cart, mess cart, G.S. wagon.
200 yds. distance will be left between sections; 200 yds between No 3 and remaining wagons.

3 **Route.** [illegible] Camp to Point Camp

4 **Baggage.** All blankets, stores, officers kits etc. will be packed by 9 a.m.

5 **Routine**
Reveille 6.30 a.m.
Breakfast 7.30 a.m.

6 **Palliasses** with straw will be handed in to Qr. Master's Stores by 8.45 a.m.

7 **Advance Party.**
Lt. H.H. Fisher & 4 N.C.O's (to be detailed by C.S.M.) will proceed at 7.30 a.m. as billeting party.

8 **Handing over.** 2/Lt. R. Rowley will hand over the camp to incoming unit.

Issued at 11.05 p.m. 7/11/17

Copy No.
1 Section officers
2 "
3 "
4 "
5 War Diary
6 File
7 Brigade
8 War Diary
9
10

[illegible] for
O.C. 106 M.G.Co.

[illegible] No 5

Operation Order No 125

106th M.G.C. plus 1 Section 241 M.G.C. will move to SIEGE Camp on the 14/11/17 Personnel by train, Transport by road.

1. TRAIN departs from PROVEN Siding at 1 pm

2 PARADE Co. will parade at 11.45 am and will march to PROVEN Station

3. ORDER OF MARCH. A. [illegible] [illegible] B. C. section

4 ROUTE. [illegible] Camp to PROVEN thence by train to ELVERDINGHE to Siege Camp No 3.

5 DRESS Fighting Order

1 TRANSPORT will Parade at 8.55 am and move off along main PROVEN road at 9.10 am.

[illegible] ORDER OF MARCH. A.B.D.C. Hd.QRS. 200 yards distance will be maintained between every 5 Vehicles

[illegible] STARTING POINT. Road junction F 3 a 7.3 which will be passed at 10.20 am 106 M.G.C. follows Bde. H.Q. and is followed by 241 M.G.Co.

9 ROUTE F 3 a, A 29 d, International Corner, [illegible] [illegible] [illegible] No 3 Siege Camp

10. BAGGAGE. All Blankets Packs, Officers Kits, [illegible] [illegible], [illegible] [illegible] will be packed on Transport [illegible] 8.30 am.

[illegible] [illegible] [illegible] call during the day and [illegible] [illegible] [illegible] [illegible] Artificers Store, Shoemakers Store and Q.M. Stores.

11 PROBABLE HOUR OF ARRIVAL. 3.50 pm.

12. ROUTINE

Reveille [illegible].30 am

Breakfast [illegible] 30 am

[illegible] arrival at new Camp.

13 BILLETING PARTY. [illegible] [illegible] Skirrington is detailed as Billeting Officer will proceed with Bicycle by first train and report to Captain Edgar [illegible] Area Commandants Office B 20 d 3.8 SIEGE CAMP on arrival.

14. 241 M.G.Co. 1 Section of 241 M G C will report at PROVEN Stn. at 12.30 pm. Time of parade, route to Station under orders of O.C. 241 M.G.C.

Transport of above section will join 106 M.G.C. transport at No 3 Siege Camp on arrival

Issued at 1.00 am 14/11/17

[illegible] [illegible] for

Copy No 1 Section Officer
2 " "
3 " "
4 " "
5 War Diary
6 File
7 Brigade
8 War Diary
9 Transport Off.
10 C.Q.M.S.
11 O.C.
12 O.C. 241 M.G.C.

5

[illegible]

[illegible] SECTIONS [illegible] M.G. Co. WILL MOVE FROM SIEGE CAMP TO KEMPTON PARK ON [illegible]/17

1 PARADE. [illegible] WILL PARADE AT 10·10 AM

2. DRESS FIGHTING ORDER – [illegible] ROLLED

3 STARTING POINT. CAMP COMMANDANTS OFFICE SIEGE CAMP WHICH WILL BE PASSED BY THE HEAD OF THE LEADING SECTION AT 10·30 AM.

4 ROUTE. CAMP COMMANDANTS OFFICE, [illegible] XROADS B 29 d 7·5, [illegible] FM. ESSEX FM ACROSS CANAL. [illegible] COTTAGE [illegible] BY CORPS ROAD TO KEMPTON PARK

5 TRANSPORT. 1 LIMBER WILL ACCOMPANY EACH SECTION TRANSPORT WILL JOIN THE COLUMN FROM THEIR TRANSP. LINES ON SECTIONS PASSING ON COMPLETION OF DUTY TRANSPORT WILL RETURN TO PRESENT TRANSP. LINES & REMAIN THERE UNTIL FURTHER ORDERS FROM BRIGADE.

6 ORDER OF MARCH –
A, B, HD. QRS. D & C SECTIONS

7 BAGGAGE. All baggage will be packed by 9.15 AM

8 BILLETING PARTY. LT. R. SKEVINGTON IS DETAILED AS BILLETING OFFICER & will be accompanied by 2 MEN of "A", 1 MAN of "B", 1 MAN OF "C" AND 2 MEN OF "D". WILL PARADE AT 9 AM & will take over 6 [illegible] HUTS.

9 HD. QRS – 106 M.G. Co. will close at SIEGE CAMP AT 10 AM & RE-OPEN AT KEMPTON PARK AT 12 AM.

Issued at 11.45 pm 11/11/17

Copy No. 1 Section Officer
2 " "
3 " "
4 " "
5 War Diary
6 File
7 Brigade
8 War Diary
9 241 M.G. Co.
10 Adjutant
11 T.O
12 C.Q.M.S.
13 [illegible]
14 [illegible]

[illegible] 106 M.G. Co.

Copy No. 5

Secret

Operation Order No. 127

Half Co. 106th M.G. Co. & 1 Sect. 241 M.G. Co. will relieve
Half Co. 198 M.G. Co. & 1 Sect. 106 M.G. Co. respectively
in the POELCAPPEL SECTOR on the 16th Nov. 1917

1. DISPOSITIONS "A" Section under Lt. H.A. FISHER on the right
Sect. HQ. GLOSTER FM. 2 guns [illegible] FM.
2 guns MEUNIER HO.
"B" Sect. under Lt. F.H. COOPER. Sect HQ. V14.c.1.1
1 gun V 14.c.1.1. 1 gun HELLES HO. 1 gun NOBLES FM.
1 " the BREWERY
1 Sub. Sect. 241 M.G. Co. under 2/Lt. JACKSON GLOSTER FM
1 Sub/Sect. 241 M.G. Co. under 2/Lt. WHEELER NORFOLK HOUSE
W. of POELCAPPEL

2. PARADE. Sect. of 241 M.G. Co. will parade at 12 noon
Half Co. " 106 " " " " 2.15 P.M.
Dress. Fighting order – Jerkins rolled on
belt, 2nd pair of socks being carried in the
haversack.
Greatcoats will be carried by 241 Co.
1 bottle of whale oil will be carried per detachment.

3 GUIDES.
1 guide will lead Section of 241 M.G. Co. to RUDOLPH FM.
where guides will be for Sub. Sect. H.Q.
2 guides per detachment section will lead
sections of 106th Co. to Sect. H.Q. where there will
be 1 guide per detachment

4 RATIONS.
3 days rations will be carried by all sections
(including the unconsumed portion of the days ration)

5 WATER.
Water bottles will be carried full. 2 petrol tins
for Sect. H.Q. & 2 tins per detachment will be
carried which will last for 3 days

6 EQUIPMENT
Tripods, belt boxes, condenser bags & tubes, S.A.A.
trench stores schemes & maps will be taken over

7 T.P.R's will be rendered by each Section 106th
& each Sub/Sect. of 241 Co. to reach H.Q. by
8.00 A.M. daily

8 COMPLETION OF RELIEF will be reported by the
outgoing sections by word "FLORENCE"

Issued at 6.00 p.m. 15/11/17

Copy No
1 Section Officer
2 " "
3 " "
4 " "
5 War Diary
6 File
7 Brigade
8 L. Army
9 D.M.G.O.
10 T.
11 198 M.G. Co.
12 } 241 M.G. Co.
13 }
14 C.Q.M.S.
15 2nd in Cd.
16 Adjutant
17 S.O.

C.W. Morrison for
Comdg 106 M.G. Co.

SECRET

Copy No 5

Operation Order No 128

Half Co 106th M.G.Co. will relieve half Co 106 M.G.C in the POELCAPPELLE Sector on the night of the 18/19th Nov 1917.

1 DISPOSITIONS. "C" Section under 2/Lt W.S. Whitehouse will relieve "A" Section on the right Sub/Sector. Section HQ GLOSTER FM. 2 guns [illegible] FM. 2 guns MEUNIER Ho.

"D" Section under 2/Lt J Eclose will relieve "B" Section. Section HQ V14 c 1.1.

1 Gun V14 c 1.1. 1 Gun HELLES House

1 " NOBLES FM. 1 " THE BREWERY

2. PARADE

Half Co will parade at 2 p.m. Dress fighting Order. – 2nd pair of socks being carried on the man. Jerkins will be taken over by the relieving Section.

1 Bottle of WHALE OIL per detachment will be carried.

3 GUIDES. 2 Guides per Section will be at Co H.Q. KEMPTON PARK to guide Sections to Sect. HQ. 1 guide per detachment will be at Sec HQ

4 RATIONS

2 Days rations will be carried in addition to the unconsumed portion of the days rations.

5 WATER Water Bottles will be carried full. 2 Petrol tins per Section HQ & 2 tins per Detachment will be carried, to last the 2 days.

6 EQUIPMENT.

Tripods, Belt boxes, Condenser bags & tube. S.A.A. Trench Stores, Schemes & Maps will be taken over.

7 T.F.R's. will be rendered by each Section to reach Co HQ by 8.00 am daily.

8 TRANSPORT 1 Limber will report to Co HQ KEMPTON PARK by 1.30 P.M.

9 COMPLETION OF RELIEF will be reported by the outgoing Sections by word "GRACE"

17/11/17

Copy No
1 Section Officer
2 "
3 "
4 "
5 War Diary
6 File
7 Brigade
8 War Diary
9 T.O.
10 CQMS.
11 Adjutant
12 2nd in C

R Skeffington Lt
for O.C. 106 MGC

SECRET

COPY No. 5

Operation Order No. 129

2 Detachments of 106th M.G.Co. will relieve 2 detachments of the 1st M.G.Co. on the right Bn. Area on the night of the 19/20th Nov 1917.

1 Detachment of 241 M.G.Co. will take up a position at Vacher Fm.

1 Dispositions. 2 Detachmts of 106 M.G.Co. & 1 Detachment of 241 M.G.Co., under 2/Lt R. [illegible] Sect H.Q. BERKS HOUSE.
2 Guns at BANFF HO. 1 Gun at VACHER Fm.

2 Parade. 3 Detachments will parade at KEMPTON PARK at 2pm.

3 Dress. Fighting Order. Greatcoats rolled in Waterproof Sheet will be carried; 2nd pr. of Socks will be carried in the Haversacks.

4 Guides. 1 Guide will be at HUBNER Fm. at 4pm.

5 Rations. 1 Days rations will be carried on the man (in addition to the unconsumed portion of the days rations).

6 Water. 1 Tin of Water per Detachment and 1 per H.Q.

7 Route. Kempton Park along Admiral Road to where Alberta track crosses. Alberta track to HUBNER Fm. where Guide will meet them.

8 Handing Over.
All Tripods, Beltboxes S.A.A. Trench Stores & Schemes will be taken over & Receipts sent to Co. H.Q.

9 Transport.
1 Limber each of 106 M.G.Co. and 241 Co. will report to Co. H.Q. by 1pm. The detachment of 241 M.G.Co. will take into the position Gun, Tripod, Spare parts & 8 Belt Boxes.

10 Completion of Relief will be reported by word by wire "[illegible]"

[illegible] Issued at [illegible]

[illegible signature]
OC/106 M.G.C.

Copy No. 1 Sect Officers
2 " "
3 " "
4 War Diary
5 File
6 Brigade
7 War Diary
8 Transport Off
9 C.Q.M.S.
10 D.M.G.O.
11 O.C. 241 M.G.C.
12 D.M.G.O. [illegible]
13 [illegible]
14 [illegible]
15 C.O.

[illegible] Order No 130 Copy No 5

[illegible] Machine Gun Coy will be relieved in the line by the 104 Machine Gun Coy on the night of the 20 [illegible] Nov [illegible]

1. Dispositions

The following dispositions will be handed over

C Section. Section HQ Foster House
2 Guns [illegible] House (Nos 5 & 6)
2 Guns Tracas Farm (Nos 3 & 4)

D Section Section HQ V 14 C 15 20
1 Gun Section HQ (No 10) 1 Gun Brewery (No 9)
1 Gun [illegible] House (No 8) 1 Gun [illegible] Farm (No 7)

Composite Section Section HQ Berks House
2 Guns [illegible] House (Nos 1 & 2)
1 Gun [illegible] Farm (No 11) Manned by [illegible] M G Coy

2. Guides

2 Guides per Section for Section HQ will be at Company Headquarters at 2.0 P

1 Guide per Detachment will be at Section HQ at 3.30pm

3. Equipment

All S.A.A. Trench Stores, Petrol Tins, Defence Schemes and Maps, Belt Boxes and Tripods will be handed over and receipts obtained

4. Withdrawals

On relief Sections will withdraw to Kempton Park by routes at discretion of Section Officers

5. Transport

1 Limber per Section for A and B Sections and Headquarters Limber will report at Coy Headquarters at 1.0 pm.

C and D Section Limbers and Officers Mess Cart will report at Company Headquarters at 3.0 pm.

6. Relief

Sections will report relief complete by word "IONE" to this office

7. Completion of Relief

On completion of relief the Company will move from Kempton Park to [illegible] Siege Camp, intervals of not less than 300x being kept between Sections.

OPERATION ORDER No 130 Contd

ROUTE

KEMPTON PARK – [illegible] COTTAGE – No 4 BRIDGE
ESSEX FARM – ISIS FARM – BRIELAN – No 3 SIEGE CAMP

HOT TEA

HOT TEA WILL BE PROVIDED AT No 3 SIEGE CAMP UNDER ARRANGEMENTS OF THE CQMS

ISSUED AT 10.0 AM
20. 11. 17

[illegible signature]
[illegible] 104 M.G.C.

FOR O C [illegible] MACHINE GUN COMPANY

Copy No.
1 Section Officer
2 " "
3 " "
4 " "
5 War Diary
6 File
7 Brigade
8 War Diary
9 Transp Officer
10 241 M.G.C.
11 C O.
12 C.Q.M.S.
13 Adjutant
14 2nd in Cd.
15 D.M.G.O.
16 104 M.G.C.
17 104 Bde.

SECRET. COPY No 5

OPERATION ORDER No 131

106th M.G.Co WILL RELIEVE 105 M.G.Co., AND 5 DETACHMENTS OF 241 M.G.Co., IN THE POELCAPPELLE SECTOR ON THE NIGHT 28/29 Nov. 1917.

1. DISPOSITIONS. RIGHT – "D" SECT. UNDER 2/LT. R. ROWLEY.
2 DETACHMENTS, BANFF HO. 1 DET. VACHER FM.
CENTRE. "C" SECT. UNDER 2/LT. E.H. HAWKES.
2 DET. TRACAS FM. 2 DET. MEUNIER HOUSE.
LEFT – UNDER LT. F.H. COOPER.
1 DET. HELLES HO. 1 DET. BREWERY. 1 DET. NOBLES FM.
1 " V 14 c 15.20.
SUPPORT. "A" SECT. – 1 SUB/SEC. UNDER 2/LT. E.A. HAWKES.
1 SUB/SEC. UNDER LT. H. FISHER M.C. NORFOLK HO.

2. PARADE Co. WILL PARADE AT 10.30 A.M. AND WILL MOVE OFF AT 300 YDS. INTERVAL BETWEEN SECTIONS.
DRESS. FIGHTING ORDER – 2ND PAIR OF SOCKS BEING CARRIED ON THE MAN – JERKINS ROLLED ON THE BELT.
1 BOTTLE WHALE OIL WILL BE CARRIED PER DETACHMENT.
THE Co. LESS 15 COMPOSITE DETACHMENTS WILL LEAVE KEMPTON PARK FOR THE LINE AT 1.30 P.M.

3. ORDER OF MARCH. D. C. B. A. H.Q.RS.
1 LIMBER FOR "D" WILL PROCEED UNDER ORDERS OF O.C. "D" SECT.
1 LIMBER FOR "C" TO MINTY FM.
1 " " "B" " RUDOLPH FM.
1½ LIMBERS " A " MINTY FM.
½ H.Q. LIMBER FOR RUDOLPH FM.

4 GUIDES FOR SECT. H.Q. will be at KEMPTON PARK AT 1.30 P.M. GUIDES FOR SEC. H.Q. ON ARRIVAL.

5 RATIONS. 2 DAYS RATIONS PLUS THE UNCONSUMED PORTION OF THE DAYS RATIONS WILL BE CARRIED ON THE PERSON.

6 WATER. WATER BOTTLES WILL BE CARRIED FULL. 1 PETROL TIN PER SEC. H.Q. – 1 PETROL TIN PER DETACHMT. WILL BE CARRIED TO LAST THE 2 DAYS.

7 EQUIPMENT.
TRIPODS, BELT BOXES, CONDENSOR BAGS & TUBES, S.A.A., TRENCH STORES, A.A. SIGHTS, SCHEMES & MAPS will be taken OVER.

8 TRANSPORT. 1 LIMBER PER SECTION, 1 LIMBER & COOKS CART FOR H.Q. WILL ACCOMPANY EACH PARTY.

9 COMPLETION OF RELIEF WILL BE REPORTED BY OUTGOING SECTION BY WORD "JEAN"

Issued AT 8 P.M. 27/11/17

[signature] O.C. 106 M.G. Co.

COPY No
1 SECT. OFFICER
2 " "
3 " "
4 " "
5 WAR DIARY
6 FILE
7 BRIGADE
8 WAR DIARY
9 D.M.G.O.
10 TRANSP. OFF.
11 105 M.G. Co.
12 241 M.G. Co.
13 C.Q.M.S.
14 2nd M.G.
15 ADJUTANT
16 C.O.

Instructions regarding War Diaries and Intelligence Summaries are contained in F. S. Regs., Part II. and the Staff Manual respectively. Title pages will be prepared in manuscript.

WAR DIARY
1st to 31 DECEMBER. 1917
~~INTELLIGENCE SUMMARY.~~
(Erase heading not required.)

106th MACHINE GUN. Co. Army Form C. 2118.

VOLUME No 20

Vol 20

Place	Date	Hour	Summary of Events and Information	Remarks and references to Appendices
In the field	2/12/17	—	1 sub-section from GLOSTER FARM + 1 sub-section from NORFOLK HOUSE co-operated in an attack by the 32nd Division (on the right) harassing fire on to special targets was carried out between 2 am + 3.30 a.m. 8,250 rounds expended.	O.O. 133
			104 M.G. Co relieved the Co. in the line	O.O. 134
	3/12/17	–	The Co. moved from KEMPTON PARK to BROWN CAMP (by bus.)	
	6/12/17	–	The Co. moved from BROWN CAMP to CARRIBOU CAMP (by road)	O.O. 135
	10/12/17	–	The Co. moved from CARRIBOU CAMP to ROAD CAMP	OO. 136
	11/12/17 to 24/12/17	}	Training at ROAD CAMP.	
	25/12/17		XMAS DAY	
	26/12/17		BOXING DAY.	
	27/12/17 to 31/12/17	}	Training at ROAD. CAMP.	

[illegible] Capt
Comdg 106 M.G. Co

A7092 Wt. W128.9/M1293 750,000. 1/17. D. D & L. Ltd. Forms/C2118/14.

SECRET

COPY No. 5

OPERATION ORDER No. 133

106th M.G.Co. WILL CO-OPERATE WITH AN ATTACK TO BE CARRIED OUT BY THE DIVISION ON THE RIGHT ON THE MORNING OF THE 2ND. DECEMBER 1917

1. GUNS IN ACTION
   1 SUB-SECTION OF "A" UNDER LT. H.E. TALBOT.
   1 SUB-SECTION OF "A" UNDER 2/LT. W.S. WHITEHOUSE
2. TARGETS
   No. OF GUN
   12, 13 } GLOSTER HOUSE. { TARGET No 2 / " No 3
   14, 15 } NORFOLK HOUSE. { TARGET. SPRIET ROAD FROM WHITECHAPEL TO SPRIET.
3. SCHEDULE OF FIRE.. AS LAID DOWN IN S.O.S. FIRE AND HARASSING FIRE SCHEME OF THE BRIGADE M.G. DEFENCE SCHEME.
4. ZERO HOUR WILL BE 1·55 A.M.
5. HOUR OF READINESS - 1·45 A.M.
6. DURATION OF FIRE - FROM ZERO + 8 TO ZERO + 90
7. RATE OF FIRE 2000 ROUNDS PER GUN PER HOUR
8. CESSATION OF FIRE. FIRE WILL CEASE AT ZERO + 90 WHEN THE GUNS WILL REMAIN ON THEIR S.O.S LINES
9. WATCHES WILL BE SYNCHRONIZED AT LEFT BATTALION H.Q. - NORFOLK HOUSE - AND Co. H.Q - GLOSTER FM. AT 12. MIDNIGHT
10. REPORTS. AT HOUR OF READINESS, WHEN THE PREPARATIONS ARE COMPLETE "O.K." WILL BE WIRED TO H.Q.
    REPORTS ON No. OF ROUNDS FIRED, PREVALENT STOPPAGES & RETALIATION WILL BE RENDERED TO H.Q. KEMPTON PARK ON COMPLETION OF FIRE BY SPECIAL RUNNER

ISSUED AT 5·00 P.M. 1/12/17

C. Skerrington Lt.
for O.C.

Copy No.
1 SECTION OFFICER
2 " "
3 " "
4 " "
5 WAR DIARY
6 FILE
7 BRIGADE
8 WAR DIARY.
9 Bn. COMMANDER
10 Co. COMMANDER GLOSTER HOUSE
11 D.M.G.O.

SECRET

Copy No 5.

OPERATION ORDER No 134.

106th M.G.Co., will be relieved in the line by 104 M.G.Co on the night 2/3rd Dec. 1917

1 DISPOSITIONS. The following dispositions will be handed over:–

RIGHT:– Sect H.Q. Burns House
2 Guns Banff Ho. 1 Gun Vacher Fm.

CENTRE:– Sect H.Q Gloster House.
2 Guns Tracas Fm. 2 Guns Meunier Ho.
2 " Gloster House

LEFT:– Section H.Q. V 14 c 15·20.
1 Gun Brewery, 1 Gun Ridles Fm.
1 " Helles Ho, 1 " Sect. H.Q.

SUPPORT:– Sect. H.Q Norfolk Ho. 2 Guns Norfolk Ho.

2. GUIDES
1 Guide per detachment will be at Sect H.Q at 4 pm.
1 " for Norfolk Ho. will be at Gloster Fm. at 4 P.M. who will know the new duckboard track between the two.

3. EQUIPMENT. All S.A.A. Trench Stores, Petrol Tins, Defence Schemes, Maps, Belt Boxes and Tripods will be handed over & receipts obtained.

4 WITHDRAWAL.
On relief sections will withdraw to Kempton Park by route at discretion of section officers.
On completion of relief the Co. plus carrying party of H.L.I. will move to Brown Camp.

5. TRANSPORT
3 Limbers will report at Kempton Park at 2 AM.
Mess Cart " " " " " " 3 P.M.
3 Limbers " " " " " " 9 AM.
Drivers for these vehicles will know the route to new camp. Remainder of Transport & Q.M. Stores will move to new camp under arrangements of C.Q.M.S & Transport Sgt.

6 RELIEF. Sections will report relief complete by word "[illegible]"

7 HOT MEAL.
A hot meal will be provided at Brown Camp under arrangements of C.Q.M.S.

8 Hd. Qrs. will close at Kempton Park on completion of relief & re-open at Brown Camp on arrival.

Issued at 10 am. 2/11/17.

H. G. [illegible] Lt.
for O.C.

Copy No.
1 Section Officer
2 " "
3 " "
4 " "
5 War Diary
6 File
7 Brigade.
8 ~~War Diary~~
9 D.M.G.O.
10 104 M.G.C.
11 C.Q.M.S.
12 Transp. Sgt.
13 2nd I–C
14 C.O.

SECRET

COPY No 5

OPERATION ORDER No 135

106th M.G. Co. will move to CARIBOU CAMP on the afternoon of [illegible] Dec 1917.

1 PARADE.
Company will parade at 1.15 P.M. — including transport.

2 ORDER OF MARCH. Battle formations A.B.C.D.
Sections & H.Q.rs. 200 yds interval will be kept between sections.

3 DRESS.
Fighting order. [illegible] water bottles filled.

4 BAGGAGE.
All baggage will be packed on limbers by 12 noon.

5 ROUTE.
Brown Camp, [illegible] main road to [illegible] corner — [illegible].

6 DINNERS.
Dinners will be served at 12 noon.

7 ARRIVAL.
Probable hour of arrival 2.30 P.M.

Issued at 10.00 am 6/12/1917

[signature] for
CAPTAIN,
O.C. 106 MACHINE GUN Co

Copy No
1 Sect. Officer
2 " "
3 " "
4 " "
5 War Diary
6 File
7 Brigade
8 [illegible] Diary
9 Transport Off.
10 C.O.

SECRET

COPY No. 5

OPERATION ORDER No. 138

106th M.G. Co. WILL MOVE TO ROAD CAMP (F25 c&d) ON THE MORNING OF 11th DEC 1917

1. PARADE. Co WILL PARADE AT 8 30 AM & MOVE OFF 8 45 AM.

2. ORDER OF MARCH
   D. C. B. A. HQ. QRS.
   No 5 LIMBERS WILL ACCOMPANY EACH SECTION IN ADDITION TO THE BATTLE LIMBERS. 200 YDS. INTERVAL WILL BE KEPT BETWEEN C AND B SECTIONS AND 200 YDS BETWEEN H.Q. AND REMAINDER OF TRANSPORT.

3. DRESS
   FIGHTING ORDER. JERKINS ROLLED ON BACK OF BELT. WATER BOTTLES FILLED

4 BAGGAGE.
   ALL BAGGAGE WILL BE PACKED, ON LIMBERS BY 8 00 AM

5 ROUTE CORNISH CORNER — WOESTEN. POPERINGHE ROAD — POPERINGHE - WATEAU ROAD TO ROAD CAMP.
   STARTING POINT CORNISH CORNER X ROADS WHICH WILL BE PASSED AT 9 20 AM

6 TRANSPORT - WILL BE DRAWN UP ON ROAD EAST OF CAMP FACING NORTH BY 8 35 A.M.

7 ADVANCE PARTY.
   2 MEN PER SECTION & 2 H.Q WILL PARADE AT 7.15 AM UNDER Lt. R. SKEVINGTON.

8 DAILY ROUTINE.
   REVEILLE 6 30 A.M.
   BREAKFAST 7 15 A.M.
   DINNERS - ON ARRIVAL AT NEW CAMP.

ISSUED AT 6.00 PM 10/12/17

COPY No.
1 SECTION OFFICER ✓
2 " " ✓
3 " " ✓
4 " " ✓
5 WAR DIARY
6 FILE
7 BRIGADE
8 WAR DIARY
9 TRANSP OFFICER
10 C.O

R Skevington Lt
for

106th MACHINE GUN COMPANY

Army Form C. 2118.

Instructions regarding War Diaries and Intelligence Summaries are contained in F. S. Regs., Part II. and the Staff Manual respectively. Title pages will be prepared in manuscript.

WAR DIARY

1st. to 31st. January 1918.

~~INTELLIGENCE SUMMARY.~~

(Erase heading not required.)

VOLUME No 21.

Vol 21

Place	Date	Hour	Summary of Events and Information	Remarks and references to Appendices
ROAD CAMP.	1.1.18 to 7.1.18.		TRAINING	
POELCAPPELLE SECTOR	8/9.1.18.		Relieved 1 Section 206 M.G.Co. and 2 section 214 M.G.Co in the Corps line POELCAPPELLE SECTOR. 1 Gun V 25d.0.2. 1. Gun DELTA HOUSE. 1. Gun U23a.9.1. 1. Gun. ROSE HOUSE 1. Gun U.24.d.6.6. 1. Gun. U.23.b.8.0. 1. Gun. U17d.0.1. 1. Gun. U.18.c.5.4. 2. Guns. OLGA HOUSE. Company. H.Q. KEMPTON PARK.	
	12/13.1.18.		Inter Section Relief	
	16.1.18.		Relieved by 241 M.G.Co in the Corps line POELCAPPELLE SECTOR. Unit withdrew to KLOBER Fm. CANAL BANK.	
KLOBER FARM.	17/21.1.18		Reorganization at KLOBER FARM.	
	21/22.1.18		Relieved 116. M.G.Co. in the WESTROOSEBEKE SECTOR of Divisional Front. Co.H.Q. ALBERTA HOUSE.	
			Left. D. Section 2 Guns. BANFF HOUSE. 4. Guns. VACHER Fm.	
			Right. B. Section 1. Gun. TOURNANT. FARM. 2. Guns. SOURCE TRENCH. 2. Guns VARLET FARM 1. Gun. YORK FARM.	
WESTROOSBEKE SECTOR.	24.1.18.		Indirect fire from VACHER Fm. to VEAL COTTAGES. 2,000 rounds fired.	
	25/26.1.18		A. Section relieved D. Section. C Section relieved B. Section.	
			Indirect fire on to VEAL COTTAGES. 1,000 rounds expended.	
	27.1.18.		Harassing fire was carried out by four guns in view of the suspected hostile relief. Pill boxes, fortified steel posts and tracks were engaged. 8,000 rounds expended.	

A7092 Wt. W128.9/M1293 750,000. 1/17. D. D & L. Ltd. Forms/C2118/14.

Army Form C. 2118.

Instructions regarding War Diaries and Intelligence Summaries are contained* in F. S. Regs., Part II. and the Staff Manual respectively. Title pages will be prepared in manuscript.

WAR DIARY
or
INTELLIGENCE SUMMARY.
(Erase heading not required.)

Place	Date	Hour	Summary of Events and Information	Remarks and references to Appendices
WESTROOSBEKE. SECTOR.	29/30.1.18		88th M.G.Co relieved the two guns at VARLET FARM. The two guns at SOURCE. TRENCH and one gun at TOURNANT. FARM were withdrawn to reay Company H.Q. CALIFORNIA DUG-OUTS. The following positions were occupied on the new Brigade front. D. Section 2. GUNS. BANFF HOUSE. 4. GUNS VACHER FARM. B. SECTION 1. GUN. YORK. FARM. 1. GUN. WINCHESTER FARM. 1. GUN GENOA. 1. GUN. VON. TIRPITZ FM. Indirect fire was carried out on to CAMERON HOUSES and PAPA. FM. 1,000 rounds expended.	

[signature] Lt. for.
O.C. 106 MACHINE GUN CO

106 ... GUN CO.
Date 31.1.18.
ORDE...

A7092 Wt. W 128 9/M1293 750,000. 1/17. D. D & L. Ltd. Forms/C2118/14.

OPERATION ORDER Nº 137.

Copy No. 5

106 MACHINE GUN COMPANY WILL MOVE TO SOLFERINO CAMP B22 B55 ON THE MORNING OF THE 8th JANUARY 1918.

PARADE

COMPANY LESS TRANSPORT WILL PARADE AT 6·15 AM AND MOVE OFF AT 6·30 AM.

ORDER OF MARCH

HEADQUARTERS, A B. C. D

DRESS

FIGHTING ORDER. JERKINS ROLLED ON BACK OF BELTS, WATER BOTTLES FILLED.

TRAIN

Nº 1 TRAIN WILL DEPART FROM PROVEN STATION AT 9·0 AM. FOR BOESINGHE, THENCE BY ROUTE MARCH TO SOLFERINO CAMP.

BILLETS

ALL BILLETS, BILLETING AREA AND TRANSPORT LINES WILL BE LEFT SCRUPULOUSLY CLEAN.

BAGGAGE

ALL BAGGAGE WILL BE PACKED ON LIMBERS BY 5·45 AM.

TRANSPORT

THE TRANSPORT WILL MOVE UNDER ORDERS OF TRANSPORT OFFICER LEAVING TRANSPORT LINES NOT LATER THAN 5·45 AM.

DAILY ROUTINE

REVEILLE 4·30 AM
BREAKFAST 5·0 AM.
DINNERS ON ARRIVAL AT NEW CAMP.

ARRIVAL

PROBABLE HOUR OF ARRIVAL 11·30 AM.

Issued at 7·0 pm. 7·1·18.

Copy No 1 Section Officer
2 " "
3 " "
4 "
5 War Diary
6 File
7 Brigade
8 War Diary
9 Transport Officer
10 C.O
11 D.M.G.O.

Lieut
Commanding 106 Machine Gun Company

SECRET. COPY No. 5.

OPERATION ORDER No. 138.

THE 106th M.G. Co WILL RELIEVE 4 DETACHMENTS OF THE 206th M.G.Co. AND 6 DETACHMENTS OF THE 214th M G Co. IN THE POELCAPPELLE SECTOR ON THE NIGHT OF THE 8th/9th JANUARY 1918.

1. DISPOSITIONS. THE FOLLOWING DISPOSITIONS WILL BE TAKEN OVER:–
RIGHT. "B" SECTION UNDER 2/LT. R. ROWLEY. SECTION H.QRS. U.3.0 A.9.1. (PHEASANT TR.) 1 GUN V.25. D.0.2., 1 GUN U.30 A.9.1. (PHEASANT TR.) 1 GUN DELTA HOUSE, 1 GUN ROSE HOUSE.
TAKEN OVER FROM 206th M.G.Co.
CENTRE. 3 DETACHMENTS OF "D" SECTION UNDER 2/LT. J. SEDDON. SECTION H.QRS. LOUVIE FARM. 1 GUN U.24 D.6.6., 1 GUN LOUIE FARM, 1 GUN U.23 B.8.0. (EAGLE TR)
LEFT. "A" SECTION UNDER LT. H.N. FISHER M.C. SECTION H.QRS. LOUIE FARM. 1 GUN U.17. D.0.1, 1 GUN U.18. C.5.4. 1 GUN OLGA HOUSES.
2 ADDITIONAL GUNS WILL BE PUT IN OLGA HOUSES.
TAKEN OVER FROM 214th M.G.Co.

2. GUIDES. 1 GUIDE FOR "B" SECTION WILL BE AT Co. H.QRS 206 M.G.Co. (HUT 27, KEMPTON PARK) AT 3.00P.M.
1 GUIDE FOR LIMBER WILL BE AT Co. H.QRS. 206 M.G.Co. AT 3.00P.M.
1 GUIDE PER DETACHMENT WILL BE AT SECTION H.QRS. ON ARRIVAL.
"A" AND "D" SECTIONS. 1 GUIDE FOR SECTION H.QRS. WILL BE AT KEMPTON PARK CORNER AT 3.00P.M.

3. PARADE. THE Co. WILL PARADE AT SOLFERINO CAMP AT 12 NOON.

4. DRESS. FIGHTING ORDER. JERKINS ROLLED ON BELT. SECOND PAIR OF SOCKS WILL BE CARRIED IN THE HAVERSACK.

5. RATIONS. TWO DAYS RATIONS WILL BE CARRIED ON THE MAN, IN ADDITION TO THE UNCONSUMED PORTION OF THE DAYS RATIONS. ONE BOTTLE OF WHALE OIL PER DETACHMENT WILL BE CARRIED.

6. WATER. WATER BOTTLES WILL BE CARRIED FULL, PETROL TINS WILL BE TAKEN UP UNDER ARRANGEMENTS OF SECTION OFFICERS CONCERNED.

7. EQUIPMENT. ALL BELT BOXES, S.A.A., TRENCH STORES, AEROPLANE PHOTOGRAPHS AND MAPS WILL BE TAKEN OVER.

8. ROUTE. SOLFERINO CAMP, DAWSON'S CORNER, BRIELAN, ISLEY FARM, ESSEX FARM, No. 4. BRIDGE, AND TO KEMPTON PARK.

9. TRANSPORT. 1 LIMBER "A" "B" "C" SECTIONS, HEAD QRS AND MESS CART WILL ACCOMPANY EACH PARTY.

10. DETAILS. THE DETAILS OF THE Co WILL BE ACCOMODATED AT KEMPTON PARK, AND WILL PROCEED THERE UNDER 2/LT. E.A. HAWKES, 2 LIMBERS WILL ACCOMPANY THIS PARTY TO CARRY WATER, RATIONS, 1 BLANKET AND 1 GREATCOAT PER MAN. ON COMPLETION OF DUTY, TRANSPORT WILL RETURN TO SOLFERINO CAMP.

11. RELIEF. SECTIONS WILL REPORT RELIEF COMPLETED BY THE OUTGOING SECTIONS TO Co. H.QRS. BY MESSENGER, BY WORD "LIZZIE"

12. T.P.R's. WILL BE RENDERED BY ALL CONCERNED, TO REACH COMPANY H.QRS. AT KEMPTON PARK BY 7.00 A.M.

ISSUED AT 7.00P.M. 7/1/18.

COPY No. 1. SECTION OFFICER.
" " 2 " "
" " 3 " "
" " 4 " "
" " 5 WAR DIARY.
" " 6. FILE.
" " 7. BRIGADE.
" " 8. WAR DIARY.
" " 9. T.O.
" " 10. D.M.G.O.
" " 11. C.O.
" " 12. ADJUT.
" " 13. 206. M.G.Co.
" " 14 214 –do–
" " 15 D.M.G.O. 58th DIV.

R Skevington Lt
O.C. 106 M.G.Co.

SECRET. COPY No. 5

OPERATION ORDER No. 139.

PERSONNEL OF THE 106TH M.G.Co. WILL RELIEVE PERSONNEL OF THE 106TH M.G.Co. IN THE CORPS LINE POELCAPPELLE SECTOR, ON THE NIGHT OF THE 12/13TH JANUARY 1918.

1. DISPOSITIONS. THE FOLLOWING DISPOSITIONS WILL BE TAKEN OVER:-

RIGHT 4 DETACHMENTS UNDER 2/LT. W. S. WHITEHOUSE.
SECTION HEAD QRS. PHEASANT TRENCH.
1 GUN V.25 C 00.45 1 GUN U30 D 15.90
1 GUN V19 C 30.00, 1 GUN U24 D 90.20

CENTRE 3 DETACHMENTS UNDER 2/LT. J. TAYLOR.
SECTION HEAD QRS. LOUIE FARM.
1 GUN U24 D 40.65 1 GUN U24 C 50.45
1 GUN U23 B 80.00.

LEFT 4 DETACHMENTS UNDER 2/LT. R. J. UTTING.
1 GUN U17 D 00.15, 1 GUN U18 C 50.40
2 GUNS U18 B 55.25.

2 GUIDES. 1 GUIDE PER DETACHMENT AT SECTION HEAD QRS. AT 1.00PM.

3 PARADE. THE RELIEVING DETACHMENTS WILL PARADE AT KEMPTON PARK CAMP AT 12.00 NOON.

4 DRESS. FIGHTING ORDER. JERKINS ROLLED ON BELT. SECOND PAIR OF SOCKS WILL BE CARRIED IN THE HAVERSACK.

5. RATIONS. 2 DAYS RATIONS WILL BE CARRIED ON THE MAN IN ADDITION TO THE UNCONSUMED PORTION OF THE DAYS RATIONS. ONE BOTTLE OF WHALE OIL PER DETACHMENT WILL BE CARRIED.

6. WATER. WATER BOTTLES WILL BE CARRIED FULL. PETROL TINS WILL BE TAKEN UP UNDER ARRANGEMENTS OF SECTION OFFICERS CONCERNED.

7 EQUIPMENT. ALL BELT BOXES S.A.A. TRENCH STORES, AEROPLANE PHOTO'S AND MAPS WILL BE TAKEN OVER.

8 RELIEF. RELIEFS WILL BE REPORTED COMPLETED BY OUTGOING SECTIONS BY THE CODE WORD "MAUD".

ISSUED AT 10.0 PM. 11-1-18.

COPY No. 1 SECTION OFFICER
" " 2. " "
" " 3.
" " 4
" " 5. WAR DIARY
" " 6. FILE
" " 7. BRIGADE
" " 8. WAR DIARY
" " 9. TRANSPORT OFFICER
" " 10. C.Q.M.S.

R Skevington Trait

O.C. JERK

SECRET

Copy No. 5

OPERATION ORDER No 11-0

106th M.G. Co. will be relieved by 241 M.G. Co. in the Corps Line Poelcappelle Sector on the afternoon of the 16.1.18

1 DISPOSITIONS The following dispositions will be handed over:

Right Section Section H Qrs Pheasant Trench
1 Gun Pheasant Tr. 1 Gun near [illegible] House
1 " Delta House 1 " Rose House

Centre Section Section H Qrs Louie Farm
1 Gun Louie Farm 1 Gun Eagle Trench
1 " U24 a 10.65

Left Section Section H Qrs Louie Farm
1 Gun Dean Trench 1 Gun [illegible] House
2 Guns Oxen Houses

2 GUIDES 1 Guide per Section H.Qrs will be at Co. H.Qrs Kempton Park at 12 noon

3 EQUIPMENT All belt boxes, S.A.A., Trench Stores, Defence Schemes, Maps, Aeroplane Photographs will be handed over and Receipts obtained.
Petrol Tins will be brought out of the Line

4 WITHDRAWALS On relief Sections will withdraw to Billets Canal Bank

5 DETAILS The Details at Kempton Park will move back to Canal Bank on relief under the orders of Sgt J [illegible]

6 TRANSPORT G.S. Wagon, H.Q. Limber and 1 other Limber will Report at Co. H.Qrs at 10.0 am.
1 Limber each for the Right & Left Sections together with the Mess Cart will report at Co. H.Qrs at 1.30 pm.

7 RELIEF Sections will report 'Relief complete' to Co. H.Qrs by code word "MELLIE"

Issued at 6.00pm 15.1.18

Copy No 1 Section Officer
2
3
4
5 War Diary
6 File
7 Brigade
8 War Diary
9 Transport Off
10 C.Q.M.S
11 D.M.G.O
12 C.O. 241 M.G. Co.

R Skerington
Lieut
O.C. 106 M.G.C.

5

SECRET. COPY No. ...

OPERATION ORDER No. 141.

106th M.G.Co. WILL RELIEVE 116 M.G.Co. IN THE RIGHT SECTOR OF THE DIVISIONAL FRONT ON THE NIGHT OF THE 21/22 JANUARY 1918.

1. DISPOSITIONS. THE FOLLOWING M.G. POSITIONS WILL BE OCCUPIED.

LEFT. 2 DETACHMENTS "D" SECTION UNDER 2/LT. R. ROWLEY. SUB. SECT. H.Q. NEAR BURNS HOUSE
2 GUNS BAIFF HOUSE.
4 DETACHMENTS OF "D" UNDER 2/LT. J. SEDDON SECTION H.Q. NEAR BURNS HOUSE.
4 GUNS VACHER FARM.
1 DETACHMENT OF "B" UNDER 2/LT. J. SEDDON
1 GUN YORK FARM.

RIGHT. 5 DETACHMENTS OF "B" UNDER LIEUT. P.H. COOPER.
SECTION H.Q. SOURCE TRENCH (V 28 c 8.8)
2 GUNS VARLET FARM.
2 " SOURCE TRENCH.
1 " TOURNANT FARM.

2 GUIDES.

LEFT. 1 GUIDE FOR YORK FARM WILL BE ON TRACK AT 4.30 P.M.
RIGHT. 2 GUIDES FOR SECTION HD.QRS. WILL BE AT "CORNER COT" SOUP KITCHEN (C 17.b 6.4) AT 4.00 P.M.
GUIDES FOR GUN TEAMS WILL BE AT SECTION HD.QRS. ON ARRIVAL

3. PARADE.

"B" AND "D" SECTIONS WILL PARADE AT 2.15 P.M.
"A, C AND DETAILS PARADE AT 2.45 P.M.

4 DRESS.

FIGHTING ORDER, JERKINS ROLLED ON BELT. SECOND PAIR OF SOCKS WILL BE CARRIED IN THE HAVERSACK.

5 RATIONS

TWO DAYS RATIONS WILL BE CARRIED ON THE MAN, IN ADDITION TO THE UNCONSUMED PORTION OF THE DAYS RATIONS. ONE BOTTLE OF WHALE OIL PER DETACHMENT WIL BE CARRIED.

6. WATER

WATER BOTTLES WILL BE CARRIED FULL, PETROL TINS WILL BE TAKEN UP UNDER ARRANGEMENTS OF SECTION OFFICERS CONCERNED,

7. EQUIPMENT

ALL BELT BOXES. S.A.A. TRENCH STORES, AEROPLANE PHOTOGRAPHS AND MAPS WILL BE TAKEN OVER. 5 DETACHMENTS OF "B" SECTION WILL TAKE OVER TRIPODS

8. ROUTE

WILL BE AT DISCRETION OF SECTION OFFICERS

9. TRANSPORT

AS PER SEPARATE ORDERS GIVEN TO TRANSPORT OFFICER.

10 DETAILS. THE DETAILS OF THE COY TOGETHER WITH 4 GUNS OF C-SECT WILL BE ACCOMODATED IN DUG-OUTS AT C.22.B 9.1 C.22.B 8.5 AND C.22.B 7.3.

11 CO.HQ WILL BE ESTABLISHED AT "ALBERTA" (C 11 c.9.6)

12 T.P.Rs WILL BE RENDERED TO CO. HQ BY 7.30 AM.

13. RELIEF SECTIONS WILL REPORT RELIEF COMPLETED BY THE OUT-GOING SECTION TO CO H.Q BY MESSENGER BY WORD "OLIVE"

ISSUED AT 7.0 PM 20/1/18

1 SECTION OFFICER	7 BRIGADE
2 " " "	8 WAR DIARY.
3 C.O	9 T.O.
4 2nd IN COMMAND	10 C.Q.M.S.
5 WAR DIARY	11 D.M.G.O
6 FILE	12 O.C. 116 Co.

R.R. Wright LIEUT
COMDG 106 MACHINE GUN COMPANY

SECRET

COPY No. 5

OPERATION ORDER No. 142

THE PERSONNEL OF A & C SECTIONS WILL RELIEVE THE PERSONNEL OF 'D' & 'B' SECTIONS RESPECTIVELY, IN THE RIGHT SECTOR OF THE DIVISIONAL FRONT ON THE NIGHT 25/26th JANUARY 1918

1. DISPOSITIONS. THE FOLLOWING M.G. POSITIONS WILL BE TAKEN OVER.

LEFT. 2 DETACHMENTS OF "A" SECTION UNDER 2/LT. H.H. BUCKLEY – SUB/SECTION H.Q. NEAR BURNS HOUSE
2 GUNS BANFF HOUSE.
4 DETACHMENTS OF 'A' SECTION UNDER 2/LT. R.J. UTTING
SECTION H.Q. NEAR BURNS HOUSE.
4 GUNS VACHER FARM.
1 DETACHMENT OF 'C' UNDER 2/LT. R.J. UTTING
1 GUN YORK FARM.

RIGHT. 5 DETACHMENTS OF 'C' SECTION UNDER 2/LT. W.S. WHITEHOUSE. SECTION H.Q. SOURCE TRENCH (V28 c 8.8)
2 GUNS YARLET FARM, 2 GUNS SOURCE TR. 1 GUN TOURNANT TR.

2 GUIDES. THE RUNNERS FROM THE LINE WILL ACT AS GUIDES TO SECT. H.Q.
GUIDES FOR DETACHMENTS WILL BE AT SEC. H.Q. ON ARRIVAL.

3 PARADE.
A & C SECTIONS WILL PARADE AT 3.45 P.M.

4 DRESS. FIGHTING ORDER – JERKINS ROLLED ON BELT.
SECOND PAIR OF SOCKS WILL BE CARRIED IN THE HAVERSACK.

5 RATIONS
2 DAYS RATIONS will be CARRIED ON THE MAN, IN ADDITION TO THE UNCONSUMED PORTION OF THE DAYS RATIONS. ONE BOTTLE OF WHALE OIL PER DETACHMENT WILL BE CARRIED.

6 WATER
WATER BOTTLES will be CARRIED FULL. PETROL TINS will be TAKEN UP UNDER ARRANGEMENTS OF SECTION OFFICERS CONCERNED.

7 T.P.R's. – will be RENDERED TO Co. H.Q. BY 4.30 AM DAILY.

8 RELIEF.
SECTIONS will REPORT RELIEF complete by THE OUTGOING SECTIONS TO Co. H.Q. BY MESSAGE BY WORD "PSYCHE"

9 EQUIPMENT. All Guns, Trench Stores etc. will be TAKEN OVER.

ISSUED AT 3.00 P.M. 24-1-18.

Copy No.
1 SECT. OFFICER 'A' SECT
2 " " 'B' "
3 C.O.
4 2ND-IN-C
5 WAR DIARY
6 FILE
7 BRIGADE
8 WAR DIARY
9 C.Q.M.S.
10 SECT. OFFICER 'C' SECT
11 " " 'D' "

[illegible]

SECRET COPY No. 5

OPERATION ORDER No. 143.

The personnel of B & D Sections will relieve the personnel of A Section plus 1 detachment of "C" Section & 2 detachments of 241 M.G.C., in the right Section of the Divisional front on the night 29/30 Jany 1918

1. **DISPOSITIONS.** The following M.G. positions will be occupied.

2 Detachments of "D" Section under 2/Lt. J. Taylor.
Sub. Section H.Q. near BURNS Ho.
2 GUNS BANFF HOUSE.

4 Detachments of D Section under 2/Lt. J. Seddon
Section H.Q. near BURNS Ho.
4 GUNS VACHER FARM.

4 Detachments of B Section under Lt. P. H. Cooper
Section H.Q. YORK FARM.
1 Gun YORK FM. 1 Gun WINCHESTER FM.
1 " GENOA. 1 " VON TIRPITZ FM.

2 **GUIDES.**
The runners from the line will act as guides to Section H.Q. for D Section.
Guides for GENOA & VON TIRPITZ Fm. will be at GENOA at 4.30 pm.
1 Guide for YORK FM. & WINCHESTER FM. will be at YORK DUMP at 5 pm.

3 **PARADE.**
B and D Sects. will parade at 4 pm.

4 **DRESS.**
Fighting Order - Jerkins rolled on belt - second pair of socks will be carried in the Haversack.

5. **RATIONS**
2 Days rations will be carried on the man in addition to the unconsumed portion of the days rations. 1 Bottle of Whale oil per detachment will be carried.

6 **WATER.** Water-bottles will be carried full. Petrol tins will be taken up under arrangements of Section Officers concerned.

7 **EQUIPMENT.**
All belt-boxes S.A.A. trench stores etc. will be taken over and receipts obtained.

8 **RELIEF.**
Sections will report relief complete by the outgoing sections to Co. H.qrs by message by word "QUEENIE"

Issued at 6 pm. 28/1/18

Copy No.
1 Sect. Officer
2 " "
3 " "
4 " "
5 War Diary
6 File
7 Brigade
8 War Diary
9 O.C. 241 M.G.Co.
10 C.Q.M.S.
11 T.O.
12 Comdg Officer
13 2/Lt J Taylor
14 2/Lt H. Buckley

R S Kelsington [?] Lieut
O.C. 106 M.G.Co.

18th H. L. I.

106

Vol. I

35

Feb '16.

Feb '19

1916

I. D.

9 Hus

www.ingramcontent.com/pod-product-compliance
Lightning Source LLC
Chambersburg PA
CBHW080848230426
43662CB00013B/2051